DATE

D1565471

The Praeger Handbook of Mental Health and the Aging Community

The Praeger Handbook of Mental Health and the Aging Community

Doreen Maller and Kathy Langsam, Editors

An Imprint of ABC-CLIO, LLC

Santa Barbara, California • Denver, Colorado

Library of Congress Cataloging-in-Publication Data

Names: Maller, Doreen, editor. | Langsam, Kathy, editor.
Title: The Praeger handbook of mental health and the aging
      community / Doreen Maller and Kathy Langsam, editors.
Description: Santa Barbara, California : Praeger/ABC-CLIO, [2018] |
      Includes bibliographical references and index.
Identifiers: LCCN 2017032316 (print) | LCCN 2017036250 (ebook) |
      ISBN 9781440853357 (ebook) | ISBN 9781440853340 (alk. paper)
Subjects: | MESH: Mental Health | Aged—psychology | Mental Health Services |
      Health Services for the Aged
Classification: LCC RC454.4 (ebook) | LCC RC454.4 (print) | NLM WT 145 |
      DDC 616.89—dc23
LC record available at https://lccn.loc.gov/2017032316

ISBN: 978-1-4408-5334-0 (print)
      978-1-4408-5335-7 (ebook)

22 21 20 19 18   1 2 3 4 5

This book is also available as an eBook.

Praeger
An Imprint of ABC-CLIO, LLC

ABC-CLIO, LLC
130 Cremona Drive, P.O. Box 1911
Santa Barbara, California 93116-1911
www.abc-clio.com

This book is printed on acid-free paper (∞)

Manufactured in the United States of America

Dedication and Gratitude

Producing this volume was a lesson in patience and resilience. Many of our contributors (both potential and final) are themselves living with the realities of the impacts of aging in their families as well as their practices. To those who made it to final stages of this volume and others who did not, we offer thanks. And to our own aging parents, those with us and those we have lost along the way, we share this work with you.

As individuals, clinicians, and especially family members, we learned as we researched, wrote, edited, and compiled these entries. It is our hope that our readers will as well.

Contents

Foreword

Thomas Prohaska

The aging of the baby boomer generation presents new and unique challenges to the health care system. This is especially true for providing mental health services to a generation of older adults who are acutely divergent on so many levels including gender identity, ethnic diversity, deteriorating cognitive processes, sexual expression, and substance abuse disorders. This is further complicated when comorbid chronic diseases and disability are considered. For example, the prevalence of dementia is estimated to be 1.4 percent among adults aged 65 to 69 years but reaches 37.4 percent among those 90 years and older (Karel, Gats, and Smyer, 2012). When dementia is combined with other mental disorders, it is estimated that one in five adults aged 65 and older meet the criteria for a mental disorder (Karel et al., 2012). With the growing number of individuals entering the ranks of 65 years and older and their complex and unique challenges, the demands on geriatric mental health service workforce providers have never been greater.

The Praeger Handbook of Mental Health and the Aging Community addresses the complexity and challenges of mental health care services to the newest group of the aging population, the baby boomers. Each chapter addresses diverse populations, therapeutic perspectives, and treatment settings and provides recommendations for the practicing mental health therapist. The book is designed for seasoned mental health practitioners as well as master's level students entering into the geriatric mental health care workforce. Researchers in mental health and aging will also find the chapters useful for generating research questions while practitioners may discover insights to incorporate into their practice. While there are multiple themes that can be identified across the chapters, three themes emerge: the use of the ecological perspective and holistic approach in the various forms of mental health services, the occasion of self-reflection on the assumption biases of the therapist, and the case flow and the creativity and diversity of the therapeutic strategy the authors present.

The Ecological Perspective

In the publication *Epidemiology of Aging: An Ecological Approach*, Satariano (2006) identified how patterns of health and well-being among older adults are influenced by an interplay of bio-psychosocial and environmental factors including families, neighborhoods, and communities. The authors in *The Praeger Handbook of Mental Health and the Aging Community* have incorporated elements of the ecological approach by implementing programs across settings, stressing the social determinants of health and identifying root causes such as stressful communities due to crime and the lack of access to healthy choices. The full spectrum of mental health from wellness and well-being to addiction and end-of-life care is addressed. Broader ecological factors such as poverty, social stigma, neighborhood crime, and violence are recognized as contributors to mental health problems among older adults. For example, the chapter on the stressful community environment for members of the lesbian, gay, bisexual, and transgender (LGBT) community and its impact on mental health documents the unique challenges presented to older LGBT adults. *The Praeger Handbook of Mental Health and the Aging Community* provides multiple examples of mental health therapies and programs in various settings. Additionally, examples of mental health services are provided at the individual, family, and group sessions in community settings.

Self-Reflection

The Praeger Handbook of Mental Health and the Aging Community provides valuable insights on self-examination and reflection. Authors urge the readers to consider their own assumptions, stereotypes, and biases that may impede the progress of the therapy and the flow of the therapy. We are reminded that ageism and lack of cultural competency exist in all fields of health care. For example, the chapter by Boston on cultured-centered hospice care stresses the importance of incorporating appropriate cultural and family values into the hospice experience. In this case, the lack of cultural humility and the inability to incorporate African American cultural family values and rituals in the hospice setting led to deep dissatisfaction by the family. The chapter by Fritchle cautions therapists against the belief that sex is something belonging only to the young. Similar assumptions are expressed in the chapter on mental health among LGBT older adults.

Creative Therapeutic Treatments

An impressive array of creative and innovative forms of therapy are provided throughout the book. For example, the chapter by Bernstein on dance/movement therapy were offered dance, therapy imagery to older adults to promote healthy aging and as a tool to work through life challenges. Speiser echoed the connection between the visual and performing arts and well-being and expanded its application to community settings. Creative applications of the use of mindfulness were noted across multiple chapters. A somewhat new and unique example of animal-assisted therapy for elderly is equine-facilitated psychotherapy. This case study successfully used horse therapy to connect the client's past experience of caring for horses to stimulate positive memories and promote communication.

Conclusion

The Praeger Handbook of Mental Health and the Aging Community is an example of the emergence of a holistic approach to mental health and aging. The authors stress the need to expand treatment of mental health of older adults to include an ecological perspective that recognizes the broader influences of bio-psychosocial and environmental factors on the mental health of older adults. It was also stressed that the therapist should be aware of policy, ageism, legal issues, and the interaction between the courses of chronic diseases including Alzheimer's disease on mental health of the older adult.

Collectively, the chapters reflect a movement toward an interdisciplinary perspective that harmonize psychology, geriatrics and public health. The primary objective of mental health practitioners is to improve and maintain mental health and to prevent and treat dysfunction and disorders of their older patients. *The Praeger Handbook of Mental Health and the Aging Community* is a resource to meet this objective by providing greater context to the challenges that confront the older adult and additional strategies to address their mental health concerns. The creative interventions are an inspiration. The challenge is real but the opportunities are vast.

References

Karel, Michele J., Margaret Gatz, and Michael A. Smyer. "Aging and Mental Health in the Decade Ahead: What Psychologists Need to Know." *American Psychologist* 67, no. 3 (2012): 184–198. doi:10.1037/a0025393.

Satariano, W. *Epidemiology of Aging: An Ecological Approach*. Sudbury, MA: Jones and Bartlett, 2006.

Introduction: Ensuring Dignified Support of the Mental Health of an Aging Population

Doreen Maller and Kathy Langsam

Demographic research of the aging American populations shows both an increase of potential clients with specific and complex issues and a lack of training in the care provider community (CDC, 2013). As the stigma around therapy and mental health support lessens (as it surely will with more and more baby boomers who have used therapeutic services throughout their lives entering into late-life care), family and individual therapists will find that issues related to age and aging, the complexity of diagnosis and care, and the stressors on the family system will impact their case load and show up in their client care. As editors of support and training materials for therapist training, the editors of this book are happy to include this volume of materials to address this growing need. It is our hope that this volume will serve as a powerful training tool for future generations of therapists.

In March 2014, the U.S. Census Bureau issued a report noting that "America's 65-and-over population is projected to nearly double over the next three decades, ballooning from 48 million to 88 million by 2050" (Ortman, Velkoff, and Hogan, 2014). In 2013, the Centers for Disease control issued a report, "The State of Aging and Health in America," which cited a need to consider the effect of the influx of aging baby boomers' "profound effects on our nation's public health, social services, and health care systems, the significant increase in racial and ethnic diversity in the aging population" (CDC, 2013) and the "need for caregiving for older adults by formal, professional caregivers or by family members—and the need for long-term care services and supports (which) will increase sharply during the next several decades, given the effects of chronic diseases on an aging population" (CDC, 2013).

The concern about the needs of a growing population and noted in the April 2016 fact sheet on mental health and aging adults, where the World Health Organization noted that "older adults, those aged 60 or above, make important contributions to society as family members, volunteers and as active participants in the workforce. While most have good mental health, many older adults are at risk of developing mental disorders, neurological disorders or substance use problems as well as other health conditions such as diabetes, hearing loss, and osteoarthritis" and that in fact, as people age, they tend to experience several conditions, both physical and emotional, at the same time. The report indicates that globally, elders are experiencing a complexity of issues, with layers of social, psychological, and biological factors which can impact mental health, as well as the typical life stressors which may include "limited mobility, chronic pain, frailty or other mental or physical problems" which may require some form of long-term care as well as "experience events such as bereavement, a drop in socioeconomic status with retirement, or a disability." The report notes that "all of these factors can result in isolation, loss of independence, loneliness and psychological distress in older people."

In 2008, the Institute of Medicine (IOM) issued a report expressing fear of an overwhelmed health care system, where too few people are trained to manage the particular needs of an again population. The Institute of Medicine (2012) and the Substance Abuse and Mental Health Service Administration (2007) note that few training programs exist for graduate-level training and few practitioners trained or interested in the special needs of this population. With the projection of elderly growing to a projected 72.1 million by 2030, there is a need to train care providers to address the particular needs, including the financial impact, of this growing and vulnerable population (IOM, 2012).

In a later report, the Institute of Medicine (2012) noted that at least 5.6 to 8 million Americans aged 65 and older are suffering from mental illness, substance abuse, or a combination of both. Noted as a "gray tsunami," these numbers will continue to increase as more and more baby boomers move into old age. The study notes that the nation is woefully lacking in doctors, nurses, and other mental health workers specifically trained in the complex needs of our aging population. The report noted the complexity of the mental health care needs of older adults, and specifically how general health, mental health, and substance use can impact the lives and well-being of a rapidly growing and underserved population.

Other issues when considering the mental health and emotional support of an aging population include the following:

- There is complexity in discerning the differences between the reactions to grief, depression, and isolation and addressing each appropriately with medication or other forms of therapy (IOM, 2012). While there may be a prevalence of decline in major depression over that in midlife, there are subsets of the aging population where depression is substantially higher, including medical outpatients (5–10%, though estimates vary widely), medical inpatients (10–12%), and residents of long-term care facilities (14 to 42%) (Fiske, Wetherell, and Gatz, 2009).

- Depression can be triggered by illness, loss of a spouse, a sense of purposelessness, or moving out of the family home (National Alliance on Mental Illness, 2009). A 2015 Gallup survey reports one in seven baby boomers are currently being treated for depression, with one in five having been diagnosed within their lifetime (McCarthy, 2015).

- Lifestyle issues associated with baby boomers will move with them into older age. In 2010, at least 5.6 million to 8 million older adults were identified as dual-diagnosed with substance and other mental health issues (IOM, 2012) with a growing number in need of rehabilitation programs (Gfroerer, Penne, and Folsom, 2003).

- Medications that are used to address physical health (particularly steroid medications) may impact mood and require close monitoring and use of antidepressants as part of a generalized health management plan (IOM, 2012).

- Age-related changes in people's bodies affects metabolism, which can impact diet and well-being as well as metabolizing of drugs and alcohol, including prescription medication, which may lead to overmedication and overdose (IOM, 2012, p. 4).

- Age-related cognitive decline, dementia, and Alzheimer's disease impact mental abilities and increase stressors on the family system and care providers. Approximately, 5.4 million older Americans may be impacted by various stages of Alzheimer's (Alzheimer's Association, 2012) including mental and physical deterioration.

- Long-term personality disorders may be exacerbated by health challenges, substance use, medication side effects, or cognitive decline (Gabriel and Jones, 2000).

- Increased diversity of the growing elderly population presents other unique challenges, which would require practitioners trained to include culturally inclusive engagement in their work with clients and patients (APA, 2009).

- The 2012 census (Department of Health and Human Services, 2014) notes 15 percent of American adults, 65 and over, live in poverty.

- Elder adults tend to underutilize mental health treatment for a variety of reasons including stigma, costs, lack of coordination of care, complicated medical billing, and lack of transportation (Bartels et al., 2005).

- Issues of physical health including incontinence and insomnia rank high in reasons families move loved ones into managed care facilities (APA, n.d.; SAMHSA, 2007). These issues can impact mood as well and contribute to depression in the aging population.

- Issues of diversity and culture as well as geographical locations can have an impact on care. The vast majority of care professionals are non-Hispanic whites, which raises concerns about the training of young professionals to serve this diverse and growing population with cultural sensitivity (Duffy et al., 2004). Geographical location can also impact care; 85 percent of the federally designated shortage areas are rural in nature (Bird, Dempsey, and Hartley, 2001). Adequate access to primary care services is essential to a well-functioning health care system. Racial and ethnic minorities and low-income individuals face more barriers when trying to access care and receive a lower quality of care (Edmunds, 2011).

- Families are now expected to provide care to their aging relatives; nearly 25 percent of American households are providing care to people aged 50 years and over. Hospital stays are shorter than ever and family caregivers are often expected to do what health care professionals once did, and do so without training, including monitoring symptoms and administer complex medication regimens; assisting with personal care; performing housekeeping tasks; providing emotional support; managing difficult behaviors such as wandering, aggression, and hallucinations; dealing with health care providers and insurance companies; managing finances; coordinating care; and dealing with uninvolved or unhelpful family members (Flori, n.d.).

With a specific focus on substance abuse and the elderly, the Institute of Medicine's 2012 report on the support workforce needed for this growing population, "The Mental Health and Substance Use Workforce for Older Adults: In Whose Hands?" cites the following effective delivery models for mental health and substance use (IOM, 2012):

- Systematic outreach and diagnosis
- Patient and family education and self-management support
- Provider accountability for outcomes
- Close follow-up and monitoring to prevent relapse

The study notes, "these elements are best obtained when care is patient-centered, in a location easily accessed by patients (such as in primary care, senior centers, or individuals' homes), and coordinated by trained personnel with access to specialty consultation." Another point in the study is the use of care managers, which are mentioned as critical to effective care (IOM, 2012).

In 2013, when we worked together as editors of the *Praeger Handbook of Community Mental Health Practice*, we were aware and concerned that we had not included a specific chapter on working with the aging population. Over time, we felt that our work in providing resources for training and preparing students and early practitioners for the work of community mental health was incomplete without a deeper inquiry and focus on the needs of the aging population and their supporting families and care providers. This volume is our contribution to the field of elder care and support; following our early intention to make "complex systems more visible to the emergent practitioner so that the services provided by interns in their early years of practice were appropriate, client centered, consumer driven, and evidence-based" (Maller, Langsam, and Fritchle, 2013), our hope is to provide the same for those working with elders and their care providers.

It was our hope in creating this volume to cover a variety of complex issues, which often present in an interrelated fashion in each family served. What we have found as clinicians is that co-occurrence is to be expected when working with the elderly, making it difficult to isolate single issues for attention and care. Depression, isolation, physical and mood symptoms, grief, loss, and cognitive and physical decline are all holistically connected as well as issues related to comfort, faith, and hopefulness. The impact on clients, their families, and care providers requires an appreciation of the complexities of diverse communities, access to care, individual family systems, and the predominance of loss. Clients may be familiar with therapy, or may be arriving as elders for support for the first time in their lives. In the included chapters and case studies, we hope to have included a breadth of possible issues that may show up in a therapist's practice, both as presenting issues and as options for interventions.

We begin this volume with a chapter that invites a structural view of case management. In Chapter 1 "Aging and the Therapist," Doreen Maller explores the complexities and practical therapeutic applications of working with aging clients, their caregivers, and their families. Insight into managing life transitions, support, referrals, and working with the complexity of feelings at later life stages for the therapist, care community, and the client are explored. This chapter is supported by two case studies, "Adjusting to Illness: A Couple's Story" in which Alexandra Kennedy shares her work with a couple working with physical challenges and "A Life in Review: Sylvia's Journey" where Kathy Langsam recounts her work with a family's aging matriarch Sylvia as the family grapples with the tensions of later life.

In Chapter 2 "The Aging Brain: New Frontiers in Neuroscience and Medicine," Gerardo Rodriguez-Menendez introduces neuroscience and cognitive impacts in the aging community. This chapter is followed by the case study, exploring "Animal-Assisted Therapy and the Elderly" by Martha McNeil who shares her work with AAT and elderly clients.

Introduction

Chapter 3 "The Impact of Physical Challenges on the Mental Health of the Aging Population" authored by Caroline D. Bergeron and Matthew Lee Smith, considers the impact of physical challenges on mental health and vice versa. Best practices for positive outcomes are shared. It is followed by "Dance/Movement Therapy with Elders: Dance for Health and Healing" by Bonnie Bernstein, which recounts her work with elders using dance to create community and connection.

Chapter 4 "Diversity in the Aging Community" by Tamara A. Baker, Darlingtina K. Atakere, Jacquelyn A. Minahan, Araba A. Kuofie, and Thomas Dirth provides an understanding of the influence of diversity on the aging population and how better knowledge of how we include this understating may impact health across the life course.

This chapter is followed by Vivien Marcow Speiser's case study, "Moving toward Connection: Using Expressive Arts Approaches to Enhance the Well-Being of Elders," which recounts her work using art to connect elders at a community care center in Massachusetts.

Chapter 5 "LGBTQ Seniors and Mental Health: Providing Compassionate Care to Age with Dignity," by Scott Valentine addresses issues specific to the LGBTQ community.

In Chapter 6, "Invisible and Overlooked: Substance Use Disorders in Aging Adults," Annie Fahy explores substance use as baby boomers move into elder care.

In Chapter 7 "Supporting Our Elders on Their Sexual Journey," Melissa Fritchle discusses the need for therapists to include sexuality in their consideration of quality of life for elder clients.

Chapters 8 and 9 focus on issues related to hospice and end-of-life care. Chapter 8 "Dignity and Companionship at the End of Life: Two Contemplations of Hope, Fear, and Human Flourishing" by John Eric Baugher shares his early work in hospice care as well as some contemplative exercises for the reader. This chapter is followed by Chapter 9, "Culture-Centered Hospice Care: Welcoming Our African American Elders Home" by Denise Boston, which discusses culturally appropriate hospice care and the use of the expressive arts in end-of-life care.

We next move toward legal and ethical considerations while working with an aging population in Chapter 10 "Aging and the Law: The Legal Aspects of Aging and Care Provision" by Pamela Zimba. In our final Chapter 11, Kathy Langsam explores "Supervision: Competencies and Special Issues" and how working with the specific needs of this population may impact trainees and interns.

We hope that our readers will learn as much as we did as we worked to create this volume. We hope that this collection will help train and support the next generation of clinicians and provide specific and useful information for working with this most deserving population.

References

Alzheimer's Association. 2012. "Alzheimer's Disease Facts and Figures." https://www.alz.org/downloads/facts_figures_2012.pdf.

American Psychological Association. n.d. "Mental and Behavioral Health and Older Adults. Fact Sheet." http://www.apa.org/about/gr/issues/aging/mental-health.aspx.

American Psychological Association. Committee on Aging. 2009. "Multicultural Competency in Geropsychology." http://www.apa.org/pi/aging/programs/pipeline/multicultural-competency.pdf.

Bartels, S. J., Blow, F. C., Brockman, L. M., and Van Citters, A. D. 2005. *Substance Abuse and Mental Health Care among Older Americans. The State of the Knowledge and Future Directions*. Rockville: WESTAT.

Bird, D. C., Dempsey, P., and Hartley, D. 2001. *Addressing Mental Health Workforce Needs in Underserved Rural Areas: Accomplishments and Challenges*. Portland: Maine Rural Health Research Center, Muskie Institute, University of Southern Maine.

Centers for Disease Control and Prevention. 2013. *The State of Aging and Health in America 2013*. Atlanta: Centers for Disease Control and Prevention, U.S. Department of Health and Human Services.

Duffy, F. F., West, J. C., Wilk, J., Narrow, W. E., Hales, D., Thompson, J., et al. 2004. "Mental Health Practitioners and Trainees." In *Mental Health, United States 2002* edited by R. W. Manderscheid and M. J. Henderson, pp. 327–368; DHHS Publication No. SMA04–3938). Rockville, MD: U.S. Department of Health and Human Services, Substance Abuse and Mental Health Services Administration, Center for Mental Health Services.

Edmunds, Margaret. 2011, July 17. "Evidence of Geographic Variation in Access, Quality, and Workforce Distribution." Geographic Adjustment in Medicare Payment: Phase II: Implications for Access, Quality, and Efficiency. Accessed April 22, 2017. https://www.ncbi.nlm.nih.gov/books/NBK207343/.

Fiske, Amy, Wetherell, Julie Loebach, and Gatz, Margaret. 2009. "Depression in Older Adults." *Annual Review of Clinical Psychology*. Accessed April 22, 2017. https://www.ncbi.nlm.nih.gov/pmc/articles/PMC2852580/.

Flori, Denise E. n.d. "Caregiving for the Elderly." American Association for Marriage and Family Therapy. Accessed April 22, 2017. https://www.aamft.org/iMIS15/AAMFT/Content/consumer_updates/caregiving_for_the_elderly.aspx.

Gabriel, C., and Jones, A. 2000. "The National Nursing Home Survey: 1997 Summary. National Center for Health Statistics." *Vital Health Statistics*, 13, 147.

Gfroerer, J., Penne, M., and Folsom, R. 2003. "Substance Abuse Treatment Need among Older Adults in 2020: The Impact of the Aging Baby-Boom Cohort." *Drug and Alcohol Dependence*, 69 (2), 127–135.

Institute of Medicine. 2008. *Retooling for an Aging America: Building the Health Care Workforce.* Washington, DC: The National Academies Press. http://www.nationalacademies.org/hmd/Reports/2008/Retooling-for-an-Aging-America-Building-the-Health-Care-Workforce.aspx.

Institute of Medicine. 2012. *The Mental Health and Substance Use Workforce for Older Americans: In Whose Hands?* Washington, DC: The National Academies Press. https://www.nationalacademies.org/hmd/~/media/Files/Report%20Files/2012/The-Mental-Health-and-Substance-Use-Workforce-for-Older-Adults/MHSU_olderadults_RB_FINAL.pdf.

Maller, D., Langsam, K., and Fritchle, M. (Eds.). 2013. *The Praeger Handbook of Community Mental Health Practice.* Santa Barbara: Praeger.

McCarthy, Justin. 2015. "Reports of Depression Treatment Highest among Baby Boomers." http://www.gallup.com/poll/181364/reports-depression-treatment-highest-among-baby-boomers.aspx.

National Alliance on Mental Illness. 2009. "Depression in Older Persons: Fact sheet." https://www.naminh.org/sites/default/files/NAMI%20Depression%20Older%20Adults%20Fact%20sheet.pdf.

Ortman, J. M., Velkoff, V. A., and Hogan, H. 2014. "An Aging Nation: The Older Population in the United States." U.S. Census Bureau. https://www.census.gov/prod/2014pubs/p25-1140.pdf.

Substance Abuse and Mental Health Administration. 2007. "An Action Plan on Behavioral Health Workforce Development: Executive Summary." http://www.mentalhealthconnection.org/pdfs/annapolis-report.pdf.

U.S. Department of Health and Human Services. 2014. *A Profile of Older Americans: 2014.* Administration on Aging (AoA), Administration for Community Living, U.S. Department of Health and Human Services. http://www.aoa.acl.gov/aging_statistics/profile/2014/docs/2014-profile.pdf.

World Health Organization. 2016, April. "Mental Health and Older Adults. Fact Sheet." http://www.who.int/mediacentre/factsheets/fs381/en/.

CHAPTER ONE

Aging and the Therapist

Doreen Maller

The United States is growing older.

The country's health care system is facing the impact of a shifting demographic and will require health care policies, research, and practitioners who can provide "real world views about the practicality of different services and programming options" (Ory and Smith, 2015). The U.S. Department of Health and Human Services' Administration for Community Living (2015) acknowledges that services and support may involve navigating an "often disjointed maze of eligibility criteria, forms, programs, and agencies which can prevent even the most determined individuals from obtaining these critical supports."

Even when a family finds support, professionals may be undertrained. In his 2014 book *Being Mortal*, surgeon Atul Gawande explored his challenges as a family member and a member of the medical community. He writes that "97 percent of medical students take no courses in geriatrics," and that to train future doctors, existing geriatric specialists should be employed to "teach rather than provide patient care."

The U.S. Department of Health and Human Services, Administration on Aging (SAMSA), issued a report in 2015 which noted that the American population aged 65 and over numbered 46.2 million in 2014 (an increase of 28% since 2004), and that between 2004 and 2014, the population aged 60 and over increased 32.5 percent from 48.9 million to 64.8 million. One in every seven, or 14.5 percent, of the population is an older American and will continue to get older; persons reaching age 65 have an average life expectancy of an additional 19.3 years. Of this cohort, 22 percent of persons aged 65+ were members of racial or ethnic minority populations and many are fairly independent; about 29 percent of noninstitutionalized older persons live alone, and half of older women aged 75+ live alone. In fact, many are quite active and may be actively involved in caring for others; in 2014, over half a million grandparents aged 65 or more had the primary responsibility for their grandchildren who lived with them. This demographic shift has implications for care of the elders themselves, and also on those providing them care and support. The study indicates that primarily family caregivers support many of these older individuals. These caregivers are considered the backbone of America's long-term care system, and are described as "selfless, tireless and courageous," and are "not immune to stress, fatigue, burnout or illness. In fact, research shows they may be more vulnerable in this regard." They are at risk for burnout and will require breaks and self-care to continue in their roles (Walker, 2016).

My work as a family therapist began with a focus on children. Over time I evolved my practice to work systemically with children in reimagining their place in their social environments, and in training and supporting their parents. As the children became more skilled at social navigation and behavioral control, their parents often chose to stay with me. As a result, my practice expanded to include parent education and child-advocacy training and support of the parents themselves, and often their stories expanded to include the pressures of caring not only for their children, but also for their aging parents, friends, partners, and in-laws at the same time. Pew Research states that "nearly half (47%) of adults in their 40s and 50s have a parent age 65 or older and are either raising a young child or financially supporting a grown child (age 18 or older). And about one-in-seven middle-aged adults (15%) is providing financial support to both an aging parent and a child" (Parker and Patton, 2013). The challenges of managing both took a physical and emotional toll on these clients as they juggled the needs of their children, aging parents, partners, friends, neighbors, and themselves. Symptoms that presented as depression may have actually been exhaustion: the daily challenge of care provision, financial responsibilities, and worry.

At the same time, I experienced another shift in my practice: elders were being referred to me for care and support by their family members or clergy or they self-referred for additional support. Today, my practice is increasingly populated with clients over 80 years old. My family practice now encompasses all generations in the family system.

My goals in this chapter are to introduce a general model of client case management, to explore three specific intervention and assessment models, and to explore the complexity of direct client services, family support, and resourcing to support the needs of all affected by this historic demographic shift.

Case Management

Working with elders provides some unique challenges for the therapist. Some issues may be unsolvable such as the loss of friendships or life partners, a loss of independence, challenging health issues, and a sense of isolation. Social isolation can become a health risk on its own, and can "increase depression, neurosis, pessimism, alcoholism and suicidal thoughts. It can also disrupt sleep and reduce self-esteem" (Perry, 2012). Often connection to the therapist can provide a much-needed point of contact and social connection which can lift spirits, and provide a much needed change in routine. "Older adults who maintain or increase social connections can slow both physical and cognitive decline" (Perry, 2012).

A comprehensive case management plan should be drafted for clients of all ages. Particularly when working with family systems and complex cases, a solid case conception can help the therapist focus on the work, optimize support, and provide structure, which can among other things help avoid caregiver burnout. While this case management model is specific for the therapist–client relationship, having a sense of structure can ease the overwhelm practitioners, care provides, and family members face when dealing with difficult issues. In this case management model, the therapist is encouraged to have clear goals, boundaries, and understandings in place, all with the objective to best serve the client's needs. These plans, while needed for insurance payments as well for providing structure, are not rigid; diagnosis and treatment planning can change as the client's experiences change and can be fluid throughout the course of treatment.

Case Conceptualization and Flow

Once initial contact is made, it is best to consider the "flow" of therapy, and form your initial case conceptualization. Over time, this may shift as you gather more information about the individual or family and their social support and connections, but sound, effective, ethical practice should include a case management plan. Case flow consists of five steps of thought and process organization. Each will be explored in this section: presenting problem, unit of treatment, goals of therapy, interventions, and termination.

Presenting Problem

Insurance practices often require early diagnosis in order to begin payment cycle, and as a result, there is often a sense of pressure to get a correct early assessment, based on the client's input and your personal observations. The presenting problem may be the issue that is pressing for the client or it may be the most comfortable issue the client is able or willing to discuss with you as your relationship begins. The nature of the presenting issue will color the time you spend together (short or long term), the interventions you choose, and the resources and additional services you might suggest for your clients and their families. A thorough intake may include a mental status exam, or a series of questions asked and answered combined with your own clinical observations. Additionally you are ethically bound in your initial contact with the client to advise regarding informed consent, your professional mandates, and your compliance with HIPAA (Health Insurance Portability and Accountability Act) regulations. It is important for the therapist to remember that while assessment is imperative in the first session or two, ongoing assessment is required to address client safety, abuse, exploitation, and mental health. Some things to consider in this initial assessment period are as follows:

- How would you diagnose this family issue?
- Are there any professional limitations you should consider before taking on this case (scope of practice, bias [age-ism or other], and any countertransference)?
- Are there cultural considerations in this family that you should be aware of?
- How would you test your theories and support your work with this family (supervisors, consultation, Internet, books)?

Unit of Treatment

Unit of treatment is the term used to help you define who might be included in therapy. Individual therapy refers to working one-on-one with an individual client. When working with caregivers, this unit can provide a place of respite, and replenishment for the ongoing challenges of care provision for a family member or loved one. Family therapy regards the family itself as the unit of treatment. It is important to remember that elder care can create stressors and conflicts within the family system and among family members and support team. The unit of treatment can help you determine your role in client support: Are you amplifying the voice of your clients or helping them understand the concerns of other family members? Are you helping the family work collectively toward a consensus? Are you helping a family member better communicate with his or her parent or partner?

When working with an elder in individual therapy, you may consider asking for releases to speak with family members, support persons, or even neighbors should you become concerned for your client's health and safety and to support the client in the unique decisions that are made at this life stage. Connection to a trusted support person allows you to connect with family should you have concerns regarding the client's cognitive abilities or changes in their physical health or safety needs.

When working with a family unit, the therapist has an opportunity to support the family in the difficult decisions and passages of this time of life; death of a partner, grief and loss, a move to assisted living, loss of independence (including driving), and the loss of friends. Quite often in family work, clients remark that these issues would have been shared with friends in the past, but now, their friends have either died or moved away, and their feelings of isolation are impacted by their own longevity. Psychological theorist Erik Erikson described this later adult life stage as one that is defined by integrity versus despair, where people struggle to find meaning in the challenges of late life, which can exacerbate a feeling that life is meaninglessness or that the end is near, and a fear or wish for death can impact the mood of the aging person. Advances of old age can create a sense that it is too late to change, further feeding a sense of gloom and depression (Newman and Brummel, 1989, p. 48).

Lastly, considering the unit of treatment allows you to consider your scope of practice and other resources that may be beneficial for the client. Marriage and family therapists focus on relational and communication issues within the family unit; should the client present with issues beyond your scope of practice, this is a good time to refer to other practitioners or clarify for the client what issues you will take on and which issues may work best with other support. For instance, referrals for legal support, financial concerns, medical support, substance abuse, and medication review can be referred to other professionals, while the client and their family may remain in your practice to process feelings of loss and grief.

Treatment Goals

Clarity around the client's or his or her family's goals of therapy help both the client and the therapist stay on track, check in regarding progress, and consider termination. Bearing therapeutic goals in mind helps the therapist maintain a healthy clinical distance from the client, one that is necessary as the client proceeds through the process of aging. Gail Sheehy (2010) notes that at this stage issues of death and dying are "real and present" (p. 315); she notes that "even for the most loving and dutiful family members, the financial and emotional and burdens of long-term care giving can be unbearable" (p. 359). The goals of therapy, then, may very well be to make this time of life easier to bear.

Working strategically with individual or family goals can pave the way for certain life transitions: a successful move to assisted living or bearing the grief of the passing of a spouse, partner, friend, or beloved pet. Goals can be organized around finding insight about loss of faith or a sense of isolation or coming to terms with a loss of independence. Behavioral goals can include creating a regimen for regular eating, sleeping, and socialization, or managing the anxieties of the social complexities of assisted living and communal meals after a lifetime of autonomy. Some of these issues are inherently related to loss, and may not be fixable. Working with a depth of compassionate understanding, the therapist can support the client as his or her eyesight, hearing, and dexterity fail. Acceptance of and adjustment to a natural decline are excellent uses of the therapeutic relationship. In my work, I have supported clients though despair regarding decline, and also through resilience. Sheehy (1995) notes, "as we grow older, we become less and less alike" (p. 419), which creates challenges and opportunities for interesting and supportive therapeutic work.

As goals are set in collaboration with your clients, sound practice requires you to review your work together and consider the following:

- Are goals within your capacity, and if not, how might you help the individual or family address them?
- Do you need more support, either in supervision, training, or consultation?
- Are there cultural considerations or spiritual practices that may bring comfort to the client's family and may inform their experiences?
- Might you be experiencing issues of countertransference or bias?

Interventions

Interventions are the main core of your work with clients, informed by theoretical orientation and client need. The flow and assessment of progress are based on the success of your interventions and their relevance to your goals. For instance, supporting a family through a move into assisted living might include: support in decision-making, support in planning the move, support through the transition, and support as the client adjusts to his or her new community. The interventions might include regulating anxiety, creating an environment where the client can share his or her fears, role-playing socialization choices, and supporting the feelings related to loss of freedom. End-stage interventions may include an end to therapy as the client successfully adjusts to a new care team.

Effective interventions for late-life depression include bibliotherapy, life review, problem-solving treatment, and antidepressant medication (Singh and Okereke, 2015, p. 141) and also brief learning-based approaches that have shown effectiveness for depressive disorders, pain, and insomnia disorders. Problem-solving therapy, behavioral therapy, and coping skills to enhance resilience and diminish a sense of loss have been shown to be effective as well (Reynolds, 2015, p. 3). While antidepressant medication has been seen to have a positive effect, a good use of therapy is to monitor the side effects of this intervention, which may include low sodium levels, risk of falls, bone demineralization, and cataracts (Reynolds, 2015, p. 3), and partnering with the client's medical team to determine proper patient care.

This stage might also include referrals to outside agencies for specific services such as health and housing, meals, and visiting nurses. In the intervention stage of therapy, it is important that the therapist consider clinical progression:

- Be mindful of client progress, and be curious and supportive of snags and setbacks.
- Rethink interventions if they are not effective or progressive, get support, do research, refer for a higher level of care or additional services, or add team members if the client needs more support than your weekly meetings.
- Check in with the client to get his or her own assessment of progress and any input as to changing goals, needs, or direction of your work together.

Termination

Termination is the final stage of client work. With elderly clients, termination can be impacted by client decline (they may be no longer able to participate in therapy), death, or change of circumstance. Working toward meaningful termination and self-care in the termination period is crucial for the therapist and client alike.

If the termination is abrupt, consider significant changes in the client's abilities or circumstances as contributing to the change in his or her relationship with you, and if you have a release, consider checking in with a family member. Abrupt termination that is not based on client's health or ability can give pause for you to consider choices you have made clinically. In these cases, you may want to assess your ability to form a strong alliance with the client or his or her family, assess client capacity, or assess your treatment plan (too aggressive, too slow, incorrect goals or diagnosis).

Winding down therapy toward termination should include interventions which:

- Move the client toward self-support
- Wean off sessions
- Encourage appropriate client independence
- Ensure services are in place as desired/needed
- Explain a return policy should the client or family members want to come back for additional support

A client care orientation that includes a carefully considered flow and structure will support the client's needs for growth, understanding, and comfort as he or she navigates the unique challenges of aging and caretaking. However, structuring the case "flow" is not enough to support families in this late life stage. In the following sections of this chapter, I will introduce three models that can help the therapist connect with and better understand the challenges families and individuals face when confronted with an aging family member.

Maslow's Hierarchy

With the growing number of people moving into their final years, the health system, including therapy practices, will be impacted by a change in population and the specific needs of this cohort in terms of their living and dying. Recently, health-related quality of life is being discussed as a new perspective in medical decision making. A holistic view of patient care is suggested, including a personalized approach incorporating "Five Ps": personalized care, predictive results and responses, precise choices, preventive care, and patient participation (Ory and Smith, 2015). It is important to remember that the client is the best expert of his or her own experience and, that our therapeutic responsibilities include joining with the client in his or her places of comfort and discomfort, and sharing and witnessing his or her emotional experiences.

In the stages of client assessment, it is critical to consider the whole of the client, and his or her situation emotionally, socially, and practically. Is your client in need of permanent housing or proper nutrition? Are the client's basic needs being met? Are the needs appropriate to the client's life circumstances and have they been reevaluated as the client has aged?

While meeting of these needs may be out of your scope of practice, identifying them and discussing them with the client are not. Taking the time to know the client and identify issues that are impacting his or her quality of life requires time and care. The client him- or herself may not be aware of his or her changes in need, so your gentle prompting may bring awareness to issues he or she had not yet considered. These issues are particularly important with the elderly, and I use the practicality of Maslow's hierarchy to keep my inquiry focused. It is difficult to offer appropriate support without a clear idea of where the client is situated.

In 1943, humanistic psychology pioneer Abraham Maslow published "A Theory of Human Motivation," which defined a hierarchy of needs. This hierarchy creates a framework to understand human motivation, which has withstood the test of time and theoretical shifts of human understanding. This model can be used to provide a much-needed framework for psychotherapeutic inquiry and case management. Starting at the bottom of the pyramid, I will now offer some suggestions for the use of hierarchy in the context of aging.

Physiological needs: These are the basic needs of human existence, typically considered food, clothing, and shelter. For elders, it is wise to inquire about the following:

• Food: Is the client losing or gaining weight (could be signs of illness or depression)? Is he or she properly hydrated? Does the client have access to food (if the client no longer drives)? Does he or she have an appetite?

• Shelter: Is the client living by him- or herself, or with family, or is he or she assisted in any way? Might the client benefit from a higher level of assistance? Is there resistance to this?

• Is the client being seen by a medical professional? Is there a clear understanding of his or her medications? Is he or she taking medications or experiencing med interactions that may affect mood? Is the client drinking alcohol or self-medicating in any way?

Safety needs: These can be considered in terms of physical safety, but also exploitation.

• Has the client fallen and is his or her physical space adjusted for advanced age (grab bars, walker, cane, etc.)?

• Is the client driving, should he or she be, and what are the client's plans regarding driving in the future? The risk of a fatal car accident with an elderly driver (85 or older) is three times higher than that of a teenager (Gawande, 2014, p. 11).

- Is the client at risk for financial exploitation? Remember, often exploitation of the elderly comes at the hands of a known person or family member (California, 2010).

- Is the client at risk of other levels of abuse as stated in your mandate of care (physical, sexual, financial, emotional, and self-neglect)?

Belonging and love: These issues are complex in the elderly. Clients may be reluctant to make new friends after suffering the losses of family members and friends. Clients in home care may feel isolated. It is important to ask about relationships and assess for depression and isolation. The challenge here is to work with the "Three Plagues" of nursing home existence (although I would imagine they exist in home care as well): boredom, loneliness, and helplessness (Gawande, 2014, p. 116)

- Has the client lost important relationships, spouses, friends, and/or pets? Is the client lost to grief, feeling a sense of resilience, or does he or she desire to discuss old disappointments?

- Is the client's behavior isolative? Are there resources available to the client in his or her communities? Are there friends or family who visit or are available?

- Might you connect with the client's caretaker or family members? Unless the client is in conservatorship, his or her rights to privacy still apply. Take care to keep releases updated, and discuss including family for support as needed, as part of your work with the client.

- Is your client open to making new friends or establishing new love relationships? He or she may need coaching on how to "be" with new people, especially if navigating the social complexity of assisted living.

Esteem needs: For the elderly, these can be equated with life's accomplishments or disappointments and issues regarding medical and social dignity as the mind and body present challenges.

- With the shifts in energy, physical health, and mental clarity, self-esteem can be sorely tested. Can you help the client find perspective, participate in a life review, grieve lost opportunities, and celebrate accomplishments?

- Can you advocate and coach for client dignity? This may include psychoeducation about palliative care, a DNR (do not resuscitate) or other end-of-life choices, or an offer (with a release) to call his or her doctors or family members.

- Is the client willing and/or able to discuss the challenges of a long life? Can you create a safe and compassionate space for these conversations?

Need for self-actualization: For the elderly, there may be some paradox to this stage of the pyramid. For instance, a client who has been able to actualize may struggle with the limitations of old age or loss of facility. I have included here a sense of existential loss and a grappling with the meaning and purpose of life.

- Is there a sense of loss to be processed regarding life accomplishments and the client's current situation?
- Is there an existential element the client may want to process: life, concepts of the hereafter, and the client's relationship with death and dying?

Spiritual needs factor into the support of the elderly as well. Not only do places of worship provide opportunities for community and socialization, but also many clients will find comfort in spiritual as well as practical support. Balboni et al. (2010) notes that, "spiritual care is associated with better patient quality of life near death."

While there are issues that can affect the client which fall outside of this model, I see it and use it as a good assessment tool, and this provides a holistic view of the client. It helps me see the client as a whole person rather than a person presenting with a set of symptomatic pathology. It helps me to partner with the client in a way that is supportive as well as educational, and to understand the inter-relativity of physical, psychological, and spiritual challenges. This is the truest expression of mind-body-spirit-based client care. Whole person approaches to care are seen as on the vanguard of public health; a 2016 article outlines the need for personalized, "subjective and multidimensional approach . . . influenced by several factors that include not only psychological and emotional aspects, individual behavior, and attitudes but also personal experiences, culture, and religious beliefs" (Ory and Smith, 2015).

Grief and Loss

Often clients and family members are directed to therapy to address issues of grief and loss or may experience a loss while they are engaged with you in therapeutic practice. Perhaps the most well-known model for grief and loss is the book *On Death and Dying* originally published by Elisabeth Kübler-Ross and updated with Ira Byok (2014). Kübler-Ross prefaced her book as an opportunity for the medical community, clergy, and family to imagine death and dying as an "opportunity to refocus on the patient as a human being, to include him in dialogues, to learn from him the strengths and weaknesses of our hospital management of the patient," and as "a way to learn more about the final stages of life with all of its anxieties, fears and hopes." Her hope was to provide a holistic view of end life care, where students can value science and technology as well as "inter-human relationships . . . human and total patient care" (p. 17). Kübler-Ross suggests that the best support we can give to those dealing with issues of death and dying is to "communicate without fear and anxiety" (p. 255) and acknowledges that therapeutic support can be helpful for those grappling with issues related to fears or inability to cope with issues related to their own eventual death or to the death of others (p. 259).

Kübler-Ross presented her model in five stages, which can be interpreted as five modes of coping skills, five ways of being with the intense emotions associated with grief and loss. In my practice, I use this model to normalize clients' strong emotional responses to loss, and I find that they are comforted by the existence of a theory that explains their emotional state. This model's application is broad; it can be applied easily to loss of identity or independence, as well as loss of life. The five stages are *denial*, *anger*, *bargaining*, *depression*, and *acceptance* and they can be seen as stepping stones toward a more regulated emotional understanding of grief and loss. In the following sections, I will offer some suggestions on how these steps and stages might be introduced to the client as they move toward acceptance of loss.

Denial

Freud first introduced denial as one of the defense mechanisms that humans utilize to protect a gentle ego state. People may block external events from awareness if a situation is too much to handle, either by minimizing the aspects or implications of the situation or by simply ignoring its existence (McLeod, 1970). The client may assume information is false or overemphasized. Kübler-Ross considered denial to be a temporary defense, which could be replaced with a partial acceptance (p. 39).

In the denial stage, clients may also be unaware of what is happening to them or around them. Denial can manifest as ignorance; it is hard to see what you cannot see. In either case, there is a need in this stage for great therapeutic compassion. Often the therapist can become an explainer and helper to the client. If you are connected to the client's family or medical community, you may be able to explain or answer questions for the client that were not addressed in his or her doctor's appointments (which are often fast, confusing, and overwhelming). Psychoeducational interventions can help a client understand implications of physical/medical conditions and limitations and medication side effects, or may just give the client a longer time to ponder over and consider the implications of life changes with a caring and considerate care provider. You must take care to be aware of your own responses to denial. Kübler-Ross reflects that the practitioner may respond to this stage with an expression of frustration or even confrontation (p. 47). In its 2014 "Guidelines for Psychological Practice with Older Adults," the American Psychological Association suggests that no single form or modality of treatment is preferable for all older adults. Instead it suggests that several modes can be considered: individual, group, family, and couple, as well as modalities that are most appropriate to the nature of the problem involved. Practitioners are directed to address clinical goals, the immediate situation, and the individual client's characteristics, preferences, and gender and cultural backgrounds (American Psychological Association, 2014, p. 50), and we are reminded that many issues of late life can be chronic or recurrent, requiring symptom management, and rehabilitation rather than a focus on a cure (p. 50). When working with denial as an entry stage toward an acceptance of loss, it is important to hold with compassion the challenge of unsolvable problems.

Anger

Anger at fate, anger at the medical community, and/or anger at family members are some of the ways anger is expressed in the therapeutic relationship. Clients may even direct their anger at you, their care provider. Thinking of anger as an expression of powerlessness can help the therapist handle strong feelings. I consider anger as an expression of frustration, and sometimes, fear. Allowing the client a place to feel and vent strong feelings is a great use in therapy. Meeting anger and frustration of a failing body or life-long regret with a sense of compassion and acceptance can help a client gain insight into his or her feelings. Knowing that anger is a predictable part of the process can comfort a client and give him or her permission to both feel his or her feelings and move through them toward a more regulated state of being. Kübler-Ross notes that anger is "very difficult to cope with from the point of view of family and staff . . . anger is displaced in all directions and projected onto the environment at times almost at random" (p. 50). In my own experience, clients can become angry at both frequency and infrequency of family visits, at food choices at the retirement home, or at my building for substandard maintenance of an elevator.

Working with respect and understanding can help the client understand that he or she is a "valuable human being, cared for, allowed to function at the highest possible level for as long as he can" (p. 51). Care providers should remember that we should not take the anger personally, especially because it has "little to do with the people who become targets of the anger" (p. 51). In sitting with hostile clients nonjudgmentally, we have an opportunity to allow them to vent some of their strong feelings and relieve some of their burdens and perhaps when relieved show another side of their personality, which may include warmth, love, insight, and affection (p. 76). When considering competence in working with older adults, the American Psychological Association urges practitioners to consider "a complex interplay of factors," including developmental issues specific to later life, generational perspectives and beliefs, comorbid physical illnesses, potential for issues related to the medications they take, cognitive or sensory impairments, and personal history of mental or medical disorders (American Psychological Association, 2014, p. 36). Additionally, considerations regarding the client's "age, gender, cultural background, degree of health literacy, prior experience with mental health providers, resiliencies, and usual means of coping with life problems should inform interventions" (p. 36).

Working through issues related to aging can create stress in elders. Increased health problems, impacts on intimate relationships, discord among adult children, and increasing needs and dependence on doctors, health care, time, finances, and transportation can all negatively impact an elderly client's quality of life and frustration levels (p. 44). Therapists should consider consultation with others working in the field to stay on top of new intervention and support models, which may reduce the client's reliance on psychoactive medications and help improve the quality of life for their clients (p. 52).

Bargaining

This stage toward acceptance is marked by a need to consider ways to change the course of their destiny or to consider a level of agency and power and create a set of promises toward recovery or better behaviors. Bargains can be made with God, or care staff or family members. Kübler-Ross considered that patients may be working through issues of guilt and fear as part of their bargaining process (2014) and may become depressed when these deals do not work out.

A sense of loss and desperation can be fertile work for the therapist and the client. Kübler-Ross suggests that relief from irrational fears or fear of punishment can come when they share them with clergy or psychological team members (2014). Specific interventions such as a life review can be effective in reducing feelings of guilt and depression, and can move clients toward a more inclusive sense of both positive and negative aspects of their lives. This intervention provides an opportunity to "structure evaluation of one's own life on one hand coping with negative experiences and conflicts and on the other hand giving a positive meaning to life" (Korte et al., 2011). The narrative framework of this intervention enhances the integration of negative events and restoration of positive identity and meaning in several ways; it creates a more open conversation about curiosity and "not-knowing"; and it allows a reflection of coping skills, a more integrated and positive view of one's identity, and a reminder of positive memories (Korte et al., 2012).

The American Psychological Association notes that there are special stressors in these later years, including "a variety of losses ranging from those of persons, objects, animals, roles, belongings, independence, health and financial well-being" (p. 39), which may trigger problematic reactions, particularly to those who are predisposed to mental disorders or emotional challenges (p. 39). They suggest supporting clients in considering positive aspects to their lives to draw upon "skills and adaptations they developed over their life spans for continued psychological growth in late life" (p. 39).

Depression

The Substance Abuse and Mental Health Services Administration (SAMHSA) recognizes depression as affecting more than 6.5 million Americans aged 65 and over, with 25 percent of older adults experiencing some type of mental health problem that is not associated with normal aging. Depression in this population increases the risks of cognitive decline and suicide, and can be closely associated with other factors such as substance abuse and disability (SAMHSA, 2016). Issues of diversity can impact the quality of life and comfort with mental health support. It is important to remember that "psychological issues experienced by older adults may differ according to factors such as age, cohort, gender, race, ethnicity and cultural background, sexual orientation, rural/frontier living status, education, socio-economic status, and religion" (American Psychological Association, 2014, p. 40).

Kübler-Ross with Ira Byock (2014) differentiates two types of depression in her original model: reactive depression, which may be tied to a specific event or life challenge, and preparatory depression, which may be tied to facing the finality of death. The first, reactive depression, can be addressed in a myriad of ways and is a traditional entrée into therapy.

In some cases the therapist can help by providing "clinical outreach . . . referral and early interventions, suicide assessment, and health promotion" (American Psychological Association, 2014). Kübler-Ross recommends an individual approach when addressing depression; issues of reactive depression respond well to treatment and can be addressed with problem solving and supportive interventions (Kübler-Ross, 2014); however, "cheering up" may not be effective for depression tied to the finality of life. In these cases, she recommends a sense of physical presence and emotional support as the client shifts from his or her struggle for life toward a preparation for death.

As the elder population expands, addressing the individual and systemic challenges of depression (in cost and care utilization) is one of today's major health priorities (Okereke, 2015). As the population ages (12% currently and 20% of the total population by 2030), demand is growing for intervention and care (SAMHSA, 2011). The U.S. Department of Health and Human Services developed an evidence-based "Kit" for practitioners specifically aimed at providing effective and appropriate strategies for working with older adults and depression (2011). It includes 14 specific principles for delivering care to older adults:

Issue 1: Co-occurring physical illness is the rule not the exception.

Physical disorders can often cloud and impact emotional well-being. Awareness of the impact of medication, mental and physical functioning, anxieties, and independence as well as "low energy, poor appetite and impaired functioning, irritability, and feelings of hopelessness can be shared symptoms of congestive heart failure and cancer." Psychotherapy has been found to be as effective as medication in the treatment of depression in this population (p. 12).

Issue 2: Co-occurring anxiety can complicate the course and treatment of depression.

The co-occurrence of anxiety can make the symptoms of depression more severe including a greater use of health services, poorer social functioning, more physical symptoms, and more thoughts of suicide. Treatment of anxiety with benzodiazepines may worsen confusion and increase risk of falls (p. 13).

Issue 3: Cognitive impairment can be a risk factor and a symptom of depression.

Memory loss, disorientation, or confusion can be assumed to be part of natural aging but may in fact be symptoms of a possible dementia, small stroke, vascular dementia, or Alzheimer's. Clients should be referred for a cognitive evaluation should you have concerns regarding cognitive functioning (p. 13); however, depression can also impact cognitive functioning and successful treatment of depression may reverse some cognitive symptoms (p. 14).

Issue 4: Older adults take multiple medications. Their bodies handle medications differently than younger buddies because of normal metabolic changes of aging.

Older adults may regularly take up to six prescription medications a day and additionally one to three over-the-counter medications. Two-thirds of older adults with depression receive five or more prescriptions compared to adults without depression. Cognitive and physical changes associated with aging can create vulnerabilities for older adults, which can include medication misuse and medication interactions. Older clients benefit from medication reviews and regular scheduling (p. 14).

Issue 5: Small amounts of substances can cause serious problems for older adults.

Alcohol and substance abuse can make treatment of depression more difficult and may impact the client with both medical and social issues, including sleep disturbances, physical health, lower quality of life, lower perceived social support, greater use of medical services, and a greater likelihood of thinking about attempting suicide (p. 15).

Issue 6: Mental and physical functioning varies widely among older adults of the same age.

There is a greater variation in age and developmental capacities in this age group based on physical and mental health as well as social issues. Considering the individual needs of your client will help create the best treatment plan (p. 16).

Issue 7: Coordination and collaboration between mental health, aging, and general medical health practitioners is essential.

Health care coordination as clients navigate multiple health care providers and services can add to the complexity of client care and depression treatment, often resulting in a lack of coordinated services (p. 16).

Issue 8: Engagement of family members and other social support is critical to successful treatment.

Although inclusion of family members requires the consent of your client, their inclusion and your participation with them are critical to client care. Family members often provide care services and will benefit from your case coordination insights and recommendations. Family members often provide help with the stressors of later life, including providing transportation, medication management, navigating social and health systems, and an antidote to isolation (p. 17).

Issue 9: Maintaining independence and aging-in-place are common values of older adults.

Helping adults to thrive in their desired living setting and lifestyle can forestall issues of depression although care services may need to be installed to prolong independent living, such as in-home health care, house cleaning, meal delivery, and transportation. Mobility needs, medication, help-alert buttons, and phone check-ins should be considered. Many older adults find the loss of independence associated with nursing home care as a major fear, and these concerns can contribute to depression (p. 17). Helping your client and his or her family navigate these changes is a good use of therapy, and continuity with you can ease some of the transition-based changes in their lives.

Issue 10: Agism and stigma affect treatment access, expectations, and outcomes.

Since many consider depression a natural condition of aging, some clients may feel reluctant to seek treatment because of feeling at fault, or a notion that they should be able to handle their situation themselves. Recognizing and working with stigma are critical components of working with this population (p. 18).

Issue 11: Cultural differences can affect perceptions of depression, access to treatment, treatment preferences, and treatment outcomes.

Culturally appropriate treatment is critical in the treatment of depression in the aging population. Stigma surrounding mental health treatment, dependence on spiritual communities, physical rather than mental issues, or anxiety rather than depression can influence self-disclosure regarding care needs. The elders themselves and mental health care providers should recognize and consider the role of agism and stigma on client care (p. 18).

Issue 12: Depression can be prevented.

Depression is predictable (at time of loss or transition or as a part of a medical downturn), and proactive treatment at these crucial times should be considered as the standard of care. Problem-solving treatments and regular exercise are effective treatments for an onset of depressive disorders (p. 19).

Issue 13: Older adult depression is associated with the highest rate of suicide.

Older adults are less likely to self-disclose suicidal ideation to their care providers, and yet suicide attempts are more likely to be deliberate and lethal. Older isolated adults who have had recent losses are at high risk for suicide. It is important to assess and report should you have suicidal concerns regarding your client's behaviors (p. 19).

Issue 14: Psychotherapy can be as effective as medication.

Tailoring psychotherapy to the specific needs of your client can be very effective for clients with depression. Behavioral therapies or problem-solving treatment can be very effective for older adults with depression. Sometimes a combination of an antidepressant and psychotherapy is more effective than each approach alone.

In the Kübler-Ross model, the therapist need not fear depression in his or her client, but instead accept depression as a stage of life: purposeful, treatable, and ultimately understandable.

Acceptance

This final stage in the Kübler-Ross's model is available to those not facing sudden, unexpected changes, but those who have had the time to work through previously addressed stages, and can enter into a stage that is dominated neither by depression nor by anger (2014). This stage is available to an individual as he or she enters the final stages or as a stage of grief and loss of another. Neither happy nor hopeless, this stage can be a time of peaceful understanding. For those passing, it can be a surrender of sorts. For those integrating the loss of another, there can be a sense of settling into a new normal. This is a time where therapy can end, due to the death of a client or the acceptance of death by a client. Acceptance of the loss of a loved one may follow the same stages of grief and loss as that of a client facing his or her own decline. Moving through these stages toward an acceptance of life and its promise can be gratifying and rewarding therapeutic work. Kübler-Ross offers these words for the practitioner: "To be the therapist to a dying patient" (I would add: and their loved ones) "makes us aware of the uniqueness of each individual in this vast sea of humanity. It makes us aware of our finiteness, our limited lifespan. A few of us live beyond our three score and ten years and yet in that brief time most of us create and live a unique biography and weave ourselves into the fabric of human history" (p. 262).

The Transtheoretical Stages of Change Model

The last model to consider in the complexity of late-stage client care and family life was developed by James Prochaska and Carlo DiClemente in 1983 and has been discussed in a number of other articles authored by Prochaska and his colleagues since then. This model was first introduced to consider in addiction treatment. It suggests how adjustments to and incorporations of change can be applied to other issues of significant life changes, and particularly in this case, the changes needed to accept and move through the challenges of late life. I include it here as a reminder of process in human adjustment to change, and also as a reminder of pacing. As one of my clients remarked when we were working with this model, not only is the model true but also it is important to remember that every family member is at a different stage in his or her own acceptance. The tensions and awareness of those differences can lead to productive therapeutic experiences. Inclusion of this model can help the therapist and the client (and family) understand the process of change as a gradient. The process can have a reluctant or slow start, a longer than anticipated planning stage, a recycling of earlier behaviors, and an understanding of the work required to achieve a level of maintenance even as the client commits to making significant life changes (Cooper, 2012).

Kimberly Calderwood (2011) notes that this model is particularly useful in counseling. "It offers an evidence-based, common-sense approach to human motivation that many therapists find reassuring and comforting," and Calderwood writes that the authors' claim that this model can support "consciousness raising, social liberation (external forces), emotional arousal (also called dramatic release, dramatic relief, or catharsis), self-reevaluation (reappraisal of the problem and the clients' self-assessment toward the end of the process), self-liberation (also called commitment, occurring when the individual accepts responsibility for change), counterconditioning (or countering for learning healthier responses), environmental control (client changing his or her environment), rewards (or reinforcement management), eliciting helping relationships (other than professionals), and stimulus control (reducing triggers and enhancing healthier alternatives)."

The transtheoretical stages of change model describes a relationship to change that includes precontemplation, contemplation, preparation, action, and maintenance and although "the stages were initially and extensively applied to changing health behaviors, this model has also proven useful in conceptualizing and guiding the change that occurs in psychotherapy" (Norcross, Krebs, and Prochaska, 2011). I will describe the stages and how they may play out in therapy here:

Precontemplation

Precontemplation implies that the client does not know, care, or understand the need for change; in other words, he or she is "pre" (before) "contemplation" (thinking about it). Others in the client's life may be well aware of the problem and anxious for the client to start on his or her movement toward change. Stressors in therapy with elders at this stage can be related to independence, where a client may feel he or she is doing fine living on his or her own, but the client's family may have other thoughts about driving or self-care. The role of the therapist at this stage is to support the client in considering that there may be a reason to be in therapy, and there may be a problem of which they are aware or underaware.

Contemplation

Contemplation is the stage where the client begins to develop awareness that there may actually be a problem to consider. This is not a stage where action begins, but rather a stage where emotions attached to the change needed will need to be addressed. Fear, loss, and a sense of overwhelming, all can occur at this stage. The therapist's best strategy is to normalize the client's fears, and begin a conversation about how the client might continue to work toward change despite these strong feelings. At this stage, clients are not yet changing, but thinking about the effort that change may entail.

Preparation

When the client transitions into preparation, he or she is embarking on the initial stages of experimenting with change. This is a stage of action, where small steps might be made toward a larger life transition. In this stage, the therapist and the client together might outline small experiments of change and discuss how they went, using successes and failures as points of interest to learn from, while the client continues to move into a more broad base of change. Humor and candor around successes and failures can support positive momentum.

Action

Family members of the client often hope for action, the fourth stage, much earlier in the process. Reminding others that change is a process and that action toward change takes time is crucial for successful change. At this stage, the client is engaged in an active process toward changing behavior and circumstance, and support and recognition of the effort the client takes will help the therapeutic relationship.

Maintenance

Maintenance is no less active than the action stage. Maintenance requires the attention of the therapist and the client to celebrate the gains of change and prevent relapse or slipups as the client settles into a new way of being or a new life circumstance.

The authors of this model note that these stages offer a framework of when people change (later in the process than you might expect, and with greater effort) but not necessarily how. As the name implies, they suggest a transtheoretical model of support at each of these stages, as the client may need different interventions at different times for different reasons. They note that:

> Change processes traditionally associated with the experiential, cognitive, and psychoanalytic persuasions are most useful during the earlier precontemplation and contemplation stages. Change processes traditionally associated with the existential and behavioral traditions, by contrast, are most useful during action and maintenance, as well as a variety of interventions modes at different stages; consciousness raising in the earlier stages of change to help clients progress from precontemplation to contemplation, focus on process to increase awareness of the advantages of changing and the multiple benefits of psychotherapy, managing emotional arousal to work with strong affective responses, and self-reevaluation to help patients increase their motivation for change." (Norcross, Krebs, and Prochaska, 2011)

In later stages, the client can reap emotional benefits from successes, as well as replace negative with positive behavioral and reward elements, for instance "assertion to counter passivity, relaxation to replace anxiety, cognitive substitutions instead of negative thinking, and exposure to counter avoidance" (Norcross, Krebs, and Prochaska, 2011). The therapist in the maintenance stage can work with the client to provide internal opportunities to reinforce positive change and appreciate the fruits of their labor. This stage can include an end to the therapeutic relationship where the client is able to self-support in his or her new life circumstances.

The authors, in a meta-analysis of their own theory, provide these guidelines for practitioners (pp. 151–152):

- Assess the client's stage of change and tailor treatment accordingly.
- Beware treating all patients as though they are in action; allow for patience through the contemplative and precontemplative stages (40% are in precontemplation, 40% in contemplation, and only 20% prepared for action).
- Set realistic goals by moving one stage at a time. Help patients break out of the chronic, stuck phase of precontemplation and to see this movement as a treatment success, because it almost doubles the chances that patients will continue toward effective action.
- Treat precontemplators gingerly with kindness and patience. Your impatience with their process is likely to drive them away.
- Tailor the interventions and approaches and relational choices to the client's present stage; allow for an integrative practice, that is stage sensitive and tailored to the client's needs and process at each stage.
- Anticipate recycling, as this model, like all others, is not necessarily linear; allow for a humanistic understanding that clients may relapse to earlier thoughts and actions; meet them (and yourself) with compassion at these moments.

In all cases and at all stages, the therapist can support the client as educator, coach, and cheerleader, bringing deep compassion to the obstacles to change and the intrinsic rewards of change acceptance. Working with aging clients requires a deft hand. Changes may include an acceptance of loss, and that grief and loss of freedom are part of the aging process.

Conclusion

Providing mental health and emotional support for older clients and their family may challenge traditional approaches in case conceptualization and demand a change in clinical strategy from an expansion of life's opportunities to a mindful acceptance of the limitations of older age. As the American population ages, the individual therapist might be the first supporter in client care, or part of a treatment team to support the complexity of client and caregiver care. A strategic and organized view of client care should incorporate the goals and flow of a particular case (case management), situating the clients in their own life journey (Maslow's hierarchy), exploring aspects of grief and loss such as the loss of independence (Kübler-Ross), and the complexities of working with acceptance of change both as an individual and as a member of a family system (transtheoretical model). These tools and lenses can help the therapist better understand the complexities of later life stages, and navigate the challenges to client care.

References

ACL. (2015, October 8). "'No Wrong Door' System Grants Help Streamline Access to Services and Supports." ACL Administration for Community Living. Accessed August 13, 2017. https://www.acl.gov/news-and-events/announcements-latest-news/acl-no-wrong-door-system-grants-help-streamline-access.

Administration on Aging. (2016, May 25). "A Profile of Older Americans: 2015." Accessed January 28, 2017. https://www.acl.gov/sites/default/files/Aging%20and%20Disability%20in%20America/2015-Profile.pdf.

American Psychological Association. (2014). "Guidelines for Psychological Practice with Older Adults." *American Psychologist, 69*(1), 34–65. doi:10.1037/a0035063.

Balboni, T. A., Paulk, M. E., Balboni, M. J., Phelps, A. C., Loggers, E. T., Wright, A. A., . . . and Prigerson, H. G. (2009). "Provision of Spiritual Care to Patients with Advanced Cancer: Associations with Medical Care and Quality of Life Near Death." *Journal of Clinical Oncology, 28*(3), 445–452. doi:10.1200/jco.2009.24.8005.

Calderwood, K. A. (2011). "Adapting the Transtheoretical Model of Change to the Bereavement Process." *Social Work, 56*(2), 107–118.

California, T. S. (2010). "What Should I Know about Elder Abuse?" http://www.calbar.ca.gov/Public/Pamphlets/ElderAbuse.aspx.

Cooper, S. (2012). *Change: Models and Processes.* Springfield: Charles C. Thomas.

Gawande, Atul. (2014). *Being Mortal.* New York: Metropolitan Books.

Korte, J., Bohlmeijer, E. T., Cappeliez, P., Smit, F., and Westerhof, G. J. (2011). "Life Review Therapy for Older Adults with Moderate Depressive Symptomatology: A Pragmatic Randomized Controlled Trial." *Psychological Medicine, 42*(06), 1163–1173. doi:10.1017/s0033291711002042.

Kübler-Ross, Elisabeth, and Byock, Ira. (2014) *On Death and Dying: What the Dying Have to Teach Doctors, Nurses, Clergy and Their Own Families.* New York: Scribner, a Division of Simon & Schuster.

Maslow, A. H. (1943). "A Theory of Human Motivation." *Psychological Review, 50,* 370–396.

McLeod, S. A. (1970, January 1). *Defense Mechanisms.* http://www.simplypsychology.org/defense-mechanisms.html.

Newman, Sally, and Brummel, Steven W. (1989). *Intergenerational Programs: Imperatives, Strategies, Impacts, Trends.* New York: Haworth Press.

Norcross, J. C., Krebs, P. M., and Prochaska, J. O. (2011). "Stages of Change." *Journal of Clinical Psychology, 67*, 143–154. doi:10.1002/jclp.20758.

Okereke, O. I. (2015). *Prevention of Late-Life Depression: Current Clinical Challenges and Priorities.* New York/Cham: Springer International Publishing.

Ory, M. G., and Smith, M. L. (2015). "Research, Practice, and Policy Perspectives on Evidence-Based Programing for Older Adults." *Frontiers in Public Health, 3*, 136. doi:10.3389/fpubh.2015.00136.

Parker, Kim, and Patton, Eileen. (2013, January 30). "The Sandwich Generation." *Pew Research Center: Social & Demographic Trends.* Accessed February 7, 2017. doi:10.4324/9781315805221.

Perry, Matt. (2012, May 13). "The Health Perils of Aging: Lonely and Sick." California Health Report. Accessed February 7, 2017. http://www.calhealthre port.org/2012/05/13/the-health-perils-of-aging-lonely-and-sick/.

Prochaska, J. O., and DiClemente, C. C. (1983). "Toward a Comprehensive Model of Change." *Treating Addictive Behaviors, 51*(3), 3–27. doi:10.1007/978-1-4613-2191-0_1.

Reynolds, C. F., III (2015). "Prevention of Major Depression: A Global Priority." In O. I. Okereke (Ed.), *Prevention of Late-Life Depression: Current Clinical Challenges and Priorities* (pp. 1–4). New York/Cham: Springer International Publishing.

Sheehy, G. (1995). *New Passages: Mapping Your Life across Time.* New York: Random House.

Sheehy, G. (2010). *Passages in Caregiving: Turning Chaos into Confidence.* Detroit: Gale, Cengage Learning.

Singh, Ankura, and Okereke, O. I. (2015). "Health Policy and Economic Aspects of Late-Life Depression Prevention." In O. I. Okereke (Ed.), *Prevention of Late-Life Depression: Current Clinical Challenges and Priorities* (pp. 135–152). New York/Cham: Springer International Publishing.

Substance Abuse and Mental Health Services Administration. (2011). *The Treatment of Depression in Older Adults: Practitioners Guide for Working with Older Adults and Depression.* HHS pub. No. SMA-11–4631. Rockville, MD: Center for Mental Health Services, Substance Abuse and Mental Health Services Administration, U.S. Department of Health and Human Services.

Substance Abuse and Mental Health Services Administration. (2016, March 2). *Age- and Gender-Based Populations.* Accessed January 3, 1017. https://www .samhsa.gov/specific-populations/age-gender-based.

Walker, Edwin L. (2016, November 7). "Take Care to Give Care: ACL's Mission to Support Families and Family Caregivers." Administration for Community Living. Accessed January 28, 2017. https://www.acl.gov/news-and-events/ acl-blog/take-care-give-care-acls-mission-support-families-and-family-caregivers.

Adjusting to Illness: A Couple's Story

Alexandra Kennedy

Leslie, a warm, expressive retired nurse in her sixties, consulted with me a year before her husband Robert joined her in therapy. As a nurse, she well understood the signs of stress as she struggled to support her husband with his diagnosed Parkinson's disease. For eight months, I have been working with the couple to explore many themes pertinent to an aging couple embracing a degenerative illness: self-care, family concerns/conflicts, unresolved issues in family relationships, care-giving issues, grief, fears of the unknown, limiting concepts of dying and illness, old traumas that prevented the flow of life in the present, self-forgiveness, and acceptance of what is. In our sessions together, we explored many themes in a rapidly changing family system: communication, self-care, care-giving issues, family conflict, grief, trauma, and fear of the unknown, among many others. As this might help other therapists in their work with aging couples, they enthusiastically gave me their permission to share their story, with the understanding that I would change some identifying details.

The Emotional Impact of Degenerative Disease

Parkinson's is a degenerative disorder of the central nervous system. Early on, the motor system is affected—with shaking, slowness of movement, and difficulty walking. Later cognitive and behavioral problems may arise, sometimes involving dementia, depression, and hallucinations. At this point, Leslie's husband was in the early stages. In the course of our therapy, he would exhibit all these symptoms—along with difficulty concentrating, sleeping, excessive guilt, anxiety, and panic attacks.

For several months, Leslie and I focused our sessions on self-care as she faced the harsh reality of her husband's cognitive and physical decline. She had already educated herself about the disease. Since Parkinson's disease is a progressive disorder, she faced a long period of caring for her husband—with care-giving becoming more intense and demanding as her husband became less capable of functioning on his own. She understood that there would be periods of gradual decline, periods of rapid degeneration, and periods of relative stability—it was challenging to face a disease with so much unknown about how it would unfold. Indeed now each day was unpredictable with her husband—she never knew what she would be dealing with as she cared for him. Even as she felt overwhelmed at times by the enormity of what she was facing, she felt committed to giving her husband a good quality of life. They had had a good marriage with much enjoyment of and respect for one another; both partners have a strong sense of humor, which has served them well.

Self-care for Leslie involved taking time to nurture herself and relax. It was also important at this stage not to put her life on hold—so we identified the most meaningful parts of her daily life that she needed to keep making time for, such as seeing friends. As more and more of the household maintenance fell on her shoulders, she worked on setting up realistic goals and coping strategies for herself while exploring who in the family would be available to assist in providing care. I proposed creating and using a sanctuary, a technique I've developed and used with many grieving clients (Kennedy, 2014, p. 33) for just 10–20 minutes a day, a safe space to daily check in with herself, embrace whatever inner experiences and feelings were arising that day, and grieve the loss of her life as she had known it. These initial sessions helped her adjust to the demands of this stage of her husband's illness; she then took the next months to integrate what we had explored together.

I find poetry to be a great source of inspiration and insight as I work with clients who are struggling with illness, trauma, or grief. At this time I gave Leslie a 2008 poem "For a Friend on the Arrival of an Illness" by Irish poet John O'Donohue to share with her husband. In the poem, O'Donohue proposes that illness can be a "dark invitation" that takes you into new territory beyond anything you would expect. He then offers a prayer that as shock subsides and a new balance is restored, you accept the illness "as a teacher who has come to open your life to new worlds" and that you can discover within a brave reception to what is "difficult, painful and unknown."

This poem invited Robert and Leslie to reframe their relationship to his illness, to see this deeply challenging experience as an opportunity for expansion and growth.

Expanding the Therapeutic Circle

Several months later, her husband Robert asked to join her for couples therapy. He was a strong, hardworking, self-sufficient man in his mid-sixties who was the patriarch of his extended family; he took that responsibility very seriously, often to the exclusion of his own feelings and needs. As soon as he sat down in my office, he wanted to share a powerful dream he had had a few months before. In this dream, he was falling through a tunnel—it felt like he was dying. And then he heard the words: "You've done well. Others will take up after you." I listen closely to the dreams my clients share with me, as these often offer guidance as to what the unconscious is bringing to attention so that healing can take place. From this dream, it was clear that Robert was preparing for his death and that he needed to know that he had "done well"—to hear this in the dream was greatly comforting to him, as he often suffered from regrets and self-recrimination in looking back at his life. Furthermore it was comforting that others would carry what he no longer could. It was clear from his dream that he would need at some point in our therapy a review of his life's accomplishments. Erik Erikson, developmental psychologist known for his theory on psychosocial development of human beings, defines this review as an important task in old age (Erikson, 1998).

In our first session, we identified their goals for therapy. Robert wanted to explore his feelings around the progression of his disease, along with his worries and fears about how the illness had changed their relationship as a couple. He felt he needed to grieve the cognitive, physical, and social losses through the illness as well as grieve lost family members. He wanted to address his isolation and learn how to embrace the unknown. Leslie's goals focused on her continued self-care and concerns about Robert's isolation. She needed to feel free to pursue her own social life and was increasingly concerned that Robert was left alone and isolated in their house (isolation is a big issue for people who have Parkinson's disease). She wanted them to create a plan for regular lunch dates with his male friends; this would provide the needed stimulation for Robert.

The next sessions were difficult for both as the cognitive aspects of the disease (such as memory loss and disorientation) were showing up. Robert had trouble following through with his phone calls (it was now difficult for him to use a phone or the computer). Leslie proposed ways she could help but he resisted her help as he was so used to being self-sufficient. On her side, Leslie got frustrated that the weeks went by with so little progress in Robert reaching out to friends. Finally through persistent communication about this issue and experimenting with different approaches with kindness and compassion, slowly progress was made and Robert began to get out more—not just with friends but to swimming class, yoga, support groups, church, and the like. We also explored and evaluated his personal relationships; family, friends, and community resources that would be available to them currently and as the illness progressed.

Acceptance of Life's Challenges

Acceptance of what is became an important theme we explored together in our sessions. Leslie acknowledged that she needed to move toward acceptance that she could not now get everything done that was on her to-do list; she was constantly disappointed with herself for letting things go. She had dropped many projects, papers were piling up on her desk, and their house needed cleaning and repairs. Robert wanted to come to an acceptance of the changes in his body; he was now going through a period of more rapid cognitive and physical decline that both he and Leslie noticed. They likened it to dropping many floors in an elevator.

Since both Robert and Leslie were receptive to guided meditations, I wove several into our sessions. These provided a way for them to share space together while focusing within. I find Stephen Levine's meditations to be very helpful in gaining a direct experience of the states of being we were talking about in therapy—such as compassion for oneself, self-forgiveness, staying present, and so on. Stephen Levine, an author, poet, and teacher, is best known for his work in death and dying; his books include *Gradual Awakening* and *Who Dies?* (Levine, 1991). Robert found the self-forgiveness meditations to be particularly useful, as he had always been very hard on himself. Both Leslie and Robert recorded these meditations on their iPhones so they could listen to them at home. An important part of my work as a psychotherapist is to empower clients with tools so they can continue their work at home. This way our work in the session can become grounded in their everyday life.

To help them relax into just this moment as it is, I guided them through Stephen Levine's soft belly meditation (Levine, 1991, p. 37):

Begin to soften the belly.
Make room for the breath in the belly . . .
Allow the breath to breathe itself in soft belly . . .

Let it all float in soft belly . . .
Expectation, judgment, doubt . . .
Softening allows them to disperse, to dissolve in soft belly.
Pains, fears, doubts dissolving into softness,
the spaciousness of merciful belly..

Levine's soft belly meditation was also helpful to me in our sessions. Working with aging clients struggling with degenerative diseases can be challenging to us as therapists, triggering our own fears and anxieties around disease, care-giving, death, and loss. As a new psychotherapist in the 1970s, I had the grace of Stephen Levine's presence in my life as a teacher and mentor. I meditated with him weekly and attended his death and dying retreats—these served me well in embracing my mortality and learning to stay present in my body with uncomfortable states. When I'm working with clients in challenging situations that might trigger my own fears, staying present in my own body keeps me grounded and ready to respond to what is called for in each moment. I can then access a deeper wisdom within each situation. As Martin Buber wrote: "In spite of all similarities, every living situation has, like a newborn child, a new face that has never come before and will never come again. It demands of you a reaction that cannot be prepared beforehand. It demands nothing of what is past. It demands presence, responsibility; it demands you" (Buber, 1961, p. 135).

Making Peace

At this point, we began to interweave individual sessions with the couple sessions. When I combine couple work with individual sessions, I assure both partners that anything they share with me in individual sessions will be held in confidence; if a partner wants to explore any issue discussed in a private session, he or she will need to bring that up in the couple sessions. I will only combine these two modes of therapy if both partners and myself as therapist are comfortable with the situation.

In his individual sessions, Robert made a list of the family members (both deceased and alive) where he felt unresolved—relationships plagued with regrets, anger, resentment, or a lack of forgiveness. He wanted to feel at peace in these relationships, even if it was just within himself. After he prioritized the people on his list, I suggested he take one person at a time and write a letter to each that he would not send (Kennedy, 2001, pp. 71–88). This letter-writing exercise involves expressing whatever has been held back in the relationship. Without editing his thoughts or feelings, he was encouraged to write what he appreciated resented, regretted, wanted to let go of, or carry on in the relationship. He was to let it flow and see where the letter took him. Robert also expressed a need at this time to review his life accomplishments—the first dream he had shared with me brought this to his attention; while he had been told in the dream that he had done well, he was still hard on himself.

As he started writing these letters, Robert felt the impact of posttraumatic stress disorder (PTSD) from the unexpected and tragic deaths of two close family members. He had needed to set aside his own feelings after these deaths in order to perform as a responsible family patriarch. As he described these situations in detail, it became clear to both of us that the impact of this trauma on his nervous system might have contributed to the onset of Parkinson's. I told him about EMDR (eye movement desensitization and reprocessing), a psychotherapy treatment I've been trained in and use regularly in my sessions. Developed by Francine Shapiro, EMDR therapy facilitates the accessing and processing of traumatic memories through therapist-directed lateral eye movements in brief sequential cycles (Shapiro, 2012). As the trauma is freed up and processed by the nervous system, more adaptive information can be utilized. After the EMDR sessions, Robert reported that he felt a heavy weight lift from his shoulders.

At the same time Robert was processing his feelings regarding his decline, Leslie's individual sessions focused on her grief; her best friend was moving away, which was a devastating blow to her support system. This also accentuated her grief about the lack of support from family. With increased responsibility for her husband (he was now exhibiting more disorientation and memory issues along with hallucinations), Leslie was feeling burned out, trapped, and overwhelmed. She felt ashamed that she had to ask for help and realized this was getting in the way of receiving the help she so needed at this point. We traced this pattern back to her childhood. She made a commitment to ask several friends for help; we discussed options for care for Robert as well as her household maintenance and finances that would alleviate the stress she was experiencing. Also, estate issues needed to be managed, as Robert was no longer able to handle this as he had. I encouraged her to explore other more long-term possibilities for care. However at this point, she was not open to thinking much about other options than living in their home. I brought up the subject, saw her reluctance to discuss it, and then let it go. At this time, we also explored Leslie taking some time away (a night or two) from Robert to replenish her energy; she explored several options. She acknowledged that it was important for her to take periodic breaks from care-giving.

Couple sessions at this time turned toward issues arising with a few family members. Some relationships with their adult children were draining their energy and resources; these relationships needed to be reassessed and concerns communicated, with new priorities identified and boundaries set. All this brought up Robert's grief over the unresolved issues in many of these family relationships—and his need for self-forgiveness. He continued to work on his letters; as using a pen and computer were difficult, we explored other options—such as speaking into a tape recorder.

Coming to Terms with Mortality

In one of our sessions (and after a difficult visit with his doctor), Robert shared that he was having a number of what he called "mortality dreams." This initiated a discussion about his concepts of what his life should look like when he died. He expected everything to be neatly taken care of so that his wife would have no "messy" estate issues to deal with. The idea that dying had to do more with a process of letting go and that things would inevitably be left undone was a new concept for him. To further explore the letting go aspect of dying, I guided them both through one of Stephen Levine's dying meditations. I had told Robert about this dying meditation weeks before but it wasn't until this session that he seemed ready to explore it. The recent mortality dreams seemed to lead the way, suggesting that it was time for him to explore what dying could be.

In this dying meditation, you let go of your last breath, then your body, your name, your family, and your thoughts as you expand into the vast spaciousness of your true nature. "Take each breath as though it was the last. The end of a lifetime. The last breath. Let each breath go, finally and forever . . . Let go of your name. Let go of your face. Let go of your reputation. Float free into vastness. Leave the body behind. Merging with space, vast, boundaryless, space, expanding into space. Such enormous peace . . . Let go into that spaciousness. Hold nowhere. Let go completely. Die gently into the light. Floating free in vast space" (Levine, 1991, pp. 310–315). When Robert opened his eyes, he felt energy streaming through his body and a deep sense of peace. He seemed genuinely relieved that dying could be this expansive.

A couple of weeks later when they returned, both reported that Robert was in a much more stable phase of his illness. His mental clarity, relaxed demeanor, and perky energy were noticeable to me. He told me that he no longer obsessed about the traumatic deaths of the two family members; when he closed his eyes and thought about them, his body did not contract as it used to. I wondered if the EMDR sessions had helped with this change in his condition. He then shared a dream in which he was working as the leader on a company project. He felt very effective in this position—and then noticed that he was completely naked. However, he had no reaction to this state—he just went ahead with the project full steam ahead. As he progressed with the project, certain pieces of clothing would show up—a pair of pants here, a shirt there, and so on. The lack of shame in this dream stood out, as this was a feeling that he often struggled with. In the dream he was stripped down to the bare bones, much as the disease had done. The dream seemed to be showing him that, as long as he didn't get hijacked by his old reaction of shame, he still could act effectively. Needed resources (as represented by the pieces of clothing in the dream) could then appear in the flow of life.

Leslie was feeling much less stressed; she spoke about feeling a sense of peace in her acceptance of their situation. From both their reports, it seemed clear that they were moving toward establishing more equilibrium in their family system. It helped that she had recently had an epiphany about who would care for Robert if something happened to her (one of her big concerns)—that family member had graciously accepted without hesitation. She also had a clear idea of where she would go if both she and her husband needed care. This was a huge relief; she noted that the answer to this dilemma came in its own time. Indeed both Leslie and Robert were exhibiting a trust in the flow of healing that was revealing itself both in our sessions and in their daily lives. At this point, our therapy together continues; however they have integrated much of our work into their daily lives so that they are coming in for sessions every couple of weeks, rather than the intense weekly sessions from the months before.

The Role of the Therapist

My work as a therapist is to stay present, grounded in my body, and alert to moments I was getting triggered, while needing to make adjustments to the flow of therapy as Robert's disease progressed. As certain issues in this situation are so difficult and challenging to face, timing becomes increasingly important, as to when and how to approach them. I might bring up an issue—and then need to let it go until the time was right (e.g., the dying meditation for Robert and long-term care options for Leslie). As we created a healing environment that fostered intimacy, trust, openness, curiosity, humor, and compassion, I've brought a number of resources as needed into our sessions: reflective listening, coping strategies, creating a sanctuary to grieve losses, writing letters to process unresolved issues in relationships, guided meditations (self-forgiveness, breathing/soft belly, dying), life review, mindfulness practices to bring attention to the present moment, dreamwork for feedback from the unconscious, EMDR to heal past traumas, and poetry for inspiration and new perspectives, among others. As John O'Donohue (2008) so eloquently expressed in his poem, Robert and Leslie are indeed learning to embrace what is "difficult, painful and unknown" and see how this illness can open their life into new worlds.

Many of the techniques involving grief in this case study are explored in more depth in my books *Honoring Grief* (2014) and *The Infinite Thread: Healing Relationships beyond Loss* (2001).

References

Buber, M. *Between Man and Man*. London: Rutledge, 1961.

Erikson, Erik H. *The Life Cycle Completed*. London: W.W. Norton & Company, 1998.

Kennedy, Alexandra. *Honoring Grief: Creating a Space to Let Yourself Heal*. Berkeley, CA: New Harbinger, 2014.

Kennedy, Alexandra. *The Infinite Thread: Healing Relationships beyond Loss*. Hillsboro, OR: Beyond Words Publishing, 2001.

Levine, Stephen. *Guided Meditations, Explorations, and Healings*. New York: Anchor Books, 1991.

O'Donohue, J. *To Bless the Space between Us: A Book of Blessings*. New York: Doubleday, 2008.

Shapiro, Francine. *Getting Past Your Past: Take Control of Your Life with Self-help Techniques from EMDR Therapy*. Emmaus, PA: Rodale Books, 2012.

A Life in Review: Sylvia's Journey

Kathy Langsam

Two years licensed, with adequate family therapy experience and education, based on treating numerous families as a marriage and family therapist (MFT) trainee, MFT intern, and licensed MFT, in addition to a family therapy concentration in my master's program in clinical psychology, I was still not prepared for the family that entered the therapy room of the community-based agency where I was working:

Sylvia, 83-year-old matriarch, her four adult children—Elizabeth (58), Susan (56), Alan (53), and Jennifer (43)—and three adult grandchildren (Susan's daughters)—Nicole (37), Erin (35), and Michelle (34).

Although the following family members were not physically present, their impact was felt throughout the course of family therapy:

- Sylvia's two deceased husbands whom she divorced
- Ten current and former spouses and partners of adult children and adult grandchildren
- Four additional grandchildren, ages 5–25
- Five great-grandchildren, ages 5–12

I realized very quickly that the family system was as complex as Sylvia's 83 years. For both her and me, the therapeutic process was to break down her life story and explore the following questions:

- When do once positive family members' roles, responsibilities, and boundaries become negative, causing the family to be in conflict and at an impasse?
- How do historical events and culture influence those factors?

During the intake session with Sylvia, she described the presenting problem as extreme discord in the family, stemming from allegations of inappropriate sexual touch by Nicole's husband, Hasan, on Sophie, age 5, daughter of Alan.

Sophie was receiving therapy, along with her parents, Alan and his former partner, Nancy. Child Protective Services was involved with the family; Hasan was prohibited from being around Sophie, which, in reality, extended to all of the young grand and great-grandchildren.

Sylvia easily identified her goals for family therapy: repair the rift between various family members and help her navigate through the "pull" to choose sides and believe her granddaughter's allegations of sexual abuse versus her adult granddaughter's defense of her husband's behavior. I recall thinking about the term "loyalty conflict," a situation that arises in families when two members disagree with or dislike each other, and each expects a third member to support them over the other. Although usually associated with children of divorce/separation who are caught between their parents' conflict and children and parents in blended families who often have divided loyalties between their first and second families, somehow it seemed to fit this 83-year-old woman's current situation.

Sylvia presented as a well-educated, intelligent, and articulate woman, speaking with a slight accent, walking assisted by the use of a cane. She was white, from an Eastern European, Jewish background. It was during our work together over the span of six months that I learned of her journey.

Family Therapy Sessions

We began family sessions after the initial individual intake session. My initial impression is what Salvador Minuchin would describe this family as *enmeshed* (Minuchin, 1974, pp. 54–56, 242). All except the oldest daughter lived in the community; most worked and/or were supported by the family real estate business that Sylvia founded. Family gatherings were a weekly occurrence, centering upon Sylvia's large home in the community.

At times, there were all nine of us in a very small therapy room. Heated discussions ensued without even touching upon the subject of the sexual allegation. The mere mention of Hasan's name ignited yelling by Nicole, Erin, and Michelle directed at Alan and Sylvia. I tried unsuccessfully to reduce the volume and redirect the anger into a useful conversation. I was later told that agency staff could hear these arguments and had safety concerns, prompting the executive director to stand outside the door of the therapy room. Although I never felt concerned for safety, I definitely felt powerless to create a shift in the family's dynamics.

Other therapy sessions revealed patterns of deep-seated conflict between Elizabeth and Susan and a "cutoff" between Elizabeth and Jennifer; essentially no relationship. The adult grandchildren seemed to resent Sylvia's current relationship with younger grandchildren and great-grandchildren.

It quickly became apparent that the discord among the family members went deeper than the presenting problem and had been in place for some time. But what was the origin of loyalty conflicts, jealousy, spite, and resentments?

Individual Sessions

After eight family sessions, I felt stuck and frustrated. I tried different constellations with varying members present: entire family, Sylvia and her children, and Sylvia and her adult grandchildren. Nothing worked; it seemed like these sessions were replicating the family chaos, perhaps even making it worse.

I conferred with Sylvia privately and shared my impression that we were at an impasse with the family work. I suggested individual work with her to provide support and solutions to navigate the current situation. She agreed with my appraisal and recommendation.

Genogram

Creating genograms with clients has always been a touchstone for me, with the goal to create a shared understanding of the client's family of origin and a road map forward.

Over the period of a month, Sylvia shared her life story; I transferred the information into the genogram format (McGoldrick and Gerson, 1985). The final product was four generations of history contained on a 3' × 2' sheet of paper.

Sylvia's story began in Germany, with her growing up in an affluent Jewish family, the middle child with an older brother and a younger sister. By the time that Jews were being sent to concentration camps, Sylvia was married to her first husband, Joseph. He also was from an affluent German Jewish family. They had two young daughters: Elizabeth, age 2, and Susan, 8 months. In order to spare their lives, the children were sent to live with house servants (non-Jews), and Sylvia and her husband hid in the woods for a few months. The family was reunited in England and ultimately immigrated to the United States in the late 1950s. Sylvia's and Joseph's families followed them to England and the United States. Alan was born in England, despite Joseph not wanting a third child. Sylvia said she was the driving force for leaving Germany, and aiding her husband in gaining independence from his family. She commented that she also helped her second husband gain independence from his family as well.

Sylvia described her marriage to Joseph as "battered wife syndrome," experiencing physical and psychological abuse (Walker, 1979). Throughout their marriage, there were numerous separations, and ultimately a divorce and reconciliation one year prior to Joseph's death. She also labeled him as having borderline personality disorder. Elizabeth and Susan were immediately sent to boarding school upon his death.

Within one month of Joseph's passing, Sylvia met and a few months later married her second husband, Henry. He was also from a German Jewish background. This was Henry's third marriage; he had abandoned his daughter from his first marriage when he entered into his second marriage. He insisted that Alan also go to boarding school. Despite being sent to boarding school, Alan considered Henry as his father. After one year of marriage, Sylvia gave birth to her youngest daughter, Jennifer. She was never sent to boarding school.

Sylvia described her 16-year marriage to Henry as combative, resulting in a high-conflict divorce in terms of custody of Jennifer and their financial settlement. At age 57, Sylvia was confronted with being concerned over finances for the first time in her life. She quickly rebounded and built a successful real estate business, which established financial security for herself and her family.

With financial security, Sylvia helped both Susan and Alan establish their own small businesses. When Susan was establishing her small business, Sylvia was very involved in rearing Susan's three young daughters, often being more in a mother's role as opposed to a grandmother's role. Susan's daughters currently work in this small business. Alan and Jennifer continued to work with Sylvia in the real estate business that she was actively running on a day-to-day basis.

Life Review and Reminiscence Therapy

The process of Sylvia sharing her story seemed very natural. I asked questions to elicit information about family structure and roles, sibling relationships, couples' relationships, parent–child relationships, relationships among the multigenerations, significant life events, power issues, communication and problem-solving styles, and so on. Genograms have been documented to be beneficial in working with older adults (Erlanger, 1990, p. 329).

> therapeutic benefits such as providing a comfortable forum for working alliances to emerge, empowering clients, examining presenting problems in an intergenerational family context, facilitating a life review, and emphasizing clients' identity as linking figure in both the history and the future of their families . . . genograms help counselors access valuable information for consultation, generate hypotheses related to both problems and solutions, identify strengths and resources. (Magnuson and Shaw 2003, p. 50)

At the time, I was unfamiliar with life review or reminiscence therapy. In his seminal paper, "The Life Review: An Interpretation of Reminiscence in the Aged" (1963), Robert Butler defined "life review" as a normal personal process that older adults evaluate their life as it nears its end. Butler's work extended Erik Erikson's concept of the eight stages of psychosocial development from birth to death. The last stage is known as late adulthood, integrity versus despair, whereby a person believes his or her life has significance and is fulfilled and therefore does not fear death (Lin, Dai, and Hwang, 2003, p. 298; Sandberg, 1999, p. 177). Life review is a spontaneous event especially when the person is confronted by death or a major crisis. Memories, reminiscence, and nostalgia are all part of the process. The goals of the life review may include resolution of past conflicts and issues, atonement for past actions or inaction, and reconciliation with family and friends. This process reinforces the person's strengths and self-esteem and promotes the ability to live in the present.

The term "reminiscence therapy" is often interchangeable with life review. The American Psychological Association defines "reminiscence therapy" as "the use of life histories—written, oral, or both—to improve psychological well-being the therapy is often used with older people" (VandenBos, 2006). In an extensive review of the literature, Lin et al. (2003) concluded that the specific effects of reminiscence therapy are difficult to measure, due to a lack of a standardized operational model (p. 299). Nevertheless, the intervention maybe helpful in maintaining or improving self-esteem and life satisfaction for the elderly.

Countertransference and Supervision

I recall feeling outside my comfort area from the onset of having the case assigned to me. I had no prior experience working with older adults, and actually felt uncomfortable with this population. I questioned what

I had to offer this family, in particular an 83-year-old client who was more than double my age, with a lifetime of experiences! I also learned during our individual sessions that Sylvia was a trained social worker; this only added to my newly licensed insecurities.

I took my older adult stigma and insecurities to my supervisor. My supervisor helped me explore my stigma that older adults can't or won't change, clearly based on my own family of origin issues. She also normalized my "newly licensed" insecurities.

Unbeknownst to Sylvia, she actually helped me in sorting through these issues. We developed a strong therapeutic relationship based on trust and unconditional positive regard, with time; our age difference didn't seem to matter. We joined in finding a solution to the current family dynamics.

Healing and Change

As Sylvia told her story and I created the genogram, we reflected on the patterns that emerged throughout the generations: separations between mother and child, divorce, conflict and cutoff between siblings, sibling rivalry, conflict between aunts/uncle and adult grandchildren, borderline personality disorder (Joseph and Nancy), blurred roles and boundaries, and essentially an enmeshed family system.

Sylvia's training as a social worker certainly helped her identify these patterns and understand their origin. She recognized that despite her independence from her family of origin, her children and adult grandchildren were still very dependent on her emotionally and financially. Both subsystems had not launched! Sylvia was startled by this revelation and was determined to change this dynamic.

And change she did. I recall Sylvia stating that, upon her death, she did not want her family structure to be in its current state. She wanted to "make things right," in terms of rebalancing the relational accounts: charges (hurts) and credits (benefits) accrued by family members over time (Sandberg 1999, pp. 177–178). The first two decisions she made were to sell her large family home and turn over the real estate business to her children. In therapy, we discussed and practiced what she wanted to tell her children and adult grandchildren regarding her feelings about being pulled to take sides in their disputes and her role as a grandmother. She was steadfast in articulating her boundaries.

The children and adult grandchildren were initially shocked with the changes that Sylvia made. Yet over a matter of months, they adapted to the changes and ultimately launched from the family, and some members resolved their conflicts. Sylvia once again relished in her role of being a grandmother to her young grandchildren and great grandchildren.

During the termination phase of therapy, I reflected on her strengths and accomplishments and commitment to her therapeutic goals, including understanding her family's dynamics and highlighting her ability to make changes. She was very gracious in acknowledging our therapeutic relationship and the challenges of the family sessions, and pleased with the family changes. As she left our final session, she gave me a lovely thank-you note and a bookmark. The bookmark is still on my desk these many years later.

Upon reflection, my work with Sylvia reinforced one of the tenets of General Systems Theory—it only takes one member of the family to change, thereby creating a shift within the entire family (von Bertalanffy, 1968).

References

Butler, Robert N. "The Life Review: An Interpretation of Reminiscence in the Aged." *Psychiatry* 26, no. 1 (1963): 65–76. doi:10.1080/00332747.196 3.11023339.

Erlanger, M. A. "Using the Genogram with Older Adult Client." *Journal of Mental Health Counseling* 12, no. 3 (1990): 321–331.

Lin, Y. C., Y. T. Dai, and S. I. Hwang. "The Effect of Reminiscence on the Elderly Population: A Systematic Review." *Public Health Nursing* 20, no. 4 (2003): 297–306.

Magnuson, S., and H. Shaw. "Adaptions of the Multigenerational Genogram in Counseling, Training, and Supervision." *The Family Journal: Counseling and Therapy for Couples and Families* 11, no. 1, 45–54 (2003).

McGoldrick, M., and R. Gerson. *Genograms in Family Assessment.* New York: W. W. Norton & Company, 1985.

Minuchin, S. *Families & Family Therapy.* Cambridge, MA: Harvard University Press, 1974.

Sandberg, Jonathan G. " 'It Just Isn't Fair': Helping Older Families Balance Their Ledgers before the Note Comes Due." *Family Relations* 48, no. 2 (1999): 177. doi:10.2307/585081.

van Bertalanffy, L. *General Systems Theory.* New York: George Braziller, 1968.

VandenBos, G. R. *APA Dictionary of Psychology.* 1st ed. Washington, DC: American Psychological Association, 2006.

Walker, L. *The Battered Woman.* New York: Harper and Row, 1979.

CHAPTER TWO

The Aging Brain: New Frontiers in Neuroscience and Medicine

Gerardo Rodriguez-Menendez

In this chapter, we'll examine how the brain and nervous system change as a function of age. First, an overview of healthy brain functioning is provided, discussing some important areas of the brain. We also discuss how nerve cell communication occurs in the brain and the importance of these cellular transmitters in facilitating our daily human functioning as reflected by memory and learning, planning, and language. Then we discuss how structural changes to these important areas over successive decades in the aging process typically occur and whether these changes might be due to normal senescence (advanced aging) or a disease process. Also discussed are the mechanisms underlying a variety of brain diseases that are commonly found among the elderly including dementia (e.g., Alzheimer's, vascular, and Lewy body disease [LBD]), stroke, and pathologies of movement and sensation (e.g., Parkinson's disease). The latest treatments for these degenerative conditions are described, and helpful resources are provided for the reader to better cope with these conditions. Finally, we explain the most current and exciting findings in neuroplasticity of the brain and best practices that help to prevent an abnormal brain aging process.

Overview of the Brain

The brain has been called the 3-pound universe. Although the human brain is not the largest in the animal kingdom, it is certainly the most powerful. The brain is in many respects "the Final Frontier." The brain is the crowning architectural masterpiece of biologic evolution. The fundamental building block of the brain is the neuron or nerve cell. It is generally accepted that there are over 100 billion nerve neurons in the brain and that over 100,000 synaptic transmissions occur in any given second. The number of possible combinations with 100 billion neurons firing or not is about 10 to the millionth power (equals 1 with million zeros), while in contrast, the number of atoms in the universe is estimated to be about 10 to the eighteenth power (Hanson and Mendius, 2009).

Through an orchestrated dance of neurotransmitter release and receptor interaction, sensation, movement, and thought are possible. Sensation through various modalities leads to cognitive processing and motor responses, thereby resulting in adaptive behavior and, hence, a selective advantage. Humans are the only known species to substantively modify our environment through thought and goal-directed behavior. We alone are able to project ourselves across time into the past, present, and future. The Holy Grail of neuroscience is to locate where consciousness resides. Yet surely, consciousness must be the result of a variety of brain areas and systems working synergistically and simultaneously to provide us with a view of what constitutes reality.

The basic building block of the brain is the mighty neuron or specialized nerve cells that are in turn supported by a cast of glial cells, also called neuroglia. Conceptually, neurons are similar to people. A neuron consists of three basic components: the soma or cell body (i.e., information processing), dendrites for information receipt (i.e., sensation), and an axon terminating in terminal buttons, which provide neurotransmitter secretion (i.e., movement). Think of the dendrites as the head and special senses, the soma as the body, and the axon as the arms and legs. Alone, a single neuron can't do very much. Its resting state is about−70 millivolts, and when conducting a nerve impulse, a peak potential of about +40 millivolts is reached. Yet, when you have a colony of neurons, something magical happens and higher cognitive functions occur, allowing us to feel, see, hear, move, and, most importantly, think. Similarly, think of a human being who has been stranded on a desert island (like in Robinson Crusoe). Alone over, say, a year, a person couldn't accomplish much and the island would be relatively unchanged. However, let there be a colony of people, and over a year's time, there would be remarkable and noticeable changes to the island. Of course, neurons aren't little people (and conversely, people aren't big neurons), but there are certain parallels.

Neurons communicate with one another via neurotransmitter secretion and reception. Neurotransmitters are chemical substances liberated by the terminal buttons of an axon. The total number of neurotransmitters in the body is not known, but well over 100 have been identified. Fortunately, there are a number of key neurotransmitters in the body, which influence functions such as the following:

- Movement
- Memory
- Pleasurable reward
- Behavior and cognition
- Attention and learning
- Sleep and dreaming
- Mood and emotional state
- Learning

Key neurotransmitters include acetylcholine, dopamine, epinephrine, norepinephrine, and serotonin. Additionally, there are several neurotransmitters that are amino acids. For example, glutamate is generally considered the most important transmitter for normal brain functioning, and nearly all excitatory nerve cells are "glutamatergic," with nearly half of all synapses releasing this agent. In contrast, gamma-aminobutyric acid (GABA) is the major inhibitor of neuronal firing in the brain.

Major Dementia Syndromes

Dementia refers to a syndrome, rather than a disease, in that it is a large class of *acquired, persistent* impairments of intellectual functioning that consists of multiple signs that adversely impact our higher levels of cognitive processing (WHO, 2016). Dementia must be distinguished from abrupt disruptions of consciousness (e.g., delirium, substance intoxication, or withdrawal) and from normal forgetfulness during the aging process (i.e., benign senescent forgetfulness). For a diagnosis of dementia, there must be at least three areas of cognitive decline. These cognitive areas are problem solving, memory, language, visual-spatial skills, personality, social functioning, and adaptive daily skills. Dementia is typically age-related, but can begin to occur at any point in life, from childhood through adulthood. As a group, the dementias are attributable to a host of causes: genetic, metabolic, endocrine, autoimmune, malnutrition, substance use, central nervous system (i.e., brain and spinal cord) diseases, tumors, trauma, poisoning, anoxia, and several psychological disorders (or the medications used to treat them). There are a variety of dementias that include, but are not limited to:

- Alzheimer's disease
- Vascular accidents (i.e., stroke)
- Frontotemporal dementia (i.e., Pick's disease)
- LBD
- Parkinson's disease

The dementias are often slowly progressive, and mostly, a confirmatory diagnosis can be provided only through autopsy. Other dementias include those that are caused by head trauma (e.g., chronic traumatic encephalopathy affecting football players) and HIV disease (also known as AIDS Dementia Complex). For purposes of brevity, however, only the most common dementia types are discussed in this chapter.

Estimates of the prevalence of dementia vary considerably by the age group on which the estimates are based. The World Health Organization (WHO) estimates that 47.5 million persons suffer from dementia worldwide, with 7.7 million new cases each year (WHO, 2016). In the United States, about 5.5 million persons suffer from Alzheimer's disease (Alzheimer's Association, 2016a). Mortality from Alzheimer's disease has steadily increased during the last 30 years. Alzheimer's disease is the sixth leading cause of death in the United States. Roughly 7 percent of women and 9 percent of men aged 65 and older will receive a diagnosis of Alzheimer's disease before death, although women are at greater risk for Alzheimer's disease than men. While estimates vary, over the course of their lifetimes, women may be twice as likely to develop Alzheimer's disease as compared to men. African Americans and Latinos experience higher rates of dementia than white mainstream Americans, due to a variety of risk factors (e.g., genetic factors such as autosomal dominant mutations and apolipoprotein E, cardiovascular health, tobacco and alcohol consumption, and low educational attainment) (Alzheimer's Association, 2016a; Qiu, Kivipelto, and von Strauss, 2009).

In recent years, diagnosis and research have increasingly focused on the existence of mild cognitive disorder (MCD) or mild cognitive impairment (MCI). In the past several years, newer classifications (i.e., *DSM 5*) tend to use MCD to contrast the condition from major cognitive disorders (i.e., the dementias proper). In effect, dementia is not an "all or none" phenomenon. That is, dementia doesn't typically develop in an "all of a sudden" manner. Rather, there is a gradual cognitive decline (i.e., loss of intellectual abilities), the precursor of which is MCD. Although MCD is not technically a dementia, it may affect 10–20 percent of persons over 65 years of age. The symptoms of MCD are generally mild. However, it is thought that persons with this condition may be at greater risk for Alzheimer's disease, although a diagnosis is not necessarily followed by a progressive and disabling course. The symptoms of MCI vary and primarily affect memory or fluid thinking skills. A brief description of the major dementia subtypes follows.

Alzheimer's dementia was first discovered by Alois Alzheimer in 1906. It is the most common cause of dementia accounting for 50–80 percent of all dementias. The disease is often referred in the scientific literature as Dementia Alzheimer's Type (DAT). Onset of Alzheimer's disease may be early (before age 65), but more commonly, it occurs after the age of 65. The prevalence of Alzheimer's disease increases with age, affecting approximately one-third (33%) of persons over the age of 80. Women are at greater risk for developing Alzheimer's as compared to men. The disease is also characterized by its course as either uncomplicated, or complicated (i.e., with psychotic features).

Alzheimer's disease is often referred to as a disease characterized by aphasia, apraxia, and agnosia. Aphasia refers to a communication disorder impacting a person's ability to understand or produce language. This disturbance is caused by damage to the brain and does not involve a problem with the senses or movements involved in speech production (e.g., impaired tongue movement resulting in pronunciation difficulties). Apraxia refers to a loss of skilled movements due to brain injury or brain disease. For example, a person with this condition may forget how to use common household implements (e.g., scissors, hammer, and straws). Agnosia refers to an inability to identify and recognize objects that is not due to a visual disturbance. For example, a person can see an object (e.g., an orange or a watch) but is unable to identify the object or know its use.

Generally, three stages of Alzheimer's disease (some models cite 4–7 stages) corresponding to mild, moderate, and severe signs have been identified; but like any stage theory, this sequence varies from person to person. While it is known that persons with Alzheimer's disease have a shorter life expectancy than same-age-matched "normal seniors," the course from onset to death varies considerably and can range from 3 to over 15 years.

Stage 1: Learning is impaired impacting particularly memory, word finding, and spatial abilities. Often individuals experience reduced spontaneity, apathy, irritability, and sadness. The affected person will often realize that his or her ability to think and remember is becoming impaired, often leading to social withdrawal. The individual will often try to use memory aids (e.g., notes or other strategies), but these gradually become ineffective. Family and friends often notice the difficulties being experienced, resulting in heightened self-consciousness and greater social withdrawal. Depression often accompanies and complicates the onset of dementia.

Stage 2: In this stage, the individual continues to experience marked memory and amnestic difficulties, visual-spatial impairment, fluent aphasia, acalculia (loss of mathematical abilities), apraxia, apathy, and restlessness. A person may not be able to remember family members at times, one's address, or what day and date it is (i.e., disorientation for place and time). Hallucinations and delusions may be present, and often the person becomes highly suspicious about the actions of others who may be trying to help. "Sundowning" refers to a greater deterioration of function in the early evening hours (as compared to early day functioning), becoming more evident and problematic over time. Often, individuals in stage 2 are at greater risk for wandering and getting lost.

Stage 3: This stage is characterized by severe intellectual deterioration, motor impairment (e.g., spasticity/rigidity), bowel and bladder incontinence, neurological signs, with structural abnormalities (e.g., ventricular dilation and sulcal enlargement suggestive of neuronal cellular death) becoming very evident. Communication and memory abilities continue to deteriorate to the point that language is severely impaired. Persons become very susceptible to pneumonia and asphyxiation due to lowered immune system functioning and poor swallowing. A person in stage 3 will require 24-hour supervision, may not be able to recognize family and friends, and may eventually adopt a fetal posture. Death invariably follows.

Alzheimer's disease is thought to result from an overproduction of beta-amyloid proteins (resulting in plaques) and neurofibrillary tangles. Although amyloid proteins are normally found in the body, in this case, they abnormally break up and clump together (forming plaques), thereby impairing neural functioning between nerve cells. Neurofibrillary tangles refer to twisted fibers found inside the brain's nerve cells. The tangles result through the breakdown of a key protein called tau, which in the healthy brain is a vital component of a structure called a microtubule. The microtubule helps transport nutrients and other important substances from one part of the nerve cell to another. In this case, however, the microtubules break apart and disintegrate.

Presently, there is no cure for Alzheimer's disease. A variety of medications may be prescribed to help with symptoms. Examples are Aricept, Cognex, Exelon, Namenda, and Razadyne, but often, the results are transitory and patients (or families) will complain of medication side effects (i.e., nausea, diarrhea, muscle cramps, headaches, dizziness, liver toxicity, and seizures). Essentially, the basic mechanism that most of the medications work is through preventing the breakdown of acetylcholine, a neurotransmitter that in the forebrain is associated with attention, learning, and memory. Clinical trials are currently underway to find more effective treatments.

Vascular dementia refers to multi-infarct dementia (MID) or vascular cognitive impairment, and is second only to DAT in frequency, accounting for an estimated 20 percent of all dementias. Vascular dementia is caused by repeated strokes, that is, a sudden-onset cerebrovascular disorder. These are also called "cerebrovascular accidents (CVAs)." Repeated CVAs eventually kill off neurons or myelin, disrupting the interconnectivity of the brain. Strokes often produce "infarcts," or an area of necrotic (dead) tissue due to vascular obstruction. Strokes can co-occur with other dementias, compounding the problems experienced by patients.

In the United States, a person dies from stroke about every 4 minutes. Strokes are the fifth most common neurological illness in the United States and the most common cause of long-term disability. Diet and social factors are known contributors to the incidence of CVAs.

Hypertension is the number 1 risk factor for strokes. Every year, more than 795,000 people in the United States have a stroke. About 610,000 of these are first or new strokes. Strokes cost the United States an estimated $34 billion each year. About 87 percent of all strokes are ischemic, when blood flow to the brain is blocked. The risk of having a first stroke is nearly twice as high for African Americans as compared to whites. African Americans are also more likely to die following a stroke than are whites (Centers for Disease Control, 2016).

In recent years, the concept of "brain attack" has been used to educate the public about the dangers of stroke. This term is being used, given that most persons clearly understand that if a person may be experiencing a heart attack, emergency evaluation and treatment by medical professionals is needed. Hence, most families will rush to an urgent care center or hospital. This is often not the case with strokes, and the tendency is to wait to see if the symptoms improve. Yet, the first minutes to hours after stroke is a time of dramatic and possibly reversible change. Cerebral blood flow is invariably reduced in local brain regions depending on: (a) the distance of the brain region from the stroke epicenter and (b) mechanisms of oxygen and glucose metabolism. Repeated strokes can eventually produce all of the problems of the cortical dementias. But progression of loss is key; unlike Alzheimer's dementia in which loss of cognitive functions occur slowly over time, vascular cognitive impairment progresses in an immediate and stepwise manner. That is to say, the person sustains a stroke and loses some cognitive function, then a second stroke, resulting in the loss of more functions, and so on (i.e., cognitive decline becomes worse with each descending step). The most obvious signs are confusion, disorientation, trouble speaking or understanding speech or writing, and visual loss. These problems appear suddenly (after a CVA) but overall progression is eventually global. CVAs closer to the brainstem or in hypothalamus, basal ganglia, or limbic system produce the most obvious changes. Therefore, progression of loss is highly individual, and not always obvious when CVAs are very small.

Impaired judgment, attention, and word-finding difficulty commonly appear early in the course of MID. Pseudobulbar affect ("bulbar" refers to the medulla/brainstem) with spontaneous laughter, crying, and yelling is not uncommon. Self-concept, mood, social interactions, and occupational function are strongly affected. Depression is highly likely and is worsened by social isolation. Treatment by interdisciplinary groups (i.e., medical, neuropsychological, speech and language, and occupational and physical therapy) is usually provided after the stroke during rehabilitation, but can be of help in slowing the progression of cognitive impairment. However, by far, the best approach for stroke treatment is prevention. By the time the syndrome is recognized, irreversible damage has already occurred. Lowering blood pressure, smoking cessation, better eating habits, exercising more, lowering body weight, and limiting one's amount of alcohol consumption are highly recommended as preventative measures.

LBD is the third most common form of dementia (after DAT and vascular dementias), accounting for 10–24 percent of dementia cases. Alpha-synuclein protein, normally present in brains, aggregates into clusters (Lewy bodies), disrupting neuronal function. This pathology also appears in Parkinson's disease and DAT, but in different patterns. Conversely, DAT pathology appears in LBD as well. Cognitive and memory-related decline occur, but not at first or to the same degree. Confusion and alertness are the more dominant features with LBD. Motor signs are also prominent and frequently include tremors at rest, hunched posture, balance problems, and rigidity. Hallucinations and delusions are also common with difficulty interpreting visual stimuli. Rapid eye movement (REM) sleep phase and autonomic nervous disorders may also be present (e.g., night terrors, blood pressure fluctuations, dizziness, and postural hypotension). The cause of LBD is unknown. Often no family history exists (unlike Parkinson's disease), and no genes have as yet been identified. Moreover, there are no treatments to stop the progression of dementia and mortality occurs as with the other dementias. Aricept and other acetylcholinesterase inhibitors, second-generation antipsychotics (Risperdal, Zyprexa), antidepressants (selective serotonin reuptake inhibitors or monoamine oxidase inhibitors), and clonazepam (Klonopin) help with symptoms only (National Institute on Aging, 2013).

Fronto-temporal Dementia (FTD or Picks' disease) involves a deterioration of the prefrontal and anterior temporal lobe with the presence of

Pick's bodies (or TDP43 protein). This form of dementia is less common than DAT and principally affects younger people between the ages of 45 and 65. Memory and personality are markedly affected, and symptoms occur earlier than with Alzheimer's disease. Spatial orientation is relatively preserved until later, unlike DAT in which disorientation occurs early. Persons with FTD have notable difficulty making sense when speaking and understanding what others say (in DAT this phenomenon occurs later in disease progression). Hallucinations and delusions are common with advanced Alzheimer's disease, but not with FTD. In about one-third of cases, there is a genetic component in disease causation; otherwise, there is no known cause. Cognitive and emotional decline varies markedly from person to person. Irritability and other personality changes can be treated symptomatically with behavioral interventions. Motor problems are dramatic. Amyotrophic lateral sclerosis (Lou Gehrig's disease), corticobasal syndrome, and progressive supranuclear palsy (PSP) can also accompany FTE. The first two conditions produce progressive loss of strength and control of limbs; PSP may also impair eye movement control. Mortality frequently results from skin and lung infections, urinary tract infections, and respiratory failure. Presently, there are no treatments available for this disorder (Association for Frontotemporal Degeneration, 2017).

Parkinson's disease can also result in dementia; onset frequently occurs around the mid-sixties but can develop at any time. In younger individuals, serious neurological problems need to be ruled out. Often patients are first seen for depression, and for the development of tremors at rest, slowness of movement (i.e., bradykinesia), a masklike face (i.e., loss of facial expression), and a short shuffling gait (often termed "Petit Pas"). Memory, concentration, and judgment deficits frequently follow. Micrographic (writing becomes smaller and smaller) and decreased voice volume (i.e., hypo-vocality), sleep disruption, and REM sleep disorder, visual hallucinations, depression, anxiety, and irritability often follow. Parkinson's dementia begins typically about 10 years after the onset of motor movement signs. The earlier the onset of the disease, typically the more aggressive the course and accompanying cognitive decline. Lewy bodies are often present, and MCI is common among patients (even those who do not progress to a debilitating dementia). Treatment with L-dopa can help, but once dementia develops, most treatment is palliative with acetylcholinesterase inhibitors. Treatment with medications, antipsychotics, antidepressants, and Klonopin is common (Alzheimer's Association, 2016b; National Parkinson Foundation, 2017).

Parkinson's disease produces four cardinal signs:

1. Tremor at rest (manifested by "pill-rolling" of fingers, possibly extremities, head, and trunk)
2. Bradykinesia (slowness of movement, especially when starting, shuffling gait, festinating, reduced lateral arm swing)
3. Rigidity ("cogwheeling" effect)
4. Postural instability

Research, Prevention, and Treatment

So, this all sounds like pretty gloomy stuff, right? You might even be thinking that inside your brain there is a ticking time bomb of some type of inevitable dementia or degenerative disorder that is genetically determined, ready to explode, and beyond our ability to control. There was a time in neuroscience that it seemed that this indeed could be the case. However, neuroscience research both in the United States and abroad over the last two decades has resulted in an explosion of new information that suggests that the brain is continually interacting with the environment, and therefore, the manifestation and course of certain neurological disorders can be altered in older individuals. Much of this research centers on the concept of neuroplasticity, which may be defined as the brain's ability to reorganize itself by forming new neural connections throughout the human lifespan. In essence, neuroplasticity allows the brain's neurons and neuronal complexes to compensate for injury and disease by forming new connective patterns in response to new environmental changes. Moreover, such neuronal changes can prevent the occurrence of brain disease. More importantly, this research moves beyond theory and into the realm of our current human condition.

The Alzheimer's Association notes that, "By 2050, the number of people age 65 and older with Alzheimer's disease may nearly triple, from 5.2 million to a projected 13.8 million persons, barring the development of medical breakthroughs to prevent or cure the disease." The operative words in this prognostic statement are, "barring the development of medical breakthroughs to prevent or cure the disease. "For example, findings of the Framingham Heart Study (FHS) suggest that the rate of new cases of dementia may actually be decreasing (Satizabal et al., 2016). FHS participants have been continuously monitored for the occurrence of cognitive decline and dementia since 1975. Thanks to a rigorous collection of information,

FHS researchers have been able to diagnose Alzheimer's disease and other dementias using a consistent set of criteria over the last three decades. The researchers found that there was a progressive decline in incidence of dementia at a given age, with an average reduction of 20 percent per decade since the 1970s, when data were first collected. Similarly, researchers at the University of Michigan, led by Dr. Kenneth Langa, analyzed data on more than 10,500 Health and Retirement Study participants aged 65 or older in 2000 and 2012. The researchers found that the percentage of older U.S. adults with dementia, including Alzheimer's disease, declined from 11.6 percent in 2000 to 8.8 percent in 2012, a decrease of nearly 25 percent (Langa et al., 2017).

Interestingly, both studies found that education was a possible contributor to the decline in dementia incidence. In the University of Michigan study, the decline in incidence was only observed in persons with a high school education and above. Other factors of importance appear to include cardiovascular health and social engagement. For example, it has been widely reported that clinical depression and social isolation are risk factors for the onset of dementia in the elderly. It is also of particular importance to note that international studies (conducted most recently in Denmark, Sweden, and the United Kingdom) are also finding decreases in the incidence of dementia among the elderly, so all of this is good news.

There is also an impressive body of research in genetics that is being revealed through the study of telomeres, which consist of noncoding repeatable segments of DNA found at the ends of our eukaryotic chromosomes, much like protective caps at the end of a cylindrical object (in this case an organic one). Delving down to the inner cellular level, telomere length provides an indication of overall cellular health; the longer our telomeres, the greater probability of more cellular divisions. Therefore, telomere length is an indication of life expectancy. This research has been so instrumental that Dr. Elizabeth Blackburn, along with Dr. Carol Greider and Dr. Jack Szostak, received the Nobel Prize in 2009 in physiology or medicine for their molecular biological research on telomeres and the effect of telomerase, the ribonucleoprotein enzyme that is essential for telomere construction. More recently, Blackburn and her colleague, Dr. Elissa Epel, have published a highly acclaimed book, *The Telomere Effect: A Revolutionary Approach to Living Younger, Healthier, Longer*. The takeaway point here is that just as there is neuroplasticity, there is genetic plasticity (Blackburn and Epel, 2017). We can actually influence the length of our telomeres (and genetic expression) through our daily health habits and lifestyles. In their book, Blackburn and Epel devote much of their efforts to relaying the importance of healthy life habits such as sleep, diet, exercise, and "mindful attention" to telomerase function, and therefore telomere growth and longer life.

Research published by the American Psychological Association notes that the term "mindfulness" has been used to refer to a psychological state of awareness, or a moment-to-moment awareness of one's experience without judgment. Although such mindful practices are associated with several disciplines such as Tai Chi Chuan, Yoga, and meditation, most of the research centers on the benefits of meditation. There is now an immense body of research that has been devoted to studying the effects of meditation on physiological brain functioning. If you think this statement is written in jest, just check out for instance, James H. Austin's massive text, *Zen and the Brain* (Austin, 1998). In fact, since the 1960s, there have been well over 1,000 research publications on meditation, carried out at over 120 universities and research institutions in the United States. Increasingly, meditation is being found to be one of the best ways to reduce anxiety and stress, which is of great importance to telomere health. The benefits of meditation also include reduced mental rumination, improved working memory, better attention, reduced emotional reactivity, greater cognitive flexibility, and increased relationship satisfaction.

Physiologically, meditation appears to have many beneficial effects on health, given that the practice suppresses stress hormones (i.e., norepinephrine, epinephrine, and cortisol), which play an important role in a host of ailments including hypertension, depression, infertility, hot flashes in menopause, and insomnia. More recently, however, meditation is also being shown to have beneficial effects for brain health (i.e., increased release of nitric oxide, a neurotransmitter that helps to repair nerve cells in the brain). These brain effects go well beyond the benefits of stress reduction. For example, Dr. Sara Lazar and her colleagues at Harvard University have found that meditation can produce experience-based *structural* alterations in the brain. They also report having found evidence that meditation may delay atrophy commonly associated with advanced aging in specific areas of the brain associated with attention, learning and memory, self-awareness, emotional regulation, and even compassion, among others. By contrast, areas of the amygdala, a structure of the brain associated with the fight or flight response, were found to have decreased volume in meditation practitioners as compared to control subjects. Most impressively, the benefits of meditation on brain functioning can be measured within 8 weeks! (Schulte, 2015).

Given the advances in the field of neuroradiology and neurophysiology, improvements in measurement and resolution have resulted in a plethora of studies, indicating that meditation is beneficial to brain health. Such studies indicate that in specific brain areas, while matched control subjects display declines in gray matter volume with age, meditators do not show a significant correlation of age-related declines in brain volume. These findings also suggest that the regular practice of meditation may have neuroprotective effects and reduce the cognitive decline associated with normal aging (Brefczynski-Lewis et al., 2007; Green and Bavelier, 2008; Pagnoni and Cekic, 2007). Moreover, research published by T.L. Jacobs and colleagues at the UC Davis Center for Mind and Brain Research found that telomerase activity (remember those telomeres we talked about) was significantly greater in meditation practitioners as compared to controls at the end of a three-month retreat (Jacobs et al. 2011). For more information about the medical benefits of meditation, you can visit the websites of the National Center for Complementary and Alternative Medicine, National Institutes of Health (https://nccih.nih.gov) and the Benson-Henry Institute for Mind Body Medicine at the Massachusetts General Hospital (http://www.massgeneral.org/bhi/).

In retrospect, it shouldn't be surprising that meditation is so effective for improving brain functioning. We tend to be constantly preoccupied by our external environment and a desire to stimulate our senses. Consequently, people often have something to keep their senses busy: the television (often left on even when no one is watching it), the radio or music player, a book or magazine to read, texting, telephone, or an interactive phone app. Often there is a perceived need to hear, see, or feel this continual background chatter in order to feel comfortable or secure. It is uncomfortable for many persons to sit with only oneself in a room and no other form of stimulation to occupy our senses. For this reason, meditation has been called the pilgrimage within. At first, meditation may seem difficult because you are teaching your mind to think of nothing. The Japanese have a proverb that states "Mind like water." The idea is that if you look into a pond of water, you can clearly see your reflection. However, if you drop a pebble into the pond, your reflection will be distorted by the ripples that form. In the same manner, one must cleanse the mind of thoughts in order to perceive clearly. So, if you want to have better brain health, you might consider practicing meditation. The steps that follow are for seated meditation, although meditation can be practiced anywhere, even while walking. Reread the steps each time you practice and with a few sessions it will become a very natural process. Lastly, although meditation is often referenced in conjunction with Buddhism, anyone of any faith can practice meditation. The three essential elements of meditation are: (1) breathing, (2) posture, and (3) concentration. Note the following caveats:

Breathing Exhalation should be equal or longer than inhalation, if you find yourself becoming lightheaded, stop immediately. Always ensure that your breathing is relaxed and comfortable, never forced.

Centering There are concentration points or centering points in the body which are helpful to enhance certain abilities. In Chinese, Japanese, and Korean meditative practice, the center point used in concentration is often referred to as the "Sea of Chi" or energy, and it is located about 1 inch below the naval. Chi refers to bioelectrical energy that is manipulated in the practice of acupuncture. This point often enhances one's sense of balance and control. In India, the central point of concentration in meditation is often located between the eyes.

Following are the steps to meditation as practiced in Zen:

1. Choose a quiet place, free of noise and distractions.
2. Be sure that you are rested and have had enough sleep.
3. Avoid meditation when you have overeaten or when you have been drinking alcohol.
4. Make sure your body is clean.
5. Sit or on the floor with your legs crossed (or on a chair) with your back erect, lowering your knees as much as possible. If you like, you can place the left foot on top of the right thigh. (If very flexible, you can also place the right foot on the left thigh. Remember, however, that you should be comfortable.)
6. Place both hands together in your lap (left over right), with the palms facing up, forming a circle so that your thumbs barely touch.
7. Stretch the upper half of your body upward and place a little tension in the abdomen. Lower and relax your shoulders.
8. Draw your hips back and concentrate on a spot about 1 inch below your navel.
9. Relax the solar plexus.
10. Pull in your chin and straighten your neck.
11. Place the tip of your tongue to the roof of your mouth, just touching the front teeth.
12. Place your teeth and lips together naturally.
13. Half close your eyes (in seated practice focus your eyes on a point, such as a candle, about 1 meter away; if standing, 2 meters away).
14. Your posture should be such that your forehead and navel are in a straight line.
15. Inhale through the nose and draw the breath to your abdomen (lower lungs). Slowly exhale the breath you have taken in through your mouth, barely

parting your lips. Repeat this two or three times (short breaths at first), gradually increasing the inhalation/exhalation cycle, but be *sure* that you are comfortable.

16. When breathing, try to do so as silently as possible.
17. You may slowly rock the body front and back (this should look to an observer as hardly being barely perceptible), gradually reducing the amplitude of the swing until you are completely motionless. Avoid moving your eyes, legs, or hands.
18. Focus your mind at the point 1 inch below your navel (this is called "centering").
19. Clear your mind of all thoughts. When you find yourself thinking of something, simply relax and refocus your concentration.
20. Your position, your breathing, and your concentration are the things that will lead you to a state of relaxation and impassivity.

That's all there is to it. Begin with 10 minutes in the morning and 10 minutes in the evening. Eventually, you may increase the time to a longer period if you wish. The rest is simply practice.

Conclusion

It is especially important to understand that dementia and other neurological disorders associated with aging are not normal in the human lifespan. It is also evident that our ultimate brain state is not simply predetermined, but rather amenable to lifestyle choices. The reduced incidence of dementia across the globe may be largely due to better health habits and improved cardiovascular well-being. Meditation is a practice that can improve your overall brain health and may be associated with neuroprotective factors in the aging process. Given this information, it certainly makes sense to give meditation a shot to improve your life. May the Om be with you!

References

Alzheimer's Association. "2016 Alzheimer's Disease Facts and Figures." *Alzheimer's & Dementia* 12, no. 4 (2016a).
Alzheimer's Association. "Parkinson's Disease Dementia. TS-0096." 2016b. Updated June 2016. http://www.alz.org/dementia/downloads/topicsheet_parkinsons.pdf.
Association for Frontotemporal Degeneration. *Understanding FTD: Disease Overview*. Radnor, PA: The Association for Frontotemporal Degeneration, 2017.https://www.theaftd.org/understandingftd/ftd-overview.

Austin, J. H. *Zen and the Brain: Toward an Understanding of Meditation and Consciousness.* Cambridge, MA: MIT Press, 1998.

Blackburn, E., and E. Epel. *The Telomere Effect: A Revolutionary Approach to Living Younger, Healthier, Longer.* New York: Grand Central Publishing, Hachette Book Group, 2017.

Brefczynski-Lewis, J. A., A. Lutz, H. S. Schaefer, D. B. Levinson, and R. J. Davidson. "Neural Correlates of Attentional Expertise in Long-Term Meditation Practitioners." *Proceedings of the National Academy of Sciences of the United States of America* 104 (2007): 11483–14888.

Centers for Disease Control and Prevention. "Stroke Fact Sheet." Atlanta: Centers for Disease Control and Prevention, Department of Health and Human Services, 2013. https://www.cdc.gov/dhdsp/data_statistics/fact_sheets/docs/fs_stroke.pdf.

Green, C. S., and D. Bavelier. "Exercising Your Brain: A Review of Human Brain Plasticity and Training-Induced Learning." *Psychology and Aging* 23, no. 4 (2008): 692–701. doi:10.1037/a0014345.

Hanson, R., and R. Mendius. *Buddha's Brain: The Practical Neuroscience of Happiness, Love, and Wisdom.* Oakland, CA: New Harbinger Publications Inc., 2009.

Jacobs, Tonya L., Elissa S. Epel, Jue Lin, Elizabeth H. Blackburn, Owen M. Wolkowitz, David A. Bridwell, Anthony P. Zanesco, Stephen R. Aichele, Baljinder K. Sahdra, Katherine A. Maclean, Brandon G. King, Phillip R. Shaver, Erika L. Rosenberg, Emilio Ferrer, B. Alan Wallace, and Clifford D. Saron. "Intensive Meditation Training, Immune Cell Telomerase Activity, and Psychological Mediators." *Psychoneuroendocrinology* 36, no. 5 (2011): 664–81. doi:10.1016/j.psyneuen.2010.09.010.

Langa, Kenneth M., Eric B. Larson, Eileen M. Crimmins, Jessica D. Faul, Deborah A. Levine, Mohammed U. Kabeto, and David R. Weir. "A Comparison of the Prevalence of Dementia in the United States in 2000 and 2012." *JAMA Internal Medicine* 177, no. 1 (2017): 51. doi:10.1001/jamainternmed.2016.6807.

National Institute on Aging, National Institute of Neurological Disorders and Stroke. "Lewy Body Dementia: Information for Patients, Families, and Professionals." NIH Publication No. 13–7907. Bethesda, MD: National Institutes of Health, 2013. https://www.lbda.org/sites/default/files/lewybodydementia-final_11–6–13.pdf.

National Parkinson Foundation. "Fact Sheet: Parkinson's Dementia." Miami, FL: National Parkinson Foundation, 2017. http://www.parkinson.org/sites/default/files/PD%20Dementia.pdf.

Pagnoni, Giuseppe, and Milos Cekic. "Age Effects on Gray Matter Volume and Attentional Performance in Zen Meditation." *Neurobiology of Aging* 28, no. 10 (2007): 1623–1627. doi:10.1016/j.neurobiolaging.2007.06.008.

Qiu, C., M. Kivipelto, and E. von Strauss. "Epidemiology of Alzheimer's disease: Occurrence, determinants, and strategies toward intervention." *Dialogues of Clinical Neuroscience* 11 (2009): 111–128.

Satizabal, Claudia L., Alexa S. Beiser, Vincent Chouraki, Geneviève Chêne, Carole Dufouil, and Sudha Seshadri. "Incidence of Dementia over Three Decades in the Framingham Heart Study." *New England Journal of Medicine* 374, no. 6 (2016): 523–532. doi:10.1056/nejmoa1504327.

Schulte, B. "Harvard Neuroscientist: Meditation Not Only Reduces Stress, Here's How It Changes Your Brain." *Washington Post*, May 26, 2016. Accessed May 26, 2015. https://www.washingtonpost.com/news/inspired-life/wp/2015/05/26/harvard-neuroscientist-meditation-not-only-reduces-stress-it-literally-changes-your-brain/?utm_term=.5752650f574a.

World Health Organization. "Dementia Fact Sheet." 2016. http://www.who.int/mediacentre/factsheets/fs362/en/.

Animal-Assisted Therapy and the Elderly

Martha McNiel

"She's a kind lady," Linda* said to her adult daughter as their car pulled out of the barn driveway after their first visit to the ranch.

Earlier that week, a message left on the DreamPower Horsemanship voice mail asked if someone would be willing to meet with a woman with middle-stage (moderate) Alzheimer's disease and her adult daughter for a "horse therapy" (equine-assisted psychotherapy) session. Linda was in her mid-seventies at the time of the referral. She had been living out of state with her husband, who was her caregiver for several years following her Alzheimer's diagnosis. When he passed away, it became apparent that Linda was no longer able to live independently and she now needed more assistance and care. Her daughter Mary* moved Linda across the country so that she can live near her.

Reflecting later on that initial phone conversation, Linda's daughter Mary said, "I was surprised you said 'yes' because nobody likes the elderly. Thank you for saying yes!"

DreamPower Horsemanship is a nonprofit organization located in Gilroy, California, that offers equine-assisted activities and equine-facilitated psychotherapy for children, teens, and adults with special needs. I founded

---

*The names have been changed to protect the privacy of those mentioned. This story is told with enthusiastic permission from "Mary."

DreamPower in 2002, because I believed working outside the office setting with animal-assisted (and especially equine) therapy and ecotherapy would be more effective (and more motivating) for many clients. After 14 years of offering psychotherapy in a barn setting, that has certainly proven true.

Animal-assisted and equine-facilitated psychotherapy are relative newcomers to the psychotherapy field. If you would like to read more about working with animals as partners in therapy, a few books to check out include: *Handbook on Animal-Assisted Therapy: Theoretical Foundations and Guidelines for Practice* (4th ed.) by Aubrey Fine (2015); *Walking the Way of the Horse: Exploring the Power of the Horse-Human Relationship* by Leif Hallberg (2008); *Zen Horse, Zen Mind: The Science and Spirituality of Working with Horses* by Allan J. Hamilton, MD (2011); *Harnessing the Power of Equine Assisted Counseling: Adding Animal Assisted Therapy to Your Practice* by Kay Sudekum Trotter (2012); and *Animal Assisted Therapy in Counseling* (2nd ed.) by Cynthia Chandler (2012).

Linda, Mary, and I met every week at the barn for several years. In the beginning, Mary, Linda, and I would together give the horses their morning feed. I would measure grain and Linda would pour it into feed pans for the senior horses. Together we would carry the grain pans to their stalls. All three of us would pull the hay carts through the barn and feed all the horses. Mary said, "You learned what she was capable of, what she could do. She could relate to serving the horses breakfast. It was very tangible and very real. It was perfect for her. To me it was peaceful, I got a lot out of it, too. Always dishing out the grains. For me, the smell of the hay in the barn was 'home.' For her, the smell of the horses was 'home.'"

After feeding the horses, some mornings we would sit in the goat pen and let baby goats climb all over Linda. Some days we would sit in the chicken pen in the sunshine and feed and watch the chickens and ducks. Some days we would sit in the miniature horse pen and talk while the mini horses milled about, looking for treats. "You knew where she was coming from. Four paws and a tail, whiskers and soft fur. You knew how to reach her," Mary said. It was moving for me to see that even though she was no longer able to speak, Linda's hands remembered how to stroke the soft fur of a dog with a familiar ease.

Cali the barn cat would often come and sit on Linda's lap while we talked. We would fold several towels and place them on Linda's lap so Cali's sharp claws could not pierce through them. Within a few minutes of Linda's arriving at the barn, Cali would usually find her way onto Linda's lap. Even though she could be an independent, slightly grumpy barn cat, she appeared faithfully for her weekly petting time with Linda.

I was always trying to find new ways to stimulate Linda's memory and to reach her. One day I decided Linda should take a "hay ride." We piled many horse and saddle blankets into a soft pile in the hay wagon. Somehow we managed to get Linda into a semi-reclining position in the hay wagon, supported by Mary. Then I drove the tractor all over the ranch, pulling the hay wagon with Linda aboard, while she smiled and grinned as she bumped along over the ruts in the ranch driveway.

When Linda's mobility had declined, she could not easily get into and out of the car, and Mary would drive their compact car into the horse barn aisle. Linda would stay sitting inside the car in the barn aisle. We would open the car doors so she could see and hear all the animals and I would pull up a chair close to the open car door. A dog and/or cat would usually come and sit in her lap in the car in the barn.

Sometime in the middle of our work together, I adopted an abandoned German shepherd dog from the county animal shelter. I did not initially intend for him to become a therapy dog, but he was so naturally gifted for therapy work, and he started participating in Linda's therapy sessions almost immediately. Rucker was a huge hit with Linda and she loved petting his soft fur while he leaned against her legs.

Mary said, "Rucker was such a blessing. Coming to the ranch was the bright part of the week. A lot of things wouldn't go well during the week but coming to the ranch was always a blessing." Mary told me that one of the last words Linda said was at the ranch. With Rucker lying across her lap Linda smiled and said, "Play." "She got that one word out and she got that right," Mary said.

Part of my work with Linda involved supporting Mary as she tried to give her mother the best care possible over five and a half challenging years. This included helping Mary sort through complicated feelings about her childhood relationship with her mother, and helping her to sort through the various treatment options, medical situations, and care facility options for Linda.

Working with Linda was challenging for me because of her physical, cognitive, and communication limitations resulting from Alzheimer's disease. But I began to view Linda as a fascinating human puzzle. I have always liked puzzles. I knew a human person was still living inside her body, although her mind and body were beginning to break down. I spent a lot of time talking with Mary, learning about Linda's earlier life, relationships, her history, and her interests. Then I tried all kinds of nontraditional interventions trying to connect with some memory, some fragment of the woman who was trapped inside her own body.

After a few years, DreamPower Horsemanship moved to a new location. Mary and Linda continued to attend therapy sessions at the new ranch. But there was no longer an enclosed horse barn with a center aisle. With a decreasing ability to respond to the world around her, Rucker (the German shepherd therapy dog) became the focus of her therapy. Mary would drive the car with Linda sitting in the front passenger seat into the middle of the ranch property. We would open both front doors. Mary would get out and she and I would sit in chairs close to the passenger door. Rucker would sit in the driver's seat and, when commanded, would lie across Linda's lap. Linda would pet and stroke his fur while we talked. Mary and I would take turns sitting beside the open passenger door and feeding Rucker baked liver treats as an encouragement to stay in the down position and as a reward for his work. At this point, Linda was unable to speak at all, but Mary and I would talk to her and help her pet Rucker.

As her illness progressed, Linda spent more and more time with her mouth wide open, like a baby bird waiting to be fed. One day, while sitting in the car and petting Rucker, one of his long ears ended up inside Linda's open mouth. The angle of the car seat caused his ear to move straight up into her open mouth. Linda closed her teeth and bit down hard on the tip of Rucker's ear. This could have become a terrible disaster. Fortunately, Rucker demonstrated the poise and grace of a good therapy dog. He let out a little yelp and looked at me with distress in his eyes. But he did not react aggressively, as many dogs would have. He did not bite, snap, or react negatively toward Linda. At this point I thought we might have to end Linda's interactions with all animals, if we could not keep the animals safe from her. But we found a way to push her car seat back as far as possible and have her lean farther back, and by keeping Rucker more forward and out of the range of her mouth, we were able to safely continue Linda's visits with Rucker until she was physically no longer able to come to the ranch.

Part of our work together included learning about Linda's life before Alzheimer's and trying anything and everything to reach her. This included music. One day Linda was humming the Elvis Presley song "Love Me Tender." Neither Mary nor I knew the words to this song. So I looked it up online and printed out the words for Mary and me. After that, from time to time, we would hum or sing along with Linda when she was in the mood for "Love Me Tender."

Linda had played the organ at her church for several decades and she knew many traditional church hymns. I looked up the words and music to old hymns I thought she might know. We got out a $100 keyboard bought on eBay and played and sang old hymns in the barn. Every time we found a song she recognized or remembered, I would make note of it. Every December I would pull out the keyboard and we would sing familiar Christmas carols. Linda would smile when she recognized a tune and sometimes she would sing or hum along while pretending to play the organ.

Eventually Linda's condition deteriorated to where she was physically unable to ride in a car and she could no longer come to the barn. At that point I started taking Rucker to visit her in the assisted living facility where she lived. We continued to visit her there until she passed away about 18 months later. In the final few months, Linda was bedridden and essentially nonresponsive to anyone or anything. Even then, we visited her. Rucker would lick her hand and (when commanded) he would get up on the bed with her and lie quietly beside her.

Linda, Mary, and I met with together for five and a half years. Horses, mules, miniature horses, dogs, cats, goats, chickens, and ducks were involved in Linda's therapy. After Linda had passed, Mary said, "I owe you a debt of gratitude for walking those final years with her. Many people peel off on that part of the path and won't walk that path with you."

Mary invited Rucker and me to Linda's funeral and we went. Later Mary said, "You and Rucker even came to her funeral. You knew her better than anyone else here. It takes a certain kind of person to walk with someone at the end of life."

During the years that we worked together, I took many photos of Linda at the barn with the various animals. I sent many good photos to Mary, who printed them and shared them with her mother and her siblings. The prominent place these photos of Linda with the DreamPower animals given at her funeral showed me how important those photos were to Mary.

Mary said, "I have photos of you and Rucker watching over Linda in the nursing home. You said 'yes' when others wouldn't even have considered it. It proved you are not afraid of the end of life. You've already done your own emotional work in that field."

My work with Linda and Mary over the five and a half years included supportive psychotherapy, animal-assisted psychotherapy, music therapy, family therapy, case management, social work, memory care, and grief and loss work. Mary said, "You never made her seem like a burden. Thank you! Having someone else participate in her quality of life was important to me. Having someone else really on the same page. You brought more joy to it. You didn't ever seem burdened or like you were not happy to be there."

About her mother's therapy services at DreamPower, Mary said, "I could relax, knowing this was a good thing for her even if she couldn't articulate 'thank you.' Now—a few years later—I can feel good. I did what I could. I did my best."

In discussing the years Linda and I worked together, Mary said, "Being kind and sweet and consistent week to week with Linda was the most important thing. There's something about love and being present for someone. But being present with all your smarts."

CHAPTER THREE

The Impact of Physical Challenges on the Mental Health of the Aging Population

Caroline D. Bergeron and Matthew Lee Smith

In the process of aging, adults can expect to see gradual changes to their bodies. Physically aging can represent important challenges for older adults, ultimately impacting their mental health and well-being. In this chapter, we argue that, as people age, physical health and mental health are directly interconnected, where one affects the other, and vice versa. These constructs can also be modified, worsened, or improved through the use or lack of clinical care, evidence-based interventions, and social support. We present a model that depicts the cyclical association between physical and mental health among the older population. The purpose of this chapter is to describe this cycle by: (1) providing a general overview of mental illnesses among older adults, (2) describing common physical changes among the aging population and its association with mental health, (3) discussing evidence-based interventions to address physical aging and mental illness and the importance of social support, and (4) offering recommendations to promote the mental health of our aging population.

Older Adults and Mental Illness

According to Healthy People 2020, mental health is a "state of successful performance of mental function, resulting in productive activities, fulfilling relationships with other people, and the ability to adapt to change and to cope with challenges" (Office of Disease Prevention and Health Promotion, 2014). Conversely, a mental illness refers to a mental health problem or disorder characterized by changes in thinking, mood, or behavior that interferes with daily life and normal functioning (Office of Disease Prevention and Health Promotion, 2014). Although mental health is a public health priority for all age groups, it is particularly important for the older population. One in five adults aged 65 years and older experience some type of mental illness (Karel, Gatz, and Smyer, 2012). The most common mental disorders experienced by the older population include depression, cognitive impairment, stress, and anxiety (American Psychological Association, 2017b). While cognitive impairment, whether mild to severe (e.g., dementia), is formally recognized as a mental illness by the *Diagnostic and Statistical Manual of Mental Disorders, Fifth Edition* (*DSM-5*; American Psychiatric Association, 2013). In this chapter, it is considered more as a neurological disorder than a mental disorder and therefore will not be addressed in subsequent sections.

Depression

Depression is not a normal part of aging; grief, temporary sadness, or blues are normal; however, persistent feelings of sadness lasting for weeks are abnormal. Other symptoms of depression include feeling pessimistic, guilty, worthless or helpless, and irritable or restless; losing interest in enjoyable activities or hobbies; feeling fatigued; having difficulty concentrating and remembering details or making decisions; overeating or losing appetite; experiencing persistent aches or pains, and/or having suicidal thoughts (Centers for Disease Control and Prevention, 2017a). Older adults are at an increased risk of suffering from depression (Centers for Disease Control and Prevention, 2017a). Depression is more common among people with chronic diseases, and half of all older adults experience one or more chronic conditions such as cardiovascular disease and diabetes (Centers for Disease Control and Prevention, 2017a; Fiske, Wetherell, and Gatz, 2009). Depression, therefore, makes it more difficult for older adults with chronic conditions to take care of themselves and seek professional help (National Institute of Mental Health, 2016).

While depression among older adults can generally be treated through antidepressant medication, psychotherapy, or a combination of both (U.S. Department of Health and Human Services, 2011), it is often undiagnosed or misdiagnosed, and subsequently left untreated. Several reasons account for this lack of proper diagnoses. Older individuals may not want to talk about their feelings (National Institute of Mental Health, 2015);

may attribute their sadness to grief, disability; or another life event; or may deny that they are suffering from a mental illness due to fear of being stigmatized (Bartels, 2004). Conversely, health care providers may also misdiagnose depression when sadness is not the main symptom (National Institute of Mental Health, 2015) or may attribute some of the symptoms (e.g., fatigue) to a physical health condition (U.S. Department of Health and Human Services, 2011). If left untreated, depression can lead to suicide (National Institute of Mental Health, 2015). Older Caucasian men commit suicide more often than any other age or racial group (U.S. Department of Health and Human Services, 2011).

Stress

Everyone experiences stress, although the nature and types of stressors vary depending on the person's age and stage in life (Pearlin and Skaff, 1996). As individuals age, stressors, such as illnesses and deaths, become more common (Jeon and Dunkle, 2009). The Geriatric Scale of Recent Life Events (Kahana, Fairchild, and Kahana, 1982) and the Geriatric Hassles Scale (Kanner et al., 1981) provide a good overview of potential stressors experienced by older adults, including losing hearing and vision, stopping to drive, experiencing age discrimination or economic strain, losing physical and cognitive abilities, and surviving the death of a family member or friend (Jeon and Dunkle, 2009). The 2014 Stress in America Survey conducted by the American Psychological Association revealed that older adults generally report lower levels of stress compared to younger age groups (American Psychological Association, 2015). This may be due to resilience acquired over time through their lived experiences (Almeida, 2005; Long, 2010). However, increasing stressors such as declining health and independence or losing a spouse may cause older adults to be more vulnerable to stress (Dunkle, Roberts, and Haug, 2001). Experiencing ongoing difficulties may also deplete personal resources that enable older individuals to react appropriately to new stressors (Almeida, 2005).

Symptoms of stress include being worried; being anxious; experiencing panic attacks; feeling sad; feeling pressured and hurried; being irritable or moody; feeling overwhelmed and helpless; having difficulty concentrating and making decisions; eating too much or not enough; abusing alcohol or drugs; and experiencing stomach issues, headaches, chest pain, allergic reactions, or sexual dysfunctions (American Psychological Association, n.d.). Stress can increase the risks of developing depression (Hall-Flavin, 2014; Jeon and Dunkle, 2009), while depression can also be considered a chronic stressor (Bruno, 2017).

Stress can be treated using one of three effective therapeutic techniques (American Psychological Association, n.d.). Relaxation training including meditation and breathing exercises can help someone manage stress. Cognitive behavioral therapy can be applied to identify and change negative thoughts that cause and prolong stress. Finally, supportive therapy, where a therapist listens to and validates the older adult's feelings, can help to reduce levels of stress (American Psychological Association, n.d.).

Anxiety

Feeling anxious or nervous is a common human emotion across the life course. Anxiety is diagnosed as a disorder when an older person frequently feels anxious or becomes overwhelmed by excessive worry or fear, which ultimately interferes with his or her daily activities (Geriatric Mental Health Foundation, n.d.). Approximately 14 percent of older adults have an anxiety disorder (Mental Health America, 2017), but the prevalence of anxiety symptoms not leading to a diagnosis is much higher. A 2008 study published in the *Journal of Affective Disorders* revealed that up to one in two older adults experience symptoms of anxiety (Bryant, Jackson, and Ames, 2008), making symptoms of anxiety more common than symptoms of depression (Bryant et al., 2008).

Symptoms of anxiety include excessively worrying or being afraid, having a racing heart, shallow breathing, having nausea, trembling, sweating, sleeping poorly, having tensed muscles or feeling weak and shaky, hoarding, refusing to do routine activities or being overly preoccupied with a routine, avoiding social situations, being overly concerned about safety, and self-medicating through alcohol or other depressants (Geriatric Mental Health Foundation, n.d.).

Considering the onset of anxiety disorders primarily occurs between the late teens and late twenties (Roux, Gatz, and Wetherell, 2005), it is possible that older adults who are living with anxiety suffered from anxiety when they were younger, but were not diagnosed or treated (Anxiety and Depression Association of America, 2016; Geriatric Mental Health Foundation, n.d.). Types of anxiety disorders that affect older adults include generalized anxiety disorder (e.g., constantly worrying about health, money, family), specific phobias (e.g., fear of falling and fear of death), social phobia (e.g., fear of being judged by others), posttraumatic stress disorder (e.g., reliving a past trauma such as war), obsessive-compulsive disorder (OCD) (e.g., continuously putting things in order), and panic disorder or attacks (Fortner and Neimeyer, 1999; Geriatric Mental Health Foundation, n.d.; NIHSeniorHealth, n.d.).

Several factors can contribute to an anxiety disorder, such as experiencing extreme trauma or having a family history of anxiety; however, stressors experienced as people age can also cause anxiety disorders (or at least symptoms of anxiety), such as bereavement, poor health, and memory problems (Geriatric Mental Health Foundation, n.d.). Consequently, anxiety commonly co-occurs with other mental and physical illnesses including depression, stress, and substance abuse (Friedman et al., 2013; Geriatric Mental Health Foundation, n.d.).

Anxiety can be treated with medication, psychotherapy (e.g., cognitive behavioral therapy or supportive psychotherapy), or a combination of both (Mental Health America 2017; National Institute on Aging, n.d.; Stanley, Beck, and Glassco, 1996). Nonetheless, anxiety often goes untreated. Similar to other mental illnesses, older adults may avoid talking about their feelings with health care providers (Mental Health America, 2017). They may have experienced symptoms of anxiety their entire lives and consider them normal (Mental Health America, 2017). Alternatively, physicians may misdiagnose anxiety due to the presence of comorbidities (Mental Health America, 2017). If left untreated, anxiety can lead to cognitive impairment, disability, and poor quality of life (Mental Health America, 2017).

Physical Aging and Mental Health

Individuals experience important physical changes as they age. The most common age-graded physical changes are vision loss, hearing loss, bone loss, and incontinence (National Institutes of Health, Medline Plus, 2007). The process of aging can also be accelerated—through what is entitled the "weathering effect"—as a consequence of having accumulated repeated experiences of social or economic adversity and discrimination throughout the life course (Geronimus et al., 2006). Some age-related diseases, including cataracts and macular degeneration, heart disease, cancer, hypertension, arthritis and osteoporosis, chronic obstructive pulmonary disease (COPD), stroke, Parkinson's disease, and dementia (Elsawy and Higgins, 2011), may cause stress, anxiety, or depression, which in turn can affect an older person's normal functioning.

Researchers at the Institute on Aging at Portland State University created a review of evidence, which supported the association between comorbid physical conditions and late life depression and reported the prevalence of depression among older adults living with these illnesses (Portland State University, n.d.). For example, depression was experienced among up to

89 percent of stroke patients, about 58 percent of adults with cancer, and up to 60 percent of patients with COPD (Portland State University, n.d.).

Falls and other frequent events in older adulthood tend to occur due to age-related physical changes, including poor vision and lower body weakness (Centers for Disease Control and Prevention, 2017b). Approximately one in three older adults experience a fall every year (Lord, 2013). It has been found that falls can have a profound effect on older adults' physical, emotional, spiritual, and social independence (Bergeron et al., 2016). Older individuals may feel embarrassed, stressed, or shocked from their fall experience, may feel helpless after a fall, and may even become afraid of experiencing another fall (Bergeron et al., 2016).

In any of these contexts, losing one's functional ability to perform basic activities of daily living (ADLs) and/or instrumental activity of daily living (IADL; Katz et al., 1963; Lawton and Brody, 1969) is associated with mental health issues (Ormel et al., 2002; Yang and George, 2005). ADLs are daily self-care activities and include eating, bathing, dressing, using the toilet, and transferring from a bed or a chair (Katz et al., 1963). IADLs are more complex activities such as shopping, cooking, taking medication, managing money, and doing house chores (Lawton and Brody, 1969). One in two older Americans aged 85 and older need assistance with some of these daily tasks (American Psychological Association, 2017c). A change in functional ability can leave older adults feeling stressed, anxious, and depressed (Ormel et al., 2002; Yang and George, 2005). Conversely, experiencing depressive symptoms can also impact older adults' functional abilities (Ormel et al., 2002).

The physical changes that accompany normal aging are inevitable. However, how older adults process and cope with these physical changes, as well as their perceived levels of control toward these changes, will significantly impact their subjective quality of life and life satisfaction (Maher and Cummins, 2010; Pennington, Saywell, and Stephens, 2005; Thompson et al., 1998). In fact, individuals with important physical limitations can report high life satisfaction (Thomas, 2001). Some, on the other hand, may have difficulty accepting and adjusting to this sense of loss over their own bodies and lives, potentially resulting in low self-esteem, social withdrawal, anxiety, and depression (American Psychological Association, 2017c; Marshall, Lengyel, and Utioh, 2012; Thompson, et al., 1998). Being exposed to ageist stereotypes and internalizing these negative views can also affect older adults' self-perceptions and mental well-being (Diehl and Wahl, 2009; Hess, Birrin, and Schaie, 2006). Older adults need interventions and support to address both physical and mental challenges that are associated with their experiences of aging. See Figure 3.1 as a guiding framework for these relationships.

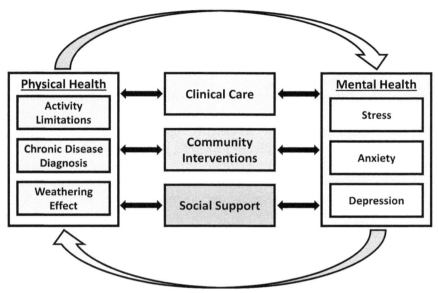

Figure 3.1   The cyclical association between physical aging and mental health with associated interventions.

Interventions for Physical Aging and Mental Illness

In the United States, a collection of evidence-based interventions has been developed to improve the health and well-being of older adults (Boutaugh et al., 2014; Boutaugh and Lawrence, 2015). A variety of topics are addressed by these interventions including physical activity, chronic disease self-management, mental health, fall prevention, medication adherence, and caregiving (National Council on Aging, 2016). Each of these interventions has been selected for grand-scale dissemination and community embedment based on their documented efficacy as randomized controlled trials. After their efficacy was established (often in clinical settings), these programs were translated so they could be delivered in community settings and organizations through the aging services network in senior centers, health care organizations, residential facilities, faith-based organizations, and tribal centers, among others. While some of these interventions require the involvement and supervision of trained professionals (e.g., nurses, physical therapists, social workers, and occupational therapists), many use lay-leaders (i.e., nonprofessionals who have undergone training) to promote widespread delivery to engage more older adult participants at a lower cost.

The proliferation of these interventions throughout the nation has been made possible by the support of many national stakeholders such as the Administration for Community Living, National Council on Aging, Centers for Disease Control and Prevention, and Archstone Foundation (Ory and Smith, 2015). Beyond financial support for these interventions, networks such as the Evidence-Based Leadership Council (Haynes et al., 2015), the FallsFree© Initiative (Beattie, 2014; Schneider and Beattie, 2015), and the Centers for Disease Control and Prevention, Healthy Aging Research Network (Belza et al., 2015) have been integral to providing guidance and technical assistance to enhance successful program delivery, scalability, and sustainability.

Given this chapter's emphasis, Table 3.1 provides basic information about selected evidence-based programs that address physical activity (directly and as a way of influencing mental health) and mental health (directly and as a way of influencing physical health). Furthermore, the small group format of these intervention workshops are beneficial to participants' mental health because of the ability to socialize and interact with other older adults.

Importance of Social Support

It is well documented that having access to a social network that provides social support is beneficial for older adults' physical and mental well-being (Cornwell and Waite, 2009; Everard et al., 2000; Fiori, Antonucci, and Cortina, 2006; Rausa, 2008; Thoits, 2011). Social support is defined as various types of help (e.g., emotional, instrumental, informational) that individuals can receive from others, including family, friends, neighbors, and community members (Reblin and Uchino, 2008; Seeman, 2008). Two models may explain the relationship between social support and mental and physical health: (1) the stress-buffering model and (2) the main effect model (Cohen and Wills, 1985). The stress-buffering model describes how perceived availability of social support and perceived or received support can help reduce negative emotions in stressful situations (Kawachi and Berkman, 2001). The main effect model presents different pathways in which participation in social networks can bring about physical and mental well-being. For example, social network members can influence each other to engage in healthy behaviors, which in turn can impact both their physical and mental health. An older adult who is integrated in a social network may be more likely to have a sense of purpose and belonging, which can increase his or her self-worth, increase motivation for self-care, and improve his or her responses to life stressors. Being part of a social network can also provide access to diverse forms of social support, which can protect against distress (Fiori et al., 2006; Kawachi and Berkman, 2001).

Table 3.1 Selected Examples of Evidence-Based Programs for Older Adults

Program Name	Goals	Audience	Duration	Delivered By	Website
PHYSICAL ACTIVITY					
Active Choices	Help individuals incorporate preferred physical activities in their daily lives	Adults aged 50 years and older	6-month telephone-based individualized program	Trained activity coach/peer counselor/facilitator	http://hip.stanford.edu/ organizational-consulting/
Active Living Every Day	Evoke behavior change by reducing barriers to physical activity	Adults interested in incorporating physical activity into their daily lives	12 weekly sessions	Trained facilitators (at least 1 per session)	www.ActiveLiving.info
EnhanceFitness	Improve the overall functional fitness and well-being	Sedentary older adults	Ongoing; 1-hour sessions; 3 times/week (group physical activity)	Certified fitness instructor	www.projectenhance .org/EnhanceFitness .aspx
Fit & Strong!	Manage lower-extremity osteoarthritis	Sedentary older adults with lower-extremity joint pain and stiffness. Participants must be cleared by a physician to participate in exercise	8 weeks; 3 times per week; 90 minutes per session	Trained facilitator	www.fitandstrong.org
Walk with Ease (community-based version)	Reduce pain and discomfort of arthritis, increase balance and strength, build confidence in the ability to be physically active and improve overall health	Community-dwelling older adults with arthritis and other chronic conditions	6 weeks; 1 hour, 3 times a week	Certified instructor	http://www.arthritis .org/wwe

(*Continued*)

Table 3.1 (*Continued*)

Program Name	Goals	Audience	Duration	Delivered By	Website
FALL PREVENTION					
A Matter of Balance	Reduce fall risk and fear of falling; Improve falls efficacy and management; Promote physical activity	Adults 60+ who are ambulatory, able to problem solve	8 sessions (meeting weekly or twice weekly); 2 hours per session	2 trained lay-leaders	www.mainehealth.org/mob
Otago Exercise Program	Increase strength, balance, and endurance	Community-dwelling frail older adults	4–5 home visits over 8 weeks; monthly phone calls for a year; optional follow-up visits (6, 9, and 12 months)	Physical therapist	http://www.med.unc.edu/aging/cgec/exercise-program
Stepping On	Increase self-confidence in making decisions and changing behavior (e.g., exercise) to reduce falls	Community-residing, cognitively intact, older adults at risk for falling	7-week program; 2 hours per session; home or telephone visit; booster session after 3 months	1 trained leader; 1 peer leader	http://wihealthyaging.org/stepping-on
Tai Chi: Moving for Better Balance	Improve balance, strength, and physical performance to prevent falls	Adults 65+	24- to 26-week program; 3 classes per week; 1 hour per session	Qualified instructors	www.tjqmbb.org

DISEASE SELF-MANAGEMENT

Chronic Disease Self-Management Education Programs	Build self-confidence to take part in maintaining their health and managing their chronic health conditions	Adults with chronic conditions	6 sessions; about 2 hours per session	2 trained lay-leaders	http://patienteducation.stanford.edu/programs/cdsmp.html
HomeMeds	Enable community agencies to address medication-related problems and errors that endanger the lives and well-being of community-dwelling elders	Area Agencies on Aging, care management programs, and home care agencies with community-dwelling elder clients	Ongoing	Care managers, physician, and pharmacist	www.HomeMeds.org

MENTAL HEALTH

Healthy IDEAS (Identifying Depression, Empowering Activities for Seniors)	Reduce the severity of depressive symptoms in frail, high-risk and diverse older clients of community agencies	Ethnically and socioeconomically diverse populations of older adults and family caregivers who are living in the community and are at high risk for depressive symptoms	3- to 6-month program (minimum of 3 in-person visits in the client's home and 5 or more telephone contacts)	Trained case manager or other social service provider in the client's home or other private location	www.careforelders.org/healthyideas

(Continued)

Table 3.1 (*Continued*)

Program Name	Goals	Audience	Duration	Delivered By	Website
IMPACT (Improving Mood-Promoting Access to Collaborative Treatment)	Develop and administer a course of treatment	Adult patients who have a diagnosis of depression, often in conjunction with another major health problem	1- to 3-day training required (online materials available)	Trained depression care manager (nurse, social worker, or psychologist)	http://impact-uw.org/
Program to Encourage Active, Rewarding Lives for Seniors	Reduce symptoms of depression and improve health-related quality of life	Adults 60+ with depression and are receiving home-based social services	8 sessions; 50 minutes per session (occurs over 19 weeks)	Trained social service worker	www.pearlsprogram.org

Source: Table adapted from: https://www.ncoa.org/resources/highest-tier-evidence-based-health-promotiondisease-prevention-programs/ and Smith, M. L., M. G. Ory, and T. R. Prohaska (2017). "Healthy Aging and Its Implications for Public Health: Social and Behavioral Interventions." In W. A. Satariano and M. Maus (Eds.). *Aging, Place and Health: A Global Perspective.* Jones and Bartlett Learning; Burlington, MA, USA.

While disabilities in older adulthood may lead to mobility restrictions and consequently lower levels of social support (Rosso et al., 2013), quality social support can significantly contribute to buffer the effects of functional limitations on depression among older adults (Yang, 2006). Social support has also been found to be beneficial to lower symptoms of anxiety, stress, and depression among cancer patients (Wang et al., 2012; Ng et al., 2015), COPD patients (Dinicola et al., 2013), and diabetes patients (Coffman, 2008; Sacco and Yanover, 2006), among other chronic conditions experienced by older adults. It is important to note that depression can also have a negative impact on social support (Sacco and Yanover, 2006; Wade and Kendler, 2000) through decreased social interactions, which highlight the need to provide greater opportunities for older adults to socialize as well as the need for early detection, diagnosis, and treatment of mental illness.

Recommendations to Promote Mental Health

Several recommendations can be made to promote the mental health of older adults. First, it is crucial to raise awareness about mental health among the older population. It is not widely understood that depression, stress, and anxiety can be treated and that effective treatment can significantly improve older adults' overall health and quality of life (National Institute of Mental Health, 2015). While raising awareness, aiming to reduce perceived public stigma associated with having a mental illness could significantly help to increase screening and detection of these issues and encourage older adults to seek treatment (Conner et al., 2010; Golberstein, Eisenberg, and Gollust, 2008; Mackenzie, Gekoski, and Knox, 2006; World Health Organization, 2016). Screening and diagnosis can be the responsibility of a range of health professionals from different disciplines, including primary care providers, psychologists, psychiatrists, mental health counselors, marital and family therapists, nurse practitioners, and social workers (Mental Health America, 2016). Non–mental health professionals who regularly interact with older adults, such as optometrists for vision loss, audiologists for hearing loss, and physical therapists for physical limitations, should also be trained to recognize the signs of the most common mental illnesses among the aging population. Subsequently, a strong local network of clinical and community organizations would be needed to ensure effective referrals to needed mental health services as well as appropriate care coordination between the different providers. Local or state resources could also be supplemented by mental health programs and services offered at the national and international levels. Table 3.2 lists potential national and international partners that promote mental health among older adults.

Table 3.2   Organizations Providing Mental Health Programs and Services to Older Adults

Administration for Community Living	International OCD Foundation
American Counseling Association	Mental Health America
American Psychiatric Nurses Association	Mental Health Foundation
American Psychological Association	National Alliance on Mental Illness
American Public Health Association	National Council on Aging
Anxiety and Depression Association of America	National Institute of Mental Health
Association of Black Psychologists	National Mental Health Association
Association of LGBTQ Psychiatrists	Pan American Health Association
Centers for Disease Control and Prevention	Society for Public Health Education
Depression and Bipolar Support Alliance	Substance Abuse and Mental Health Services Administration
Evidence-Based Leadership Council	U.S. Department of Health and Human Services
Indian Health Services	World Federation for Mental Health
International Association of National Public Health Institutes	World Health Organization

Conclusion

Despite the prevalence of mental health issues among the aging population, few older adults with mental disorders use mental health services. The lack of perceived need for mental health care may contribute to low rates of mental health service use among older adults (Klap, Unroe, and Unutzer, 2003). While mental health issues include an array of conditions and symptomology (e.g., depression, stress, and anxiety), the complexities of their occurrence (e.g., social and environmental) support the need for a multitude of resources and services offered in community and clinical settings. Because physical health can influence (and can be influenced by) mental health, interventions to address older adult health need not solely focus on psychological factors. Rather, interventions that include physical activity, that improve efficacy to manage conditions (thus alleviating fear and stress), and that provide social interactions and support can be effective to improve mental health outcomes and status among older adults. It is recommended that marriage and family therapists/professionals utilize existing organizations, programs, and resources to link their older clients with needed services and offerings. While many of these services are available to older adults free of charge, others require the older adult to meet eligibility requirements. Regardless, deliberate efforts are needed to increase the availability, accessibility, and affordability of mental health services to improve utilization rates among the aging population. Furthermore, awareness-raising efforts are critical to reduce social stigma surrounding mental health disorders as well as give older adults "permission" to recognize/admit they have a condition so they can be linked to necessary mental health interventions and resources.

References

Almeida, David M. "Resilience and Vulnerability to Daily Stressors Assessed via Diary Methods." *Current Directions in Psychological Science* 14, no. 2 (2005): 64–68. doi:10.1111/j.0963-7214.2005.00336.x.

American Psychiatric Association. *Diagnostic and Statistical Manual of Mental Health Disorders.* (2013). Accessed May 17, 2017. https://www.psychiatry .org/psychiatrists/practice/dsm.

American Psychological Association. "Aging and Depression." (2017a). Accessed May 17, 2017. http://www.apa.org/helpcenter/aging-depression.aspx.

American Psychological Association. "Coping with Stress and Anxiety." (n.d.). Accessed May 17, 2017. https://www.apa.org/pi/aging/09-33-coping-with-stress-fin.pdf.

American Psychological Association. "Mental and Behavioral Health and Older Americans." (2017b). Accessed May 17, 2017. http://www.apa.org/about/ gr/issues/aging/mental-health.aspx.

American Psychological Association. "Older Adults' Health and Age-Related Changes." (2017c). Accessed May 17, 2017. http://www.apa.org/pi/aging/ resources/guides/older.aspx.

American Psychological Association. "Stress in America: Paying with Our Health." (2015). Accessed May 17, 2017. https://www.bing.com/cr?IG=6F9F917 7D28A47F997AA12BC4AA89DAA&CID=035042A84230672E326A482 D43A066FE&rd=1&h=uMEAy-0g6lA2oRZ6_gXUAQ1hU6ePA04PqCd0 Vl7kQbc&v=1&r=https%3a%2f%2fwww.apa.org%2fnews%2fpress%2fre leases%2fstress%2f2014%2fstress-report.pdf&p=DevEx,5060.1.

Anxiety and Depression Association of America. "Older Adults." (2016). https:// www.adaa.org/living-with-anxiety/older-adults.

Bartels, Stephen J. "Caring for the Whole Person: Integrated Health Care for Older Adults with Severe Mental Illness and Medical Comorbidity." *Journal of the American Geriatrics Society* 52 (2004). doi:10.1111/j.1532-5415.2004.52601.x.

Beattie (Bonita) Lynn. "Effective Fall-Prevention Demands a Community Approach." *Journal of Geriatric Physical Therapy* 37, no. 1 (2014): 31–34. doi:10.1519/jpt.0b013e31828835f4.

Bergeron, Caroline D., Daniela B. Friedman, Deanne K. Hilfinger Messias, S. Melinda Spencer, and Susan C. Miller. "Older Women's Responses and Decisions after a Fall: The Work of Getting back to Normal." *Health Care for Women International* 37, no. 12 (2016): 1342–1356. doi:10.1080/07399332.2016.1173039.

Boutaugh, Michele L., Susan M. Jenkins, Kristie P. Kulinski, Kate R. Lorig, Marcia G. Ory, and Matthew Lee Smith. "Closing the disparity gap: The Work of the Administration on Aging." *Generations* 38, no. 4 (2014): 107.

Boutaugh, Michele L., and Laura J. Lawrence. "Fostering Healthy Aging through Evidence-Based Prevention Programs: Perspectives from the Administration for Community Living/Administration on Aging." *Frontiers in Public Health* 2 (2015). doi:10.3389/fpubh.2014.00236.

Bruno, K. "Stress and Depression." WebMD. 2017. Accessed May 17, 2017. http://www.webmd.com/depression/features/stress-depression#1.

Bryant, Christina, Henry Jackson, and David Ames. "The Prevalence of Anxiety in Older Adults: Methodological Issues and a Review of the Literature." *Journal of Affective Disorders* 109, no. 3 (2008): 233–50. doi:10.1016/j.jad.2007.11.008.

Centers for Disease Control and Prevention. "Depression Is Not a Normal Part of Aging." (January 31, 2017a). Accessed May 17, 2017. https://www.cdc.gov/aging/mentalhealth/depression.htm.

Centers for Disease Control and Prevention. "Important Facts about Falls." (February 10, 2017b). Accessed May 17, 2017. https://www.cdc.gov/homeandrecreationalsafety/falls/adultfalls.html.

Coffman, Maren J. "Effects of Tangible Social Support and Depression on Diabetes Self-Efficacy." *Journal of Gerontological Nursing* 34, no. 4 (2008): 32–39. doi:10.3928/00989134-20080401-02.

Cohen, Sheldon, and Thomas A. Wills. "Stress, Social Support, and the Buffering Hypothesis." *Psychological Bulletin* 98, no. 2 (1985): 310–57. doi:10.1037//0033-2909.98.2.310.

Conner, Kyaien O., Valire Carr Copeland, Nancy K. Grote, Gary Koeske, Daniel Rosen, Charles F. Reynolds, and Charlotte Brown. "Mental Health Treatment Seeking among Older Adults with Depression: The Impact of Stigma and Race." *The American Journal of Geriatric Psychiatry* 18, no. 6 (2010): 531–543. doi:10.1097/jgp.0b013e3181cc0366.

Cornwell, Erin York, and Linda J. Waite. "Social Disconnectedness, Perceived Isolation, and Health among Older Adults." *Journal of Health and Social Behavior* 50, no. 1 (2009): 31–48. doi:10.1177/002214650905000103.

Diehl, M. K., and H. W. Wahl. "Awareness of Age-Related Change: Examination of a (Mostly) Unexplored Concept." *The Journals of Gerontology Series B: Psychological Sciences and Social Sciences* 65B, no. 3 (2009): 340–350. doi:10.1093/geronb/gbp110.

Dinicola, Gia, Laura Julian, Steven E. Gregorich, Paul D. Blanc, and Patricia P. Katz. "The Role of Social Support in Anxiety for Persons with COPD." *Journal of Psychosomatic Research* 74, no. 2 (2013): 110–115. doi:10.1016/j.jpsychores.2012.09.022.

Dunkle, Ruth E., Beverly Roberts, and Marie R. Haug. *The Oldest Old in Everyday Life: Self Perception, Coping with Change and Stress.* New York: Springer Publishing Company, 2001.

Elsawy, B., and K. E. Higgins. "The Geriatric Assessment." *American Family Physician* 83, no. 1 (2011): 48–56.

Everard, K. M., H. W. Lach, E. B. Fisher, and M. C. Baum. "Relationship of Activity and Social Support to the Functional Health of Older Adults." *The Journals of Gerontology Series B: Psychological Sciences and Social Sciences* 55, no. 4 (2000). doi:10.1093/geronb/55.4.s208.

Fiori, K. L., T. C. Antonucci, and K. S. Cortina. "Social Network Typologies and Mental Health among Older Adults." *The Journals of Gerontology Series B: Psychological Sciences and Social Sciences* 61, no. 1 (2006). doi:10.1093/geronb/61.1.p25.

Fiske, A., J. L. Wetherell, and M. Gatz. "Depression in Older Adults." *Annual Review of Clinical Psychology* 5, no. 1 (2009): 363–389.

Fortner, Barry V., and Robert A. Neimeyer. "Death Anxiety In Older Adults: A Quantitative Review." *Death Studies* 23, no. 5 (1999): 387–411. doi:10.1080/074811899200920.

Friedman, M. B., L. Furst, Z. D. Gellis, and K. Williams. "Anxiety Disorders in Older Adults." *Social Work Today* 23, no. 5 (2013): 387–411.

Geriatric Mental Health Foundation. "Anxiety and Older Adults: Overcoming Worry and Fear." (n.d.). Accessed May 17, 2017. http://www.aagponline.org/index.php?src=gendocs&ref=anxiety.

Geronimus, Arline T., Margaret Hicken, Danya Keene, and John Bound. "Weathering and Age Patterns of Allostatic Load Scores among Blacks and Whites in the United States." *American Journal of Public Health* 96, no. 5 (2006): 826–833. doi:10.2105/ajph.2004.060749.

Golberstein, E., D. Eisenberg, and S. E. Gollust. "Perceived Stigma and Mental Health Care Seeking." *Psychiatric Services* 59, no. 4 (2008): 392–399. doi:10.1176/appi.ps.59.4.392.

Hall-Flavin, M. D., and K. Daniel. "Chronic Stress: Can It Cause Depression?" Mayo Clinic. (November 25, 2014). Accessed May 17, 2017. http://www.mayoclinic.org/healthy-lifestyle/stress-management/expert-answers/stress/faq-20058233.

Haynes, Margaret, Susan Hughes, Kate Lorig, June Simmons, Susan J. Snyder, Lesley Steinman, Nancy Wilson, Roseanne Distefano, Jennifer Raymond, Stephanie Fallcreek, Martha B. Pelaez, and Don Smith. "Evidence-Based Leadership Council: A National Collaborative." *Frontiers in Public Health* 2 (2015). doi:10.3389/fpubh.2014.00136.

Healthy People 2020. "Mental Health and Mental Disorders. (2014). Accessed May 17, 2017. https://www.healthypeople.gov/2020/topics-objectives/topic/mental-health-and-mental-disorders.

Hess, T., J. Birrin, and K. Schaie. "Attitudes toward Aging and Their Effects on Behavior." *Handbook of the Psychology of Aging* 6, (2006): 379–406. doi:10.1016/b9-78-012101-2/64950-0203.

Jeon, H.-S., and R. E. Dunkle. "Stress and Depression among the Oldest-Old: A Longitudinal Analysis." *Research on Aging* 31, no. 6 (2009): 661–687. doi:10.1177/0164027509343541.

Kahana, E., T. Fairchild, and B. Kahana. "Clinical and Social Psychology." In *Research Instruments in Social Gerontology*, edited by David J. Mangen. Minneapolis: University of Minnesota Press, 1982.

Kanner, Allen D., James C. Coyne, Catherine Schaefer, and Richard S. Lazarus. "Comparison of Two Modes of Stress Measurement: Daily Hassles and Uplifts versus Major Life Events." *Journal of Behavioral Medicine* 4, no. 1 (1981): 1–39. doi:10.1007/bf00844845.

Karel, Michele J., Margaret Gatz, and Michael A. Smyer. "Aging and Mental Health in the Decade Ahead: What Psychologists Need to Know." *American Psychologist* 67, no. 3 (2012): 184–198. doi:10.1037/a0025393.

Katz, Sidney, A. B. Ford, R. W. Moskowitz, B. A. Jackson, and M. W. Jaffe. "Studies of Illness in the Aged." *Journal of the American Medical Association* 185, no. 12 (1963): 914. doi:10.1001/jama.1963.03060120024016.

Kawachi, I., and L. F. Berkman. "Social Ties and Mental Health." *Journal of Urban Health: Bulletin of the New York Academy of Medicine* 78, no. 3 (2001): 458–467. doi:10.1093/jurban/78.3.458.

Klap, R., K. T. Unroe, and J. Unutzer. "Caring for Mental Illness in the United States: A Focus on Older Adults." *American Journal of Geriatric Psychiatry* 11, no. 5 (2003): 517–524. doi:10.1176/appi.ajgp.11.5.517.

Lawton, M. Powell, and Elaine M. Brody. "Assessment of Older People: Self-Maintaining and Instrumental Activities of Daily Living." *Gerontologist* 9, no. 3 (1969): 179–186.

Long, James "Chip," Dr. "Stress in Older Adults." Your Mind Your Body. 2010. Accessed May 17, 2017. http://www.yourmindyourbody.org/stress-in-older-adults/.

Lord, Stephen R. *Falls in Older People: Risk Factors and Strategies for Prevention.* Cambridge: Cambridge University Press, 2013.

Mackenzie, C. S., W. L. Gekoski, and V. J. Knox. "Age, Gender, and the Underutilization of Mental Health Services: The Influence of Help-seeking Attitudes." *Aging & Mental Health* 10, no. 6 (2006): 574–582. doi:10.1080/13607860600641200.

Maher, Elise, and Robert A. Cummins. "Subjective Quality of Life, Perceived Control and Dispositional Optimism among Older People." *Australasian Journal on Ageing* 20, no. 3 (2010): 139–146. doi:10.1111/j.1741-6612.2001.tb01776.x.

Marshall, Catherine, Christina Lengyel, and Alphonsus Utioh. "Body Dissatisfaction: Among Middle-aged and Older Women." *Canadian Journal of Dietetic Practice and Research* 73, no. 2 (2012). doi:10.3148/73.2.2012.e241.

Mental Health America. "Anxiety in Older Adults." (April 28, 2017). Accessed May 17, 2017. http://www.mentalhealthamerica.net/anxiety-older-adults.

Mental Health America. "Types of Mental Health Professionals." (March 30, 2016). Accessed May 17, 2017. http://www.mentalhealthamerica.net/types-mental-health-professionals.

National Council on Aging. "Key Components of Evidence-Based Programming Archives." (2016). Accessed May 17, 2017. https://www.ncoa.org/resources/highest-tier-evidence-based-health-promotiondisease-prevention-programs/.

National Institute of Mental Health. "Older Adults and Depression." (2015). Accessed May 17, 2017. https://www.nimh.nih.gov/health/publications/older-adults-and-depression/index.shtml.

National Institute of Mental Health. "Older Adults and Mental Health." (2016). Accessed May 17, 2017. https://www.nimh.nih.gov/health/topics/older-adults-and-mental-health/index.shtml.

National Institutes of Health. "8 Areas of Age-Related Change." Medline Plus (2007). Accessed May 17, 2017. https://medlineplus.gov/magazine/issues/winter07/articles/winter07pg10-13.html.

Ng, Chong Guan, Salina Mohamed, Mee Hoong See, Faizah Harun, Maznah Dahlui, Ahmad Hatim Sulaiman, Nor Zuraida Zainal, and Nur Aishah Taib. "Anxiety, Depression, Perceived Social Support and Quality of Life in Malaysian Breast Cancer Patients: A 1-year Prospective Study." *Health and Quality of Life Outcomes* 13, no. 1 (2015). doi:10.1186/s12955-015-0401-7.

NIHSeniorHealth. "Anxiety Disorders—About Anxiety Disorders—About." (n.d.) Accessed May 17, 2017. https://nihseniorhealth.gov/anxietydisorders/about anxietydisorders/01.html.

Office of Disease Prevention and Health Promotion. "Mental Health and Mental Disorders." (2014). Accessed May 17, 2017. https://www.healthy people.gov/2020/topics-objectives/topic/mental-health-and-mental-disorders.

Ormel, J., F.V. Rijsdijk, M. Sullivan, E. Van Sonderen, and G.I.J.M. Kempen. "Temporal and Reciprocal Relationship between IADL/ADL Disability and Depressive Symptoms in Late Life." *The Journals of Gerontology Series B: Psychological Sciences and Social Sciences* 57, no. 4 (2002): P338–P347. doi:10.1093/geronb/57.4.p338.

Ory, M.G., and M.L. Smith, eds. *Evidence-Based Programming for Older Adults.* Lausanne, Switzerland: Frontiers Media, 2015.

Pearlin, L.I., and M.M. Skaff. "Stress and the Life Course: A Paradigmatic Alliance." *The Gerontologist* 36, no. 2 (1996): 239–247. doi:10.1093/geront/36.2.239.

Pennington, H., M. Saywell, and C. Stephens. "Perceived Control over Physical Aging: An Exploratory New Zealand Study." *New Zealand Journal of Psychology* 36, no. 2 (2005): 157.

Portland State University. "Comorbid Physical Conditions and Late Life Depression." (n.d.). https://www.pdx.edu/ioa/sites/www.pdx.edu.ioa/files/Comor bid%20Physical%20Conditions%20and%20Late%20Life%20Depres sion-2%20(1).pdf.

Rausa, B. A. "Social Support." In *Encyclopedia of Aging and Public Health*, edited by Sana Loue and Martha Sajatovic. Berlin: Springer-Verlag, 2008.

Reblin, Maija, and Bert N. Uchino. "Social and Emotional Support and Its Implication for Health." *Current Opinion in Psychiatry* 21, no. 2 (2008): 201–205. doi:10.1097/yco.0b013e3282f3ad89.

Rosso, Andrea L., Jennifer A. Taylor, Loni Philip Tabb, and Yvonne L. Michael. "Mobility, Disability, and Social Engagement in Older Adults." *Journal of Aging and Health* 25, no. 4 (2013): 617–637. doi:10.1177/0898264313482489.

Roux, Hillary Le, Margaret Gatz, and Julie Loebach Wetherell. "Age at Onset of Generalized Anxiety Disorder in Older Adults." *The American Journal of Geriatric Psychiatry* 13, no. 1 (2005): 23–30. doi:10.1097/00019442-2005 01000-00005.

Sacco, William P., and Tovah Yanover. "Diabetes and Depression: The Role of Social Support and Medical Symptoms." *Journal of Behavioral Medicine* 29, no. 6 (2006): 523–531. doi:10.1007/s10865-006-9072-5.

Schneider, Ellen C., and Bonita Lynn Beattie. "Building the Older Adult Fall Prevention Movement: Steps and Lessons Learned." *Frontiers in Public Health* 2 (2015). doi:10.3389/fpubh.2014.00194.

Seeman, T. "Support and Social Conflict: Section One—Social Support." MacArthur SES & Health Network Research. (2008). Accessed May 17, 2017. http://www.macses.ucsf.edu/research/psychosocial/socsupp.php.

Stanley, Melinda A., J. Gayle Beck, and Jill Dewitt Glassco. "Treatment of Generalized Anxiety in Older Adults: A Preliminary Comparison of Cognitive-Behavioral and Supportive Approaches." *Behavior Therapy* 27, no. 4 (1996): 565–581. doi:10.1016/s0005-7894(96)80044-x.

Thoits, Peggy A. "Mechanisms Linking Social Ties and Support to Physical and Mental Health." *Journal of Health and Social Behavior* 52, no. 2 (2011): 145–161. doi:10.1177/0022146510395592.

Thomas, D. R. "The Critical Link between Health-Related Quality of Life and Age-Related Changes in Physical Activity and Nutrition." *The Journals of Gerontology Series A: Biological Sciences and Medical Sciences* 56, no. 10 (2001): M599–M602. doi:10.1093/gerona/56.10.m599.

Thompson, Suzanne C., Craig Thomas, Cheryl A. Rickabaugh, Peerapong Tantamjarik, Teresa Otsuki, David Pan, Ben F. Garcia, and Evan Sinar. "Primary and Secondary Control over Age-Related Changes in Physical Appearance." *Journal of Personality* 66, no. 4 (1998): 583–605. doi:10.1111/1467-6494.00025.

U.S. Department of Health and Human Services. *Treatment of Depression in Older Adults: Key Issues.* (2011). https://store.samhsa.gov/shin/content/SMA11-4631CD-DVD/SMA11-4631CD-DVD-KeyIssues.pdf.

Wade, Tracey D., and Kenneth S. Kendler. "The Relationship between Social Support and Major Depression." *The Journal of Nervous and Mental Disease* 188, no. 5 (2000): 251–258. doi:10.1097/00005053-200005000-00001.

Wang, Xi, Shu-Sen Wang, Rou-Jun Peng, Tao Qin, Yan-Xia Shi, Xiao-Yu Teng, Dong-Gen Liu, Wei-Qing Chen, and Zhong-Yu Yuan. "Interaction of Coping Styles and Psychological Stress on Anxious and Depressive Symptoms in Chinese Breast Cancer Patients." *Asian Pacific Journal of Cancer Prevention* 13, no. 4 (2012): 1645–1649. doi:10.7314/apjcp.2012.13.4.1645.

World Health Organization. "Mental Health and Older Adults." (2016). Accessed May 17, 2017. http://www.who.int/mediacentre/factsheets/fs381/en/.

Yang, Yang. "How Does Functional Disability Affect Depressive Symptoms in Late Life? The Role of Perceived Social Support and Psychological Resources." *Journal of Health and Social Behavior* 47, no. 4 (2006): 355–372. doi:10.1177/002214650604700404.

Yang, Yang, and Linda K. George. "Functional Disability, Disability Transitions, and Depressive Symptoms in Late Life." *Journal of Aging and Health* 17, no. 3 (2005): 263–292. doi:10.1177/0898264305276295.

Dance/Movement Therapy with Elders: Dance for Health and Healing

Bonnie Bernstein

Throughout all time and world cultures, dance has been an integral part of community life. Village elders commonly participated in traditional dances and dance rituals. In Ghana, West Africa, I have watched elders joining in the work dances of pulling fishing nets from the sea. In Kelantan, Malaysia, I have witnessed elders playing the principal role in Main Puteri, a community dance ritual performed to heal emotional distress. In these societies, dance is a vital part of daily life and a natural part of healthy aging.

For an elder in contemporary Western culture, dance can also contribute to healthy aging. Dance/movement therapy directly addresses the social, physical, and psychological needs of elders in many ways. Group dance activities provide the connecting threads for community building and social engagement. The physical activity of dance can strengthen, rehabilitate, and reinvigorate the body. The individualized expression within dance provides opportunities for freeing creativity and opens therapeutic channels for working through emotional challenges. The joy of dance encourages new learning and builds experiences of competency and purpose.

Based on a decade of leading a weekly dance/movement therapy group at the Greenwich House Senior Center in New York's Greenwich Village,

I developed a comprehensive dance/movement therapy approach for bringing health and healing to elders. Following is a brief description of my philosophy and methods.

Creating an Elder Dance Community

The Greenwich House Senior Center community consisted predominantly of Italian immigrants, with ages ranging from 65 to 90. They were "well elderly," physically mobile enough to walk to the center; however, many lived with age-related physical limitations including arthritis and heart conditions. Many lived alone and their daily visit to the center was their main source of social interaction. Some were drawn to the center's subsidized lunch program that provided the main meal of their day. This elder community had in common a culture of sturdy determination, with the physical and emotional stamina to weather their life circumstances.

When designing a dance/movement therapy program for elders, it is important to fully consider the participants' physical and mental abilities, cultural identity, and social and emotional needs and resources. Sensitivity to cultural diversity in dance/movement therapy includes recognizing the impact of culture on movement styles, group dynamics, and nonverbal communication (Chang, 2009). Importantly, dance/movement therapy can target a wide range of elder populations, from a hospitalized psychiatric population to high-functioning elders in a day center. Sandel and Hollander, in their chapter, "Dance/Movement Therapy with Aging Populations" (1995), describe elders in five subgroups, as a way of distinguishing dance/movement therapy treatment needs:

- The well elderly
- The physically challenged
- Those with psychiatric disorders
- The cognitively impaired
- The frail elderly

Setting Goals for the Dance/Movement Therapy Session

My approach was developed for the "well elderly" attending a senior center.

Setting goals for the dance/movement therapy session requires acknowledgment of the participants' strengths and challenges. Often "well elderly" have become out of touch with their own emotional resources because of their current physical limitations or life circumstances. Our Western culture often plays a role in diminishing the elders' sense of self-worth by marginalizing them and providing an inadequate social network. Breakdown of the extended family leaves many elders socially isolated. However, when offered a safe and supportive atmosphere in a dance/movement therapy group, elders most often contribute fully and provide rich and dynamic dance themes fueled by stories and wisdom drawn from their lifelong experiences.

Goals of the dance/movement therapy session include:

- Building social support to decrease loneliness and isolation.
- Providing physical rehabilitation and cognitive stimulation to improve physical health, mental health, mobility, and independence.
- Providing avenues for creative expression and new learning.
- Providing therapeutic themes for self-discovery, emotional outlet, and working through life's challenges.
- Offering joyful dance experiences to restore personal agency and build self-esteem.
- Providing emotional and physical safety through therapeutic interventions that encourage personal strengths and dance activities that are flexible to accommodate a range of abilities. Irregular attendance is common to working in senior centers; although many participants return weekly, each session must provide a stand-alone experience, without expectation of follow-through the future weeks.

Fundamental Elements of a Dance/Movement Therapy Session

Music. My dance/movement therapy sessions are empowerment-focused, always aiming toward reinvigorating the elder's emotional and physical health and resources. Music plays an important part in each session. Music from participants' culture of origin provides a welcoming environment for new members. Ethnic music can also generate positive nostalgia and associations to personal history and cultural roots. Music drawn from participants' earlier life stages can evoke body memories of times when they experienced more physical freedom, agency, and independence. In contrast, introducing contemporary rhythms or less-familiar music styles stimulates spontaneity and innovative dance explorations and the therapeutic experience of expanding horizons and new learning.

Imagery. Cultivating the creative use of imagery and metaphor for building dance themes is fundamental to this dance/movement therapy approach. The introduction of nature imagery to stimulate dances opens new outlets for creative expression and expanded movement vocabulary.

For example, dancing to the gentle patter of rain with the hands and feet, or the wildness of a storm with arms and torso, or a group dance embodying the waves of the sea opens the participants to ranges and changes in tempos and movement dynamics. Dancing out scenes and images from the participants' personal life experience can stimulate memories, sharpen memory skills, and heighten the imagination. For example, building a group dance based on activities from their teenage years or having participants teach each other dances popular when they were young adults opens doors to storytelling and story dancing.

Time Travel. Expressing life stories through dance provides many avenues for exploration and therapeutic growth. Elders may carry habitual negative self-concepts that have rigidified over time. Dance provides a unique opening to memory retrieval or what I call "time travel" back to more positive narratives from the past and forward to fantasy and hopes. Dance can awaken embodied memories and stories from times when greater agency and control were experienced and can reintroduce that sense of personal strength into an elder's present self-concept. This process is restorative for the individual storyteller; as well, witnessing and dancing each other's stories benefits all group participants. In their chapter "Dance/Movement Therapy: Partners in Personhood," Shustik and Thompson (2002) affirm "Dancing and moving with others can open hearts not only to the fears and frustrations of life, but also to the magnificent strengths and beauty manifested in bodily expression and communal bonding" (76).

Dance themes utilizing "time travel" opens doors to empowering improvisations and therapeutic explorations. I raise evocative questions, "What is something that you have done in your life that you are particularly proud of?" or "Is there an important situation in your life when you felt strong and confident?" Unfolding these stores in words and dance reminds the elder of lifelong capacities and victories that for many have sunk into the psycho-physical unconscious. This process strengthens self-esteem by bringing the participant's history into the present.

In a senior center setting, it is important to focus memory retrieval themes on empowerment-focused memories because of what may be a limited capacity for follow-up. Unless the group is a designated ongoing group that requires regular attendance, for example, a grief-focused group, only an empowerment-focused memory retrieval theme is appropriate. It is my philosophy that dance themes related to self-determination and inner capacities can also indirectly address the impacts of past traumas without the risk of opening wounds or re-traumatization.

Folk Dance. Adapted folk dance is another enriching way to utilize culture to stimulate movement and pleasurable experiences. When developing folk dances for elders, a key concern is enhancing the vitality of the dance experience within the safety requirements of the participants' physical capacity. Safe pedestrian movements such as walking, stomping, and swaying can be transformed into lively folk dances through the use of ethnic music and creative, yet cautious, choreography. A walking step becomes a dance filled with spontaneity and expressive freedom when danced to lively music and shaped into circles, lines, partner dances, or snake-like formations. Folk dance encourages dynamic social interaction while increasing stamina, physical mobility, and vitality.

Session Example

This session begins with an energizing interactive warm-up focused on strengthening and loosening joints and muscles while building initial connections among group members. To music, participants seated in a circle are directed in a rhythmic freeing of arms and torso through bending joints, twisting, reaching, and wiggling. Suggesting images, for example, "wiggle like you are a pup shaking water off his fur," introduces the use of creative imagination from the onset. I then initiate a body/voice experience, modeling yawning stretches accompanied by loud "ahh's" and releasing of the torso. Through these rehabilitation-focused activities, participants relieve tension and broaden range of motion in their spine, torso, joints, and muscles. We transition into a playful greeting of others across the circle with exaggerated gestures and words. These sound/movement greetings immediately inspire a social connection. With a cultural twist, our greetings improvisationally transform into Italian greetings, Italian phrases, and laughter.

Moving on to rhythmic drum music, I shift the group's attention to their legs. While still seated, we begin lifting knees "high," and then lowering feet into a stamp. We collectively build into a rhythmic trot, gradually increasing speed. Like running to a sprint, each participant at his or her own pace, we build to a climax and a restful self-massage of upper legs. The group repeats this action, growing in excitement each time with the uplifting joy that naturally arises from building intensity through dance.

This energetic activity is followed by a more restful focus on awakening face muscles and facial expression. The group is divided into two, creating a face/sound/hand gesture dialogue with one half initiating and the other half responding. This dramatic play and dialogue awaken new sounds and facial expressions while building social interactions and liberating spontaneity. This activity also therapeutically frees up the often-stilted facial expressions that commonly develop as people age.

The above exercise is a gateway to affect-filled dance/vocalizations, for example, the exploration of assertive statements accompanied by gestures. Together the group members come to standing in a circle, although some may participate while remaining seated. I initiate moving-out statements: "It's mine" while grabbing the arms, "go away" while pushing the arms, "It's so nice to see you" with a welcoming gesture. I ask the question "Was there anything you needed to say this week, but didn't? Might we do this together?" The session experiences thus far have helped to develop a group cohesion that encourages this intimate expression of feelings. As participants offer examples, together the group repeats the words and actions in solidarity and support. For example, "Watch out, you will knock me over!" or "I want to make my own decisions." At the close of this improvisation, I suggest a group summary through a dance statement. "Stamp as if we have something important to say!" and we fill the room with a loud and assertive stamp dance.

The standing group members join hands initiating a folk dance circle, while those seated are handed percussion instruments to heighten their participation. We begin a dance to the traditional Italian song "Oh, Marie." The group circles around in unified, stable walking steps. For this group, the music drawn from their heritage is compelling. We circle round, and then with arms held high, we dance toward the center accenting our coming together, and then out again with a collective shout. The group is brimming with vitality and a sense of well-being as we sing to the music in our loudest voices, "Oh, Oh, Marie. . . ."

Dance/movement therapy sessions become a place for elders to work through feelings related to navigating daily life circumstances. Emotional responses such as frustration with the social security office, worrying about grandchildren, or anger at a bus driver that passes them by, all can be directed outward through dance. The group becomes a supportive environment for normalizing the elder's life challenges. For example, in this group, participants returned to their seats after the active folk dance. The conversation turned to the relief of tension they felt. We created an image of throwing all tension and worries out into the center of the circle. This provided relief and further group bonding. In a future session, I might direct a therapeutic role-play of alternative responses to worry and tension. Dancing out themes from daily life thus provides therapeutic outlet and can alter behavior.

In closing the session, I bring participants' attention to increasing well-being in their daily activities. I ask, "Is there one way to take today's dance experience into your week?" Responses include taking a walk with a new friend, participating in an activity in the community rather than remaining home alone, and telling a grandchild about the need for additional help without perceiving this as diminished independence. A farewell, as the sitting group sways through a shared Italian song, keeps the session's emphasis on creative expression and offers an uplifting re-entry into the larger senior center community.

In conclusion, an empowerment-focused dance/movement therapy approach with elders contributes to healthy aging. When viewing the elder with respect and a belief in their capacity for growth, the dance experience increases psycho-physical health and vitality.

References

Chang, M. 2009. "Cultural Consciousness and the Global Context of Dance/ Movement Therapy." In *The Arts and Science of Dance/movement Therapy*, edited by S. Chaiklin, and H. Wengrower, 299–316. New York: Routledge Press.

Sandel, S., and Hollander, S. 1995. "Dance/Movement Therapy with Aging Populations." In *Dance and Other Expressive Arts Therapies: When Words Are Not Enough*, edited by F. Levy, 133–146. New York: Routledge Press.

Shustik, L., and Thompson, T. 2002. "Dance/Movement Therapy: Partners in Personhood." In *Healing Arts Therapies and Person-Centered Dementia Care*, edited by A. Innes and K. Hatfield, 49–78. London: Jessica Kingsley.

CHAPTER FOUR

Diversity in the Aging Community

Tamara A. Baker, Darlingtina K. Atakere,
Jacquelyn A. Minahan, Araba A. Kuofie,
and Thomas Dirth

The definition of "diversity" emphasizes that of being different, having variety, and the inclusion of differences (e.g., people, races, culture). Over the last 25 years, there has been an emergent emphasis in the gerontology field to examine issues related to diversity across racial and ethnic groups. While this has resulted in evident scholarship, the presumably inclusive term does not fully capture the complexities and salient differences seen among the aging communities nationally and globally. This addresses the involvedness of how diversity extends beyond one's physical characteristics (i.e., race), but more on identified selves as defined by disabilities, those with a serious mental illness (SMI), and individuals who identify as lesbian, gay, bisexual, or transgender (LGBT). These descriptions have profoundly been ignored, particularly as they address the social, emotional, physical, and mental health needs of our aging community. What must be recognized is that these identities contribute to the diverse characteristics that influence medical diagnoses, treatment, disease management, and access to resources.

It is critical that we now focus on paramount public health, social, behavioral, and biological concerns as they relate to the needs of older adults. We must distill important advances in the science of aging, while incorporating the evidence of scholars in gerontology, anthropology, humanities, psychology, public health, sociology, social work, biology, medicine, and other similarly related disciplines. It is time that our attention focus on areas pertinent to the well-being of the aging adult population such as work and retirement, social networks, neighborhood and built environments, discrimination, health disparities, long-term care, physical functioning, disabilities, caregiving, housing, end-of-life care, and quality of life.

In identifying the circumstantial reasoning of diversity, there is the need to understand how recognized determinants are intertwined with societal needs, while deciphering how these social pedigrees may successfully embrace the institutional framework of diversity. Thus, in recognizing that with diversity, there are differences, and with differences there are unfortunately disparities. Understanding the dynamics of social and health disparities provides a platform to appropriately address the needs of all aged persons.

The Impetus of Social Determinants of Health and the Aging Community

To improve health among the nation's most vulnerable communities, efforts are needed to better understand and interpret the "root causes" of not only health and well-being, but also disease and health inequalities, inequities, and disparities. It is overdue that practitioners and policy makers recognize the need to better understand the depth of how identifiable determinants embolden health outcomes in general, and among the aging community in particular. Factors, such as social determinant of health (SDoH), underscore existent evidence emphasizing the drastic change in global health outcomes (Marmot and Wilkinson, 2008; Raphael, 2006; Rubin, 2016).

Termed by the Centers for Disease Control (CDC, 2008) and the World Health Organization (WHO), SDoH is defined by five key areas (i.e., economic stability, education, health and health care, neighborhood and built environment, and social and community context). These domains allow for a better understanding as to not only (mental and physical) disease onset, but also the circumstances by which these illnesses exist. It is important to recognize that such determinants define systems by which people are born, grow up, live, work, and age (Marmot and Wilkinson 2008; Solar and Irwin, 2007; WHO, 2008). This is regarded nationally and globally, as there is an emergent recognition of the importance social determinants have in rejecting risky behaviors and harmful lifestyle practices, while assessing areas that promote healthy living and aging. Understanding the dynamics of these determinants may allow for a more theorized explanation of unequal and avoidable differences in health status within and between communities (Adler and Stewart, 2010; Rasanathan and Sharkey, 2016; Rubin, 2016; Solar and Irwin, 2007).

The WHO concedes SDoH as multifaceted, integrated, and overlapping social structures and economic systems that identify and acknowledge upstream and downstream factors that may impact disease diagnoses and management. Yet, what is important to recognize is that the details of SDoH can amass across the life course bringing about fluctuations in health trajectories. For example, neighborhood environments with access to healthy foods, quality housing, reduced exposure to crime and violence, and better environmental conditions (i.e., green space) may serve as catalysts for improved health outcomes. What cannot be dismissed is that SDoH addresses causes of (mental and physical) illness that are beyond that of the individual, but rather provides meaning of the circumstances for symptom onset.

The role of SDoH cannot be overstated. Understanding the meaning of each determinant may bring about a better knowledge of health outcomes, and how to best prioritize treatment options across a multitude of populations. Allowing for such explanations may provide programming that promotes evidence-based strategies, whereby the individual can achieve optimal symptom management, while improving his or her overall quality of life. This may endorse early detection and diagnosis, medication adherence, adequate access to health care, advanced technology, and universal health care (i.e., insurance). Identification and awareness of differences among populations are important to reducing disparities, particularly as it addresses the needs of those older adults experiencing a mental illness.

SDoH and Mental Health Outcomes

In deciphering the role of SDoH on mental health outcomes among older adults, we must first delve into the historical implications of access and opportunities among the most marginalized populations. This primarily references to that of race, by which structural opportunities are related (Phelan and Link, 2015). Race, for example, is a commonly recognized indicator that has past implications on economic and health outcomes. It is a complex and multidimensional social construct that establishes a conceptual framework for how we perceive health, illness, social demands, and environmental changes across the life course. To understand the role of race in one's lived experiences is to understand the extent to which the individual identifies with that (race or cultural) group.

The guise of racial disparities is often fueled by identifiable indices such as economic assembly, education, poverty, unemployment, and food and housing insecurity. This is also evident in the differences in prevalence rates, diagnoses, access to care, and sources of care. Emergent evidence links economic instability to increase incidences of chronic conditions such as cancers, chronic lung diseases, depression, and schizophrenia (Non et al., 2014). Another area that requires attention when addressing the needs and daily lived experiences of the older adult is that of built environment, by which access to healthy foods, quality housing, less crime and violence, discrimination and equity, and incarceration or institutionalization have bearing on mental health outcomes (Gatrell and Elliot, 2015).

Yet, it is without question that humans have diverse cultural experiences and life opportunities contingent on their place and circumstance of birth. In the context of social determinants, culture includes the values and norms that shape beliefs, attitudes, and behaviors of those within their communities. Understanding the influence of social and cultural factors such as discrimination, language, food, and communication style is paramount in the reduction of mental health disparities, as it will aid in the design, implementation, and dissemination of unbiased and culturally sensitive mental health services. An example worth considering is the stigma (and definition) surrounding a mental health diagnosis (Corrigan et al., 2014; Pescosolido, 2013; Yang et al., 2014). Stigma is reported as one of the most significant barriers to seeking help, with disclosure concerns reported as the most common barrier (Clement et al., 2014). It is without question that stigma leads to avoidance (behavior) and delay in seeking specialized mental health in- and out-patient services (Clement et al., 2014). Older adults are more likely to view mental illness as a stigmatizing condition, thereby creating a barrier to care (Cummings, 2008; Jimenez et al., 2013; Sorkin et al., 2001). Not surprising, these individuals are often too embarrassed or ashamed to report their symptoms, as they were raised in a time where such conditions were rarely discussed (Morris, 2001).

Stigma rears itself in reflecting inadequate attention given to the needs of this population, negative attitudes on behalf of treatment providers, unjust policies, exclusion from mental health treatment programs, and an absence from clinical research (Cummings, 2008). Additionally, older adults may question the efficacy of psychotherapy and other treatment measures, which may also decrease the likelihood of engaging in effective treatment (Karlin and Norris, 2005). This is further complicated by those from diverse race and ethnic populations, where the "triple stigma" of being an older adult from a diverse race group, with a mental illness, intersects and co-exists (Jimenez et al., 2013). It has been found that older adults from diverse raced and ethnic groups acknowledge mental illness as a result of internal and external stressors, such as the death of a loved one, financial stress, familial stress, cultural differences, or immigration stress (Jimenez et al., 2013; Sorkin et al., 2011). This is concerning considering that these individuals are less likely to report psychological symptoms (Lee et al., 2014; Nestor, Cheek, and Liu, 2016), to seek out or receive adequate mental health services, or to have access to psychotropic medications (Cook et al., 2013; Lee et al., 2014).

Recognizing that stigma is a product of cultural relevance, societal influences, and moderated by knowledge of the mental illness is an initial step to treatment engagement and service utilization. More importantly, understanding the cultural, biologic, and social influences of these factors is important to consider if the health care paradigm is to adequately expose the needs and vulnerability of our most diverse and marginalized patient population. This is all the more important when addressing diversities among the adult population diagnosed not only with a mental illness, but also with an SMI.

Diversity of Serious Mental Illnesses and the Adult Population

Categorized as schizophrenia, bipolar disorder, schizoaffective disorder, major depressive disorder, depressive psychosis, and treatment-refractory depression (Bartels, 2004; Penkunas, Friedman, and Hahn-Smith, 2015), an estimated 1 million older adults (2–3% of the adult population) are diagnosed with an SMI (Cummings, 2008). By 2030, 25 percent of adults 70+ years of age will be diagnosed with a mental illness, in general with 15 million (20%) reporting an actual diagnosis (Jimenez et al., 2013; Penkunas et al., 2015). In response to the increasing incidence of those diagnosed with an SMI, the federal government passed Public Law 102-321, the Alcohol, Drug Abuse, and Mental Health Administration Reorganization Act (Wang, Demler, and Kessler, 2002). This created block grants to fund community mental health services (at the state level) to provide care to those with an SMI, who are otherwise unable to afford care (Wang et al., 2002). However, these funds amount to less than $50 per year per person (Kessler, Berglund, and Walters, 1998; Kessler, Berglund, and Zhao, 1996; Wang et al., 2002), thus augmenting concerns of the appropriateness and availability of care.

Despite the financial implications, little consideration has been given to the impact these illnesses have on the well-being of the older adult (Bartels and Pratt, 2009). Yet, while slowly gaining momentum, epidemiological evidence shows consistent disparities in service utilization, with older adults being less likely to utilize provided resources (Byers, Arean, and Yaffe, 2012; Garrido et al., 2011; Karlin and Norris, 2005; Penkunas et al., 2015). When compared with younger cohorts with similar diagnoses, older adults do not benefit from the use of mental health services, and when services are sought out, they are more likely to receive treatment through a general practitioner rather than from a mental health provider/specialist (Cuffel et al., 1996).

These factors, inclusive with an SMI diagnosis, significantly influence quality of life, community integration, and physical and cognitive functioning, all of which serve as deterrents to successful aging (Bartels and Pratt, 2009; Cohen et al., 2008; Jeste, Depp, and Vahia, 2010). Factors such as underutilization of mental health services, poor access to treatment, stigma surrounding mental health diagnoses, and marginalization of race and ethnic groups are identified barriers to effective treatment. Not surprisingly, these factors are further complicated by comorbid medical conditions that are common in the aging process. It is important to address this mental and physical health dyad, as many of these chronic medical conditions (e.g., cardiovascular and respiratory diseases) co-occur with that of an SMI diagnosis (Bartels, 2004). For these adults, there is the risk of engaging in harmful health behaviors, such as drug and alcohol use, and/or physical inactivity (Bartels, 2004; Davidson, 2002; Kendrick, 1996; Lambert, Velakoulis, and Pantelis, 2003; Lawrence, Holman, and Jablensky, 2001). Theorists suggest that these risky behaviors, amalgamated with long-term use of antipsychotics, may compromise one's health in later life (American Diabetes Association, 2004; Bartels, 2004). This contends the paucity of empirical evidence underscoring the facilitators and barriers to service treatment, implicating the diversities of an SMI diagnosis (Cummings, 2008), among the aged patient. This may lead to an increasingly complex symptom presentation that must be attended to when conceptualizing their reported needs.

Despite the distribution in services, the historical milieus of "minority" groups (e.g., African Americans, Hispanics, and Native Americans) represent a population of individuals that remain underserved. Biases and race (and ethnic) discrimination solicit (un)recognized barriers to services, similar to that of socioeconomic status, immigration, education, and sexual orientation determinants (Morris, 2001). Historically, African Americans are reported being less likely to seek services (medical and psychiatric), stemming from documented distrust of the medical community. Similarly, Asian Americans are less inclined to participate in psychotherapy, given the differences intrinsic to their cultural heritage of avoiding mental health services until the condition renders as unmanageable and/or other options having been exhausted (Lee et al., 2014; Lin and Cheung, 1999; Yeung et al., 2004). Understanding the intersection of culture and race/ethnicity, with respect to the mental health needs of older adults, may facilitate care that expands across diverse groups.

It is without question that there exists a long-standing history of maltreatment among individuals diagnosed with a mental illness. Until the 1950s, the inpatient care model was considered the gold standard for treating mentally ill patients (Knapp et al., 2010). While state hospitals increased access to services, they were often understaffed and underfunded, leading to unacceptable living conditions and frequent violations of human rights (Knapp et al., 2010). While deinstitutionalization led to an increase in community-based mental health care, this contemporary paradigm shifted more responsibilities (burden) to that of the caregiver(s), who was often ill equipped to provide adequate care to the older patient (Knapp et al., 2010; Novella, 2010). Additionally, mental health services for older adults with SMI are typically provided by a variety of providers, often resulting in gaps of treatment and care (Cummings, 2008). Traditionally, older adults are more likely to approach a primary care physician or medical professional for mental health concerns. However, this presents an issue as physicians or primary health care providers often misdiagnose the psychiatric condition, and are less likely to refer their patients to clinical psychiatric care (Alvidrez and Arean, 2002; Karlin et al., 2008). This is further obscured by a lack of specialized geriatric providers, particularly in community mental health centers treating older adults with severe psychiatric disorders (Cummings, 2008; Light, Lebowitz, and Bailey, 1986; Morris, 2001). However, given the proclivity of older adults seeking mental health services in a primary care setting, mental health services are purposefully becoming available in these settings, as primary care offices move toward a health home model aimed at providing multidisciplinary care (Penkunas et al., 2015).

While the historical interpretation of service use among this adult population underscores the complex nature of diagnosis and treatment, there remain a number of unrecognized characteristics and identities that give emphasis to the diversities of older adults. While societal implications of SMIs is still in a pubescent stage, the inferences of the (older) adult ascribing to an identity as LGBT is still in its infancy. This is, beyond question, an area that has been largely ignored, as diversity in sexual orientation among older adults has been grounded by ethnicity and race, and not by their identity as an older adult.

Diversities among the Adult LGBT Community

There's an amalgam of terms used to recognize persons identifying as LGBT. For example, "sex" refers to one's biological status, where "gender" suggests the attitudes and behaviors that's associated with a person's biological sex. Similarly, "gender identity" references a person's sense of oneself as male, female, or transgender, while "sexual orientation" refers to the gender an individual is sexually and romantically attracted to (American Psychological Association [APA], 2012). Knowing these terminologies allows for appropriate national representation. Accordingly, the APA reports that nearly 2.4 million of older adults (65+) identify as LGBT. While small in number, these adults are disproportionately impacted by mental illness (Fredriksen-Goldsen et al., 2013). As with those experiencing SMI symptomatology, these individuals have similarly higher rates of depression, anxiety, and substance use due to social stressors that are often rooted in stigma and discrimination (Orel, 2013). Older LGBT adults are not only confronted with societal based stigmas of mental health (illness) and aging, but must also withstand prejudices resulting from their sexual orientation.

Born during a time where homosexuality was criminalized and viewed as a sin or mental illness in itself, the older LGBT adult has witnessed an era of deep-rooted hate, victimization, and discrimination. On average, these adults have experienced (or currently experience) victimization and discriminatory practices from verbal insults and physical violence to being threatened if their sexual orientation was revealed (Choy and Meyer, 2016). Those who "came out" at a younger age report having experienced more incidences, with greater intensity, of being verbally and/or physically victimized (D'Augelli and Grossman, 2001). This is further complicated by gradations of discrimination, disparities, racism, homophobic beliefs (National Resource Center on LGBT Aging, 2012), rejection by children and family members, and inequalities in the workplace and health care, all of which may compromise access to and seeking out mental health services and treatment (Smalley, Warren, and Barefoot, 2015). Faced with a number of challenges including high poverty (Badgett, Durso, and Alyssa, 2013), inequalities in health insurance coverages, unfavorable marriage laws, gaps in education, poor treatment by mental health care providers, lack of social support, and nondisclosure of orientation/identity (Smalley et al., 2015), older LGBT adults are yet another group bound by the adage of neither being seen nor being heard. This is evident when seeking mental health and medical services. Accordingly, LGBT adults are more likely to receive lower incomes, thus making them susceptible to higher rates of poverty (Badgett et al., 2013). With a significant number of these adults receiving social security as their only (or primary) source of income, they are placed at a disadvantage on multiple levels. An example is demonstrated in recognizing that only legally married couples (spouses) are eligible to receive/collect financial benefits from social security after the death of a spouse. These benefits, however, may not be available to (older) LGBT couples (Hughes et al., 2011).

Yet, amidst public support for the legalization of same-sex marriage, some states continue to impose bans on same-sex marriages. Failure to recognize and protect LGBT relationships has permitted discrimination in social security and other programs such as Medicaid. Prior to the implementation of the Affordable Care Act, insurance agencies could elect to deny coverage to individuals due to preexisting conditions, thus preventing these individuals from obtaining adequate insurance and care (Skopec and Long, 2015). As a result of years of denial in medical coverage, a high percentage of these adults are uninsured and refused treatment. Similarly, fear of rejection by family members and/or community and lack of social support or social isolation may negatively impact adequate care (Fredriksen-Goldsen et al., 2011), all of which may also increase the individual's risk of depression and other chronic mental illnesses (Cahill and South, 2002).

Lack of awareness about the LGBT community has led to conscious (and/or unconscious) biases among providers and health care staff members, which has resulted in inadequate treatment among this adult population (Foglia and Fredriksen-Goldsen, 2014). In such cases, providers and staff members may inadvertently display discriminatory behaviors and attitudes toward LGBT patients. These sorts of behaviors have often resulted in nondisclosure of sexual orientation of the older (LGBT) adults (D'Augelli and Grossman, 2001) since concealment of their sexual and gender identities may serve as a protective factor against being victimized and/or discriminated against (Fredriksen-Goldsen et al., 2011). Yet, while serving as a potential defense mechanism, rates of nondisclosure may have (in)direct consequential health outcomes. For example, failure to disclose sexual orientation or gender identity may negatively influence patient–provider relationships, which may lead to avoidance in care, delay in diagnosis(es), and misdiagnosis (Durso and Meyer, 2012). Providers who are unaware of a patient's sexual orientation or identity may similarly fail to educate the patient about relevant issues, regardless of their knowledge of the issues affecting the patient population (Durso and Meyer, 2012).

Fortunately, these barriers may be mitigated by other factors that may increase access to mental health services for older LGBT adults. Services that are unrestricted by prejudice and discrimination, strong patient–provider relationships, and networks of social support are culturally appropriate and sensitive for the older LGBT patients (Foglia and Fredriksen-Goldsen, 2014). Training staff to inclusive behaviors and acknowledging the emotional and identified selves of older LGBT adults must be integrated into the system of care (APA, 2012).

The APA has developed guidelines of practice for LGBT clients, by which areas of attitudes toward homosexuality, relationships and families, issues of diversity, economic and workplace issues, and education and training are addressed. Some of these guidelines include: "1) Psychologists understand that lesbian, gay, and bisexual orientations are not mental illnesses, 2) Psychologists strive to recognize the unique experiences of bisexual individuals, 3) Psychologists recognize that the families of lesbian, gay, and bisexual people may include people who are not legally or biologically related 4) Psychologists are encouraged to consider the influences of religion and spirituality in the lives of lesbian, gay, and bisexual persons, 5) Psychologists are encouraged to increase their knowledge and understanding of homosexuality and bisexuality through continuing education, training, supervision, and consultation, 6) Psychologists strive to understand the unique workplace issues that exist for lesbian, gay, and bisexual individuals" (APA, 2011). Application of these guidelines supports the evolving topics salient to working with LGBT clients. These guidelines are critical in informing professional practices and public policies. This political advocacy has similarly been witnessed among another diverse group of older adults—those with a disability.

Disabilities

Referencing to the definition of "diversity," the meaning addresses variety and the inclusion of different types of people. Beyond that of race and ethnicity, the many diversities associated with the older adult clearly shows there is no "one size fits all" paradigm to deciphering the intersection of differences and aging. This again demonstrates the many complexities as to who we are and how we interact with and respond to the specific needs of the growing adult community. An area that has received less attention in addressing issues of diversity among older adults is that of disabilities.

Although numerous, one of the common descriptions defining disability is a lack of capacity to meet the typical demands of life resulting from a mental and/or physical impairment (Iezzoni and Freedman, 2008). This growing body of literature underscores the association disability and physical and mental health have across the life course, by which this relationship being a poignant realization for a number of aging adults (Bruce et al., 1994).

An estimated 20 percent of adults 70+ years of age and 50 percent of those 85 years and older report having a disability (National Long Term Care Survey, 2004). Unfortunately, understanding disability issues in aging adults is often limited by overly individualistic conceptualizations of disability that exclude important socially determined disability experiences. Yet, what has originated from this issue is the contribution of disability activists and scholars who have audaciously (re)conceptualized how society views persons with a disability.

The social model emerged as part of the disability rights movement in the 1970s, which contends the stigmatizing representation of disability experiences, by recognizing a shared disability minority group identity/ representation (Fleischer and Zames, 2011). The social model underscores ways by which the environment and negative social attitudes have a substantial role in functional outcomes of individuals with disabilities, beyond that of a biological condition (Oliver, 1996; Shakespeare, 2014). Likewise, the model is integral in expanding the analysis of disability beyond the medical-scientific field to that of historical, cultural, and political factors influencing the disability experiences (Linton, 2010).

As one considers the assembly of disability, aging, and mental health, the social model's positioning of function from within the person to that of his/her surrounding environment provides a useful connection to the social determinants of disability and health (e.g., Marmot, 2005; Shaw, 2008). Economic insecurity, vulnerability to crime, social isolation, and perceived stigma are contrived influences that disproportionately intersect as aging and disability markers, thus leading to adverse consequences impacting the psychological well-being and quality of life among the general adult populations. For example, there are a number of individuals with a disability(ies) who are often reliant on public assistance for their day-to-day needs, with their use being three times higher than nondisabled persons. These are the very same individuals living at or below the poverty line (von Schrader and Lee, 2015). The life strain of economic deprivation and functional limitations is often predictive of psychological distress (Revicki and Mitchell, 1990).

To the degree that inclusion and group membership are important determinants of psychological health, people with disabilities are often on the outside looking in and are often restricted to certain environments (e.g., hospitals, care institutions, and charitable organizations) (Davis, 2011; Linton, 2010). This suggests that active participation in social relations/ situations is crucial to maintaining functional ability in old age (Avlund et al., 2004). Moreover, the social support that comes from this participation accounts for lower rates of depressive symptomatology (Bruce et al., 1994; Muramatsu, Yin, and Hedeker, 2010).

An area that could be a pervasive negative influence on disability and mental health outcomes is that of perceived discrimination within the disability community (Dovidio, Pagotto, and Hebl, 2014). A recent meta-analysis examining the impact of perceived discrimination on well-being found that the largest average effect size occurred in studies related to the disabilities and illnesses target groups (Schmitt et al., 2014). This suggests that exclusionary treatment received by the target groups is considered legitimate, by which those with certain abilities should not be involved in specific tasks. This may make individuals feel as if they do not have control over their life outcomes, which can profoundly (negatively) impact a person's psyche (Matheson and Anisman, 2012). When one considers the intersecting stereotypes of disability and old age, the perceived legitimacy of exclusionary treatment is only likely to increase.

The disability and aging dyad brings a change in social role, and with declining physical and/or mental functional capacities, these role changes often occur more precipitously. As social roles change, there is loss in identity and social relationships, which may lead to feelings of isolation, loneliness, and poor psychological health (e.g., depression) (Alpass and Neville, 2003). This feedback loop contributes to further social isolation, which may bring about poorer physical and declined mental health outcomes (Penninx et al., 2015).

By attending to the social model of diversity and disability(ies) in aging, practitioners are better equipped to recognize the social mediation that explains the relationship between disability and mental health. Take, for example, hearing loss in older adults. Hearing loss constitutes one of the most common functional declines (disabilities) as a person ages, thus predicting behavioral changes that precipitate social withdrawal and subsequent decline in cognitive performance and increase in depressive symptoms (Arlinger, 2003; Mener et al., 2013). While hearing loss may have a direct medical solution (e.g., hearing aids), there are several barriers that must be considered. Hearing loss is often misattributed to other psychological pathologies such as dementia (Garstecki and Erler, 1998). For this reason, there is limited support from health care providers. This lack of support may lead to a delayed diagnosis and social withdrawal. With this scenario, one has to also account for the financial burden that acquiring hearing aids brings to an aging adult, given that it is often considered an "elective" device and is not covered by one's insurance. Likewise, there continues to be a stigma attached to the use of hearing aids and a resistance to admitting that a person is losing one's hearing (Kochkin, 2000). In short, the disabilities associated with hearing loss must be understood as a socially mediated phenomenon that predicts psychological distress and social isolation.

The case of hearing loss can similarly be generalized to disabilities associated with mobility impairments and chronic illnesses, both which may decrease functioning as a person ages. While it is true that disability and declining health are risk factors for mental health issues (e.g., depression and anxiety) (Kennedy, Kelman, and Thomas, 1990), seeing beyond the impairment to adequately intervening at the patient, provider, and societal levels is imperative. As with the case of hearing loss, are older adults with disabilities given adequate medical support that is not prejudiced by stereotypical expectations? Are everyday environments and public transportation accessible in order to allow active social participation without the anxieties of falling or navigating environmental barriers? Are accommodations too financially burdensome for those subjected to disability stigma?

Moving forward, it is important for clinicians and practitioners working with aging adults to shift the paradigm of healthy aging to include aging with a disability as a viable area of diversity. Given that traditional training of mental health professionals does not include disability competency, established assumptions of disability as a source of mental health issues often makes this shift in thinking impossible (Olkin and Pledger, 2003). Regarding aging and disability through the lens of the social model provides an analytical framework to reimagine a person's ecology as a significant player that considers the ebbs and flows of functional capacities as a natural part of the aging process (Minkler and Fadem, 2002). More importantly, this model provides a connection to the greater disability community that has incredible expertise in flourishing in a non-normative and interdependent living environment (Linton, 2010). More importantly, those working with elderly populations need to understand and appreciate the role of disability, not as a determining feature of poor mental health but as a normal accommodated human experience. More attention is needed to better understand the socially mediated relationship between disability and mental health, encouraging efforts that remedy social isolation rather than focus on an individual's (physical and mental) functional status. This attention should also identify ways to accommodate declines in functional capacities by encouraging self-determined choices in care (i.e., home- and community-based supports) as opposed to institutional care.

It is often assumed that disability is synonymous with old age. However, by listening to the stories and lessons given by those in the disability community, we are encouraged to revise this assumption to see disability as one of many experiences that can be accommodated with the proper staff training and support systems, all of which speak to the diversity of our aging communities.

Conclusion

The role of diversity can never be overstated. Understanding its influence may bring about a better knowledge of how we interpret and assess health determinants (mental and physical) across the life course. An understanding of these factors implies that we can achieve better health outcomes by addressing the circumstances of the individual in promoting (prevention) intervention-based practices and self-management strategies, whereby the individual can achieve optimal symptom management and improved quality of life.

To fully appreciate the contributions of older adults, there must be a commitment to create a multidisciplinary overview for all to understand the aging process across diverse groups of individuals (race, ethnicity, LGBT, socioeconomic status, gender, etc.). Recognizing the enormity of this challenge, leaders in the gerontology field should focus more on contributing to our knowledge and insight on matters most pertinent to understanding the changing demographic tapestry of the adult population.

Yet, what must be clearly understood is that characteristics of diversity are embedded in lived experiences that reflect a biological, behavioral, and social patterning of differential treatment, rights, and privileges that are defined by the life course, which is surrounded by larger historical, geographic, social, cultural, and economic milieus. These constructs outline important factors such as socioeconomic positioning; the contextual grounding of raced, gendered, and more marginalized populations; and explanations for similarities and differences in health outcomes. This may help to identify the social, behavioral, and health-related factors that have important implications for public policy, advocacy, and long-term health (mental and physical) needs of a growing population. Bringing our current knowledge to that of future needs is achievable for future generations of scholars aiming to embrace the diversity of our aging community.

References

Adler, Nancy E., and Judith Stewart. "Health Disparities across the Lifespan: Meaning, Methods, and Mechanisms." *Annals of the New York Academy of Sciences* 1186, no. 1 (2010): 5–23. doi:10.1111/j.1749-6632.2009.05337.x.

Alpass, F. M., and S. Neville. "Loneliness, Health and Depression in Older Males." *Aging & Mental Health* 7, no. 3 (2003): 212–216. doi:10.1080/13607860 31000101193.

Alvidrez, Jennifer, and Patricia A. Areán. "Physician Willingness to Refer Older Depressed Patients for Psychotherapy." *The International Journal of Psychiatry in Medicine* 32, no. 1 (2002): 21–35. doi:10.2190/j26t-yqmj-bf83-m05d.

American Diabetes Association. "Consensus Development Conference on Antipsychotic Drugs and Obesity and Diabetes." *Diabetes Care* 27, no. 2 (2004): 596–601. doi:10.2337/diacare.27.2.596.

American Psychological Association. "Best Practices for Mental Health Facilities Working with LGBT Clients." http://www.apa.org/pi/lgbt/resources/promoting-good-practices.aspx.

American Psychological Association. "Guidelines for Psychological Practice with Lesbian, Gay, and Bisexual Clients." *American Psychologist* 67, no. 1 (2012): 10–42. doi:10.1037/a0024659.

Arlinger, Stig. "Negative Consequences of Uncorrected Hearing Loss—A Review." *International Journal of Audiology* 42, no. Supp. 2 (2003): 17–20. doi:10.31 09/14992020309074639.

Avlund, Kirsten, Rikke Lund, Bjorn E. Holstein, and Pernille Due. "Social Relations as Determinant of Onset of Disability in Aging." *Archives of Gerontology and Geriatrics* 38, no. 1 (2004): 85–99. doi:10.1016/j.archger.2003.08.003.

Badgett, M. V. Lee, Laura E. Durso, and Alyssa Schneebaum. "New Patterns of Poverty in the Lesbian, Gay, and Bisexual Community." The Williams Institute, UCLA, 2013. http://escholarship.org/uc/item/8dq9d947.

Bartels, Stephen J. "Caring for the Whole Person: Integrated Health Care for Older Adults with Severe Mental Illness and Medical Comorbidity." *Journal of the American Geriatrics Society* 52, no. s12 (2004): S249–S257. doi:10.11 11/j.1532-5415.2004.52601.x.

Bartels, Stephen J., and Sarah I. Pratt. "Psychosocial Rehabilitation and Quality of Life for Older Adults with Serious Mental Illness: Recent Findings and Future Research Directions." *Current Opinion in Psychiatry* 22, no. 4 (2009): 381–385. doi:10.1097/yco.0b013e32832c9234.

Bruce, M. L., T. E. Seeman, S. S. Merrill, and D. G. Blazer. "The Impact of Depressive Symptomatology on Physical Disability: MacArthur Studies of Successful Aging." *American Journal of Public Health* 84, no. 11 (1994): 1796–1799. doi:10.2105/ajph.84.11.1796.

Byers, Amy L., Patricia A. Arean, and Kristine Yaffe. "Low Use of Mental Health Services among Older Americans with Mood and Anxiety Disorders." *Psychiatric Services* 63, no. 1 (2012): 66–72. doi:10.1176/appi.ps.201100121.

Cahill, S., and K. South. "Policy Affecting Lesbian, Gay, Bisexual, and Transgender People in Retirement." *Generations* 26, no. 2 (2002): 49.

Centers for Disease Control and Prevention. *Health Disparities among Racial/Ethnic Populations.* Report. Atlanta: Centers for Disease Control and Prevention, 2008.

Choy, S. K., and I. H. Meyer. *LGBT Aging: A Review of Recent Findings, Needs and Policy Implications.* Report. Los Angeles: Williams Institute, 2016.

Clement, S., O. Schauman, T. Graham, F. Maggioni, S. Evans-Lacko, N. Bezborodovs, C. Morgan, N. Rüsch, J. S. L. Brown, and G. Thornicroft. "What Is the Impact of Mental Health-Related Stigma on Help-seeking? A Systematic Review of Quantitative and Qualitative Studies." *Psychological Medicine* 45, no. 01 (2014): 11–27. doi:10.1017/s0033291714000129.

Cohen, Carl I., Richa Pathak, Paul M. Ramirez, and Ipsit Vahia. "Outcome among Community Dwelling Older Adults with Schizophrenia: Results Using Five Conceptual Models." *Community Mental Health Journal* 45, no. 2 (2008): 151–156. doi:10.1007/s10597-008-9161-8.

Cook, Benjamin L., Samuel H. Zuvekas, Nicholas Carson, Geoffrey Ferris Wayne, Andrew Vesper, and Thomas G. McGuire. "Assessing Racial/Ethnic Disparities in Treatment across Episodes of Mental Health Care." *Health Services Research* 49, no. 1 (2013): 206–229. doi:10.1111/1475-6773. 12095.

Corrigan, Patrick W., Benjamin G. Druss, and Deborah A. Perlick. "The Impact of Mental Illness Stigma on Seeking and Participating in Mental Health Care." *Psychological Science in the Public Interest* 15, no. 2 (2014): 37–70. doi:10.1177/1529100614531398.

Cuffel, B. J., D. V. Jeste, M. Halpain, C. Pratt, H. Tarke, and T. L. Patterson. "Treatment Costs and Use of Community Mental Health Services for Schizophrenia by Age Cohorts." *American Journal of Psychiatry* 153, no. 7 (1996): 870–876. doi:10.1176/ajp.153.7.870.

Cummings, Sherry M. "Treating Older Persons with Severe Mental Illness in the Community: Impact of an Interdisciplinary Geriatric Mental Health Team." *Journal of Gerontological Social Work* 52, no. 1 (2008): 17–31. doi:10.1080/01634370802561919.

D'Augelli, A. R., and A. H. Grossman. "Disclosure of Sexual Orientation, Victimization, and Mental Health among Lesbian, Gay, and Bisexual Older Adults." *Journal of Interpersonal Violence* 16, no. 10 (2001): 1008–1027. doi:10.1177/088626001016010003.

Davidson, M. "Risk of Cardiovascular Disease and Sudden Death in Schizophrenia." *Journal of Clinical Psychiatry* 63, no. 9 (2002): 5–11.

Davis, L. J. "Why Is Disability Missing from the Discourse on Diversity?" *The Chronicle of Higher Education.* September 25, 2011. Accessed March 12, 2017. http://www.chronicle.com/article/Why-Is-Disability-Missing-From/129088/.

Dovidio, J. F., L. Pagotto, and M. R. Hebl. "Implicit Attitudes and Discrimination against People with Physical Disabilities." In *Disability and Aging Discrimination*, edited by Richard L. Wiener, 157–183. Place of Publication Not Identified: Springer, 2014.

Durso, Laura E., and Ilan H. Meyer. "Patterns and Predictors of Disclosure of Sexual Orientation to Healthcare Providers among Lesbians, Gay Men, and Bisexuals." *Sexuality Research and Social Policy* 10, no. 1 (2012): 35–42. doi:10.1007/s13178-012-0105-2.

Fleischer, Doris Zames, and Frieda Zames. *The Disability Rights Movement: From Charity to Confrontation.* Philadelphia: Temple University Press, 2011.

Foglia, Mary Beth, and Karen I. Fredriksen-Goldsen. "Health Disparities among LGBT Older Adults and the Role of Nonconscious Bias." *Hastings Center Report* 44, no. S4 (2014). doi:10.1002/hast.369.

Fredriksen-Goldsen, K. I., H. Kim, S.E. Barkan, A. Muraco, and C.P. Hoy-Ellis. "Health Disparities among Lesbian, Gay, and Bisexual Older Adults: Results from a Population-Based Study." *American Journal of Public Health* 103, no. 10 (2013): 1802–1809. doi:10.2105/AJPH.2012.301110.

Garrido, Melissa M., Robert L. Kane, Merrie Kaas, and Rosalie A. Kane. "Use of Mental Health Care by Community-Dwelling Older Adults." *Journal of the American Geriatrics Society* 59, no. 1 (2011): 50–56. doi:10.1111/j.1532-5415.2010.03220.x.

Garstecki, Dean C., and Susan F. Erler. "Hearing Loss, Control, and Demographic Factors Influencing Hearing Aid Use among Older Adults." *Journal of*

Speech Language and Hearing Research 41, no. 3 (1998): 527. doi:10.1044/jslhr.4103.527.

Gatrell, Anthony C., and Susan J. Elliott. *Geographies of Health: An Introduction.* Chichester: John Wiley & Sons, 2015.

Hughes, Anne K., Rena D. Harold, and Janet M. Boyer. "Awareness of LGBT Aging Issues among Aging Services Network Providers." *Journal of Gerontological Social Work* 54, no. 7 (2011): 659–677. doi:10.1080/01634372.2011.585392.

Iezzoni, Lisa I., and Vicki A. Freedman. "Turning the Disability Tide." *Journal of the American Medical Association* 299, no. 3 (2008). doi:10.1001/jama.299.3.332.

Jeste, Dilip V., Colin A. Depp, and Ipsit V. Vahia. "Successful Cognitive and Emotional Aging." *World Psychiatry* 9, no. 2 (2010): 78–84. doi:10.1002/j.2051-5545.2010.tb00277.x.

Jimenez, Daniel E., Stephen J. Bartels, Veronica Cardenas, and Margarita Alegria. "Stigmatizing Attitudes toward Mental Illness among Racial/Ethnic Older Adults in Primary Care." *International Journal of Geriatric Psychiatry* 28, no. 10 (2013): 1061–1068. doi:10.1002/gps.3928.

Karlin, Bradley E., Michael Duffy, and David H. Gleaves. "Patterns and Predictors of Mental Health Service Use and Mental Illness among Older and Younger Adults in the United States." *Psychological Services* 5, no. 3 (2008): 275–294. doi:10.1037/1541-1559.5.3.275.

Karlin, Bradley E., and Margaret P. Norris. "Public Mental Health Care Utilization by Older Adults." *Administration and Policy in Mental Health and Mental Health Services Research* 33, no. 6 (2005): 730–736. doi:10.1007/s10488-005-0003-5.

Kendrick, T. "Cardiovascular and Respiratory Risk Factors and Symptoms among General Practice Patients with Long-Term Mental Illness." *The British Journal of Psychiatry* 169, no. 6 (1996): 733–739. doi:10.1192/bjp.169.6.733.

Kennedy, Gary J., Howard R. Kelman, and Cynthia Thomas. "The Emergence of Depressive Symptoms in Late Life: The Importance of Declining Health and Increasing Disability." *Journal of Community Health* 15, no. 2 (1990): 93–104. doi:10.1007/bf01321314.

Kessler, R. C., P. A. Berglund, and E. E. Walters. "A Methodology for Estimating the 12-Month Prevalence of Serious Mental Illness." In *Mental Health, United States 1998*, edited by R. W. Manderscheid and R. W. Henderson, 99–109. Washington, DC: U.S. Government Printing Office, 1998.

Kessler, R. C., P. A. Berglund, and S. Zhao. "The 12-Month Prevalence and Correlates of Serious Mental Illness (SMI)." In *Mental Health, United States*, edited by R. W. Manderscheid and M. A. Sonnenschein, 59–70. Washington, DC: U.S. Government Printing Office, 1996.

Knapp, Martin, Jennifer Beecham, David McDaid, Tihana Matosevic, and Monique Smith. "The Economic Consequences of Deistitutionalization of Mental Health Services: Lessons from a Systematic Review of European Experience."

Health & Social Care in the Community 19, no. 2 (2010): 113–125. doi:10.1111/
j.1365-2524.2010.00969.x.

Kochkin, Sergei. "'Why My Hearing Aids Are in the Drawer': The Consumers'
Perspective." *The Hearing Journal* 53, no. 2 (2000): 34. doi:10.1097/000
25572-200002000-00004.

Lambert, T. I., D. Velakoulis, and C. Pantelis. "Medical Comorbidity in Schizophrenia." *Medical Journal of Australia* 178 (2003): 67–70.

Lawrence, David, D'Arcy Holman, and Assen Jablensky. *Preventable Physical Illness
in People with Mental Illness.* Crawley, Western Australia: Centre for Health
Services Research, Department of Public Health, University of Western Australia, 2001.

Lee, Su Yeon, Qian-Li Xue, Adam P. Spira, and Hochang B. Lee. "Racial and Ethnic
Differences in Depressive Subtypes and Access to Mental Health Care in
the United States." *Journal of Affective Disorders* 155 (2014): 130–137. doi:10
.1016/j.jad.2013.10.037.

Light, Enid, Barry D. Lebowitz, and Frank Bailey. "CMHC's and Elderly Services:
An Analysis of Direct and Indirect Services and Service Delivery Sites."
Community Mental Health Journal 22, no. 4 (1986): 294–302. doi:10.1007/
bf00754384.

Lin, Keh-Ming, and Freda Cheung. "Mental Health Issues for Asian Americans."
Psychiatric Services 50, no. 6 (1999): 774–780. doi:10.1176/ps.50.6.774.

Linton, Simi. *Claiming Disability: Knowledge and Identity.* New York: New York
University Press, 2010.

Marmot, M. "Social Determinants of Health Inequalities." *The Lancet*, 365, no. 9464
(2005): 1099–1104.

Marmot, Michael, and Richard G. Wilkinson. *Social Determinants of Health.*
Oxford: Oxford University Press, 2008.

Matheson, K., and H. Anisman. "Biological and Psychosocial Responses to Discrimination." In *Social Cure: Identity, Health and Well-Being,* edited by
J. Jetten and S. A. Haslam, 133–153. New York: Psychology Press, 2012.

Mener, D. J., J. Betz, D. J. Genther, D. Chen, and F. R. Lin. "Hearing Loss and
Depression in Older Adults." *Journal of American Geriatrics Society* 61,
no. 9 (2013): 1627–1629.

Minkler, M., and P. Fadem. "'Successful Aging': A Disability Perspective." *Journal
of Disability Policy Studies* 12, no. 4 (2002): 229–235. doi:10.1177/104420
730201200402.

Morris, D. L. "Geriatric Mental Health: An Overview." *Journal of American Psychiatric Nurse Association* 7, no. 6 (2001): 2–7.

Muramatsu, Naoko, Hongjun Yin, and Donald Hedeker. "Functional Declines, Social
Support, and Mental Health in the Elderly: Does Living in a State Supportive of Home and Community-Based Services Make a Difference?"
Social Science & Medicine 70, no. 7 (2010): 1050–1058. doi:10.1016/j.
socscimed.2009.12.005.

National Long Term Care Survey. 2004. report.nih.gov/nihfactsheets/ViewFact
Sheet.aspx?csid=37.

National Resource Center on LGBT Aging. "Inclusive Services for LGBT Older Adults: A Practical Guide to Creating a Welcoming Agencies." 2012. Accessed March 12, 2017. https://www.sageusa.org/files/NRCInclusiveSer vicesGuide2012.pdf+.

Nestor, Bridget A., Shayna M. Cheek, and Richard T. Liu. "Ethnic and Racial Differences in Mental Health Service Utilization for Suicidal Ideation and Behavior in a Nationally Representative Sample of Adolescents." *Journal of Affective Disorders* 202 (2016): 197–202. doi:10.1016/j.jad.2016.05.021.

Non, A. L., M. Rewak, I. Kawachi, S. E. Gilman, E. B. Loucks, A. A. Appleton, J. C. Roman, S. L. Buka, and L. D. Kubzansky. "Childhood Social Disadvantage, Cardiometabolic Risk, and Chronic Disease in Adulthood." *American Journal of Epidemiology* 180, no. 3 (2014): 263–271. doi:10.1093/aje/kwu127.

Novella, Enric J. "Mental Health Care and the Politics of Inclusion: A Social Systems Account of Psychiatric Deinstitutionalization." *Theoretical Medicine and Bioethics* 31, no. 6 (2010): 411–427. doi:10.1007/s11017-010-9155-8.

Oliver, Michael. *Understanding Disability: From Theory to Practice.* Houndmills: Macmillan, 1996.

Olkin, Rhoda, and Constance Pledger. "Can Disability Studies and Psychology Join Hands?" *American Psychologist* 58, no. 4 (2003): 296–304. doi:10.1037/0003-066x.58.4.296.

Orel, Nancy A. "Investigating the Needs and Concerns of Lesbian, Gay, Bisexual, and Transgender Older Adults: The Use of Qualitative and Quantitative Methodology." *Journal of Homosexuality* 61, no. 1 (2013): 53–78. doi:10.1080/00918369.2013.835236.

Penkunas, Michael J., Anne Friedman, and Stephen Hahn-Smith. "Characteristics of Older Adults with Serious Mental Illness Enrolled in a Publicly Funded In-Home Mental Health Treatment Program." *Home Health Care Management & Practice* 27, no. 4 (2015): 224–229. doi:10.1177/108482 2315571531.

Penninx, B. W., S. Leveille, L. Ferrucci, J. T. Van Eijk, and J. M. Guralnik. "Exploring the Effect of Depression on Physical Disability: Longitudinal Evidence from the Established Populations for Epidemiologic Studies of the Elderly." *American Journal of Public Health* 89, no. 9 (2015): 1346–1352.

Pescosolido, Bernice A. "The Public Stigma of Mental Illness." *Journal of Health and Social Behavior* 54, no. 1 (2013): 1–21. doi:10.1177/0022146512471197.

Phelan, Jo C., and Bruce G. Link. "Is Racism a Fundamental Cause of Inequalities in Health?" *Annual Review of Sociology* 41, no. 1 (2015): 311–330. doi:10.1146/annurev-soc-073014-112305.

Raphael, Dennis. "Social Determinants of Health: Present Status, Unanswered Questions, and Future Directions." *International Journal of Health Services* 36, no. 4 (2006): 651–677. doi:10.2190/3mw4-1ek3-dgrq-2crf.

Rasanathan, K., and A. Sharkey. "Global Health Promotion and the Social Determinants of Health." In *Introduction to Global Health Promotion*, edited by Rick S. Zimmerman, Ralph J. Diclemente, Jon K. Andrus, and Everold N. Hosein, 49. San Francisco, CA: Jossey-Bass, 2016.

Revicki, D.A., and J.P. Mitchell. "Strain, Social Support, and Mental Health in Rural Elderly Individuals." *Journal of Gerontology* 45, no. 6 (1990). doi:10.1093/geronj/45.6.s267.

Rubin, I. L., J. Merrick, D.E. Greydanus, and D.R. Patel (Eds.). *Health Care for People with Intellectual and Developmental Disabilities across the Lifespan.* Cham: Springer International Publishing, 2016.

Schmitt, Michael T., Nyla R. Branscombe, Tom Postmes, and Amber Garcia. "The Consequences of Perceived Discrimination for Psychological Well-being: A Meta-analytic Review." *Psychological Bulletin* 140, no. 4 (2014): 921–948. doi:10.1037/a0035754.

Shakespeare, Tom. *Disability Rights and Wrongs Revisited.* London: Routledge, 2014.

Shaw, D. "Social Determinants of Health: Present Status, Unanswered Questions, and Future Directions." *Clinical Medicine* 8, no. 2 (2008): 225–226.

Skopec, L., and S.K. Long. "Lesbian, Gay and Bisexual Adults Making Gains in Health Insurance and Access to Care." *Health Affairs* 34, no. 10 (2015):1769–1773. doi:10.1377/hlthaff.2015.0826.

Smalley, K.B., J.C. Warren, and K.N. Barefoot. "Barriers to Care and Psychological Distress Difference between Bisexual and Gay Men and Women." *Journal of Bisexuality* 15 (2015): 230–247. doi:10.1080/15299716.2015.1025176.

Solar, O., and A. Irwin. *A Conceptual Framework for Action on the Social Determinants of Health. Discussion Paper for the Commission on Social Determinants of Health.* Working paper. Geneva: World Health Organization, 2007.

Sorkin, Dara H., Hannah Nguyen, and Quyen Ngo-Metzger. "Assessing the Mental Health Needs and Barriers to Care among a Diverse Sample of Asian American Older Adults." *Journal of General Internal Medicine* 26, no. 6 (2011): 595–602. doi:10.1007/s11606-010-1612-6.

von Schrader, S., and C. G. Lee. "Disability Statistics from the Current Population Survey (CPS)." Disability Statistics. 2015. Accessed September 25, 2015. http://www.disabilitystatistics.org/.

Wang, Philip S., Olga Demler, and Ronald C. Kessler. "Adequacy of Treatment for Serious Mental Illness in the United States." *American Journal of Public Health* 92, no. 1 (2002): 92–98. doi:10.2105/ajph.92.1.92.

World Health Organization. *Closing the Gap in a Generation: Health Equity through Action on the social Determinants of Health.* Final report of the Commission on Social Determinants of Health, World Health Organization, Commission on Social Determinants of Health, Geneva, 2008.

Yang, Lawrence H., Fang-Pei Chen, Kathleen Janel Sia, Jonathan Lam, Katherine Lam, Hong Ngo, Sing Lee, Arthur Kleinman, and Byron Good. "What Matters Most: A Cultural Mechanism Moderating Structural Vulnerability and Moral Experience of Mental Illness Stigma." *Social Science & Medicine* 103 (2014): 84–93. doi:10.1016/j.socscimed.2013.09.009.

Yeung, Albert, Doris Chang, Robert L. Gresham, Andrew A. Nierenberg, and Maurizio Fava. "Illness Beliefs of Depressed Chinese American Patients in Primary Care." *The Journal of Nervous and Mental Disease* 192, no. 4 (2004): 324–327. doi:10.1097/01.nmd.0000120892.96624.00.

Moving toward Connection: Using Creative Arts Approaches to Enhance the Well-Being of Elders

Vivien Marcow Speiser

We have been taught in the past to fear the limitations associated with older age. But the arts can reframe our later years into a new period of discovery, and possibility. Instead of losing vision, or hearing or mobility, the arts show us that we are lifelong learners; that we are never too old to dream, create, and blossom.

—Jane Chu, at the National Center for Creative Aging Conference 2016

This case study presents a partnership between a community housing project for elders in Massachusetts and a university-based arts in health institute, infusing arts based programming funded by a National Endowment for the Arts grant to enhance the well-being of elders. Given the increased and increasing numbers of elders living longer, with varied degrees of ability and functioning, there is an increased need for creative approaches to working with this population. Personal expression through creativity and the arts has been proven to access the body, mind, spirit, and heart continuum, across the ages, and has a demonstrated efficacy in working with elders. We can safely hypothesize that the need for creative programs as well as the financial impact of caring for elders will grow and that the need for supportive services for elders will increase and that this creative arts–based approach could be expanded for use in a range of other senior community and residential settings.

Background

Carmel, Morse, and Torres-Gil (2007) in their cross-cultural study on aging argue that across the globe we are facing the challenges and the need for care solutions to address unprecedented growth in an aging population. In addition to the medical and health care issues posed by increased longevity, the long-term implications and systemic challenges will create burdens upon existing care giving and health systems. Changes in geographical circumstances may separate the elderly from family support systems at the same time as they are facing declines in health and functional capacities. This in turn may lead to feelings of disconnection and isolation, which may lead to increased incidences of depression (Black, 2015). Therefore, there is a need for initiatives to combat isolation and its attendant health and mental health consequences in the aging population. These unique challenges present opportunities for creative and innovative new strategies.

This is where arts can be brought into play.

Defining the Need

The Whitehouse Conference on Aging report of 2015 (National Endowment for the Arts, 2015) notes that:

> The United States continues to experience incredible transformation. Over 10,000 baby boomers are turning 65 every day, and the fastest growing demographic in the U.S. is women over age 85. This age wave will continue into the next decade and beyond. To help every American enjoy a longer, better, more active and independent life, our society needs to be able to effectively engage the challenges and fully embrace the possibilities inherent in an aging population.

Elder care giving is further exacerbated with an increase of people living with age-related disorders such as dementia and Alzheimer's disease. According to the Administration on Aging, "U.S. Census Bureau Projections of 2012" (p. 1), it is estimated that in 2050 there will be increases in the population above 65 years to 83.7 million people, almost double the 43.1 million in 2012.

As the proportion of older people in the population increases, so does the number of people living with dementia and the people who care for them. As the condition progresses, an individual's ability to communicate deteriorates, increasing stress and putting pressure on everyone surrounding the person. In Massachusetts, there are currently more than 120,000 individuals aged 65 and older with Alzheimer's disease or a related dementia, and more than 319,000 unpaid individuals caring for those with dementia (Alzheimer's Association, Executive Office or Elder Affairs, 2012).

Role of the Arts

Research has shown that participation in creative arts can improve self-esteem, well-being, and physical health (Cohen et al., 2006). Creative endeavors during the older years can enhance well-being by developing and maintaining problem-solving skills, symbolic expression, perception, and motivation (Abraham, 2005; Alders and Levine-Madori, 2010; Stallings, 2010; Stewart, 2004). In addition, participation in arts-based activities promote engagement in community activities and contribute toward an improvement in morale and the promotion of physical and emotional well-being (Moody and Phinney, 2012; Noice and Noice, 2008). Sixsmith and Gibson (2007) and McDermott, Orrell, and Ridder (2014) write about the improvements they noted in their studies for using music with dementia as well as its positive effects on caregivers and the widespread and systemic benefits it offers such as increasing social connections and opportunities for meaning making as well as perceived psychological and physical benefits.

Castora-Binkley et al. (2010) state that: "The aging of the population, coupled with significant increases in health care costs resulting from the proliferation of chronic health diseases and disabilities, have fostered a growing interest in health promotion and wellness interventions for older adults" (p. 353). They conclude that, "With the current emphasis on self-management of health and engagement in health promotion and disease prevention activities, arts programs can serve as an attractive and effective means to these ends for older adults from a diversity of backgrounds" (p. 365).

Hallam et al. (2014) hypothesize that "active engagement in community music supports the well-being of older people." They demonstrate in their findings that "those actively engaged with making music exhibit higher levels of well-being than those engaged in other group activities" (p. 111). They conclude "there is growing evidence that active music making in a social context has the potential to enhance well-being and physical and mental health in older people. Providing opportunities in local communities for music making has the potential to meet some of the needs, identified as important to and for older people to assist them in remaining active and enabling them to age with dignity and maintain their independence for longer" (p. 115).

The arts utilize organizational properties of artistic forms to structure, make meaning of, and express inner worlds. Engagement with the arts can provide both an enjoyable experience and a source of interpersonal contact (Keogh et al., 2009). Improved memory, alertness, reality orientation, judgment, stability, anxiety, personal insight, acceptance, mobilization, and self-esteem have all been associated with using movement with older individuals (Ashley and Crenan, 1993).

Resilience and the Elderly

A key to well-being is predicated on resilience in individuals. Resilience is a function that need not decline with age and is enhanced by factors including age, gender, health and well-being, social connections, family networks, and spirituality. The Centre for Policy on Aging defines "Resilience in older age is the ability to stand up to adversity and to 'bounce back' or return to a state of equilibrium following individual adverse episodes" (2004, p. 6).

Antonovsky (1985) postulates that stressors impact upon the individual, depending upon the disruption in coherence of factors of comprehensibility, manageability, and meaningfulness. Numerous studies focus their research on the positive effects of spirituality and belief as a factor in well-being and resilience (Cummings and Pargament, 2010; Faigin and Pargament, 2014; Pargament, 2001). All of these factors are brought into play in working with the arts with elders.

Using Creative Arts Approaches to Enhance the Well-Being of Elders

Working in collaboration with the Jewish Community Housing for the Elderly (JCHE), the Institute for Arts and Health (IAH) has been piloting a healthy aging program with a grant from the National Endowment for the Arts. The IAH has engaged 1,500 low-income JCHE residents in a series of creative experiences over a two-year period. With the NEA Art-Works grant, IAH and JCHE teamed up to deploy a range of artistic disciplines and creative modalities specifically adapted for older adults and designed to build community, enhance well-being, foster cross-cultural appreciation, increase self-esteem, improve motor and cognitive skills, and promote meaningful social connections. The participatory arts activities included in this program, creative arts opportunities, including access to playback theater performances, art and music-making workshops, mural-making, dance, creative movement, and poetry writing experiences are cited to contribute to healthy aging through an improvement in individuals' physical and psychological well-being (National Endowment for the Arts, 2013).

This project infused the arts throughout the four residences of JCHE where artists worked directly with an aging multicultural community of adults with varying abilities and backgrounds to promote enhanced engagement with the arts, healthy aging, improved well-being and social connections, and a heightened sense of community identity and place. The arts activities were designed to build a sense of community through enhanced modes of communication and expression while creating an inclusive environment that allows all participants to engage with the arts, especially these who are limited by mobility, ethnicity, language, and disability.

The JHCE populations served are on average 80 years old, and 78 percent immigrants who have had extremely difficult lives, contending with political and religious persecution, abuse, and poverty. In addition, they are from 25 countries and speak 22 primary languages. Loss, illness, depression, and increased frailty frequently result in social isolation for older adults. Research indicates that chronic loneliness can seriously impact mental and physical health. The creative arts programs were intended to use the "language of art" to build bridges of understanding between diverse residents, many of who don't even share a common language. Artistic engagement can create inspirational opportunities that engage both residents who are seasoned artists and those who have impaired vision, mobility, and cognition. These workshops were intended to build community, enhance cross-cultural appreciation, increase self-esteem, improve motor and cognitive skills, and promote meaningful social connections.

This approach is predicated upon the belief that effective engagement in the arts, through workshops specifically designed for older adults, requires participation on their part in diverse artistic creative processes across a spectrum of artistic disciplines. Each resident was given the opportunity to choose between several modalities offered at each of the four sites.

The goals of the program included the following:

1. The creation and evaluation of a model that promotes creative approaches to healthy aging through engagement in a variety of arts experiences designed for older adults residing in affordable, independent housing through creative arts and movement experiences.

2. The provision of community-building opportunities for creative meaningful connections that combat social isolation and depression for groups of up to 100 adults, depending on the activity.

3. The evaluation of the effectiveness of these sessions in promoting meaningful social connections and healthy aging.

The measures used to evaluate the outcome included observations and informal interviews and the design of survey questions for the artists/ workshop leaders. The workshop leaders and artists who participated in the program noted the interest and enthusiasm of the participants and their willingness to engage in the arts-based activities.

Outcomes

In general, both the artist leaders and participants noted an increase in social connections and self-esteem through participation in meaningful creative expression experiences with others. The surveys noted engaged participation and a felt connection to others. The participants also expressed joy and gratitude toward the program. They also noted that the activities provided a positive atmosphere, which fostered creative expression and opportunities for socialization.

Most residents appreciated the opportunity to try something new, for example, working with clay, even when the task is challenging. The fact that we can introduce new and creative activities when working with residents in their eighties and nineties, many of whom declare that they have never been able to produce any sort of artwork but are enthusiastic and excited about the program, is truly a gift. Not only were these residents able to engage in creative expression through the arts, but they also learned about artistic expression through their engagement with the materials.

One of the activities in this project resulted in a mural-making project where artist and art therapist, Tova Speter, engaged residents of JCHE's Golda Meir House in Newton in the creation of a distinctive art installation to hang prominently in the front lobby (Jewish Community Housing for the Elderly, 2016).

Ms. Speter offers these reflections on the project:

> It was an honor to work with this community to design a project reflective of the residents' interests. We took our inspiration from the colors of spring and the vibrancy of this community. Residents brain-stormed ideas during a community event and expressed interest in creating art that is colorful, welcoming, peaceful, balanced, bright and happy. As with all JCHE events,

the project included a diverse group of residents, including English, Chinese, and Russian speaking cultures—and it was very heartwarming to see them find a common language through art and the natural beauty of spring. After engaging with various materials, the project took shape with the goal of creating a unified structure focused on the colorful inspiration and memories participants had with regard to flowers and springtime. Artwork was first created individually, then in pairs, and finally, all woven together into a unified presentation. I feel the end product is entirely reflective of the values of this community. Each participant contributed a piece that is unique and plays an important role in the overall tapestry.

Residents painted leaves and pine cones as well as created a collective poem that came out of the morning check-in.

Collective Poem—Golda Meir Poetry, Art and Movement group December 17, 2015

It came to my mind, a picture of my life as a child. We have all moments, sad moments, happy moments,

But overall I feel blessed.

The acorn and the Pine cone, what beautiful ornaments & necklaces, like in our childhood.

Reminds me of tall trees: let's hope our lives are tall with love and kindness.

I have a big pine cone, I don't know who put it there, but I picked it up! I've never seen one like that before. Is this real!?

I'm having trouble hearing today so I'll pass this along.

I want to be thoughtful for things I can do and not look at the negative things in my life.

A gold pinecone. How interesting. I love this time of year, reminds me of change. Change is healthy.

It feels nice as an adult to appreciate the things when I was young.

I'm happy I woke up this morning. I'm happy to be here. I really feel blessed by all the life in my life.

This heart connects us all. I feel the connection. Each one of you will be in my heart.

Conclusion

Working with elders in this program has been a privilege. These elders are role models for overcoming adversity and finding joy in connection and self-expression. This community taught this writer never to take anything for granted. They remind "me" that we are all in this together. There are no "we" and "them." It is all "us." It is about finding the common threads of individual stories woven together within the collective artistic experience. The attribution of meaning and continuity in the face of enormous and sometimes overwhelming losses is heartwarming and inspirational. As the poem concludes:

This heart connects us all. I feel the connection. Each one of you will be in my heart.

References

Abraham, Ruth. *When Words Have Lost Their Meaning: Alzheimer's Patients Communicate through Art.* Westport, CT: Praeger, 2005.

Administration on Aging, "U.S. Census Bureau Projections of 2009." Administration for Community Living. Accessed April 25, 2014. http://www.aoa .gov/AoARoot/AoA_Programs/HPW/Behavioral/docs++2/Massachusetts+ Epi+Profile+Final.pdf+.

Alders, Amanda, and Linda Levine-Madori. "The Effect of Art Therapy on Cognitive Performance of Hispanic/Latino Older Adults." *Art Therapy* 27, no. 3 (2010): 127–135. doi:10.1080/07421656.2010.10129661.

Alzheimer's Association. Executive Office or Elder Affairs. "Massachusetts Alzheimer's Disease and Related Disorders State Plan." February 2012. Accessed April 25, 2014. http://www.alz.org/documents_custom/alz_state_ plan_mass.pdf+.

Antonovsky, Aaron. *Health, Stress and Coping.* San Francisco: Jossey-Bass, 1985.

Ashley, F. B., and M. Crenan. "Dance: The Movement Activity of the Elderly." *Nursing Homes* 42 (1993): 50–51.

Black, Kathy, Debra Dobbs, and Tiffany L. Young. "Aging in Community." *Journal of Applied Gerontology* 34, no. 2 (2015): 219–243. doi:10.1177/073346 4812463984.

Carmel, Sara, Carol A. Morse, and Fernando M. Torres-Gil. *Lessons on Aging from Three Nations.* Amityville, NY: Baywood Publishing, 2007.

Castora-Binkley, Melissa, Linda Noelker, Thomas Prohaska, and William Satariano. "Impact of Arts Participation on Health Outcomes for Older Adults." *Journal of Aging, Humanities, and the Arts* 4, no. 4 (2010): 352–367. doi:10. 1080/19325614.2010.533396.

Chu, Jane, National Center for Creative Aging Conference. "Notable Quotable: Jane Chu on the Arts and Aging." Accessed at https://www.arts.gov/art-works/2016/notable-quotable-jane-chu-arts-aging.

Cohen, G. D., S. Perlstein, J. Chapline, J. Kelly, K. M. Firth, and S. Simmens. "The Impact of Professionally Conducted Cultural Programs on the Physical Health, Mental Health, and Social Functioning of Older Adults." *The Gerontologist* 46, no. 6 (2006): 726–734. doi:10.1093/geront/46.6.726.

Cummings, J., and K. I. Pargament. "Anchored by Faith: Religion as a Resilience Factor." In *Handbook of Adult Resilience*, edited by John W. Reich, Alex J. Zautra, and John Stuart Hall, 193–210. New York: Guilford Press, 2010.

Faigin, C. A., and K. I. Pargament. "Strengthened by Spirit: Religion, Spirituality and Resilience through Adulthood and Aging." In *Resilience in Aging: Concepts, Research, and Outcomes*, edited by B. Resnick, L. P. Gwyther, and K. A. Roberto. Place of Publication Not Identified: Springer, 2014.

Hallam, Susan, Andrea Creech, Maria Varvarigou, Hilary Mcqueen, and Helena Gaunt. "Does Active Engagement in Community Music Support the Well-being of Older People?" *Arts & Health* 6, no. 2 (2014): 101–116. doi:10.1080/17533015.2013.809369.

Jewish Community Housing for the Elderly. "'Woven Welcome' Adorns Golda Meir House Lobby." July 18, 2016. Accessed November 11, 2016. http://www.jche.org/stories-from-jche-reader/items/woven-welcome-adorns.shtml.

Keogh, Justin W. l., Andrew Kilding, Philippa Pidgeon, Linda Ashley, and Dawn Gillis. "Physical Benefits of Dancing for Healthy Older Adults: A Review." *Journal of Aging and Physical Activity* 17, no. 4 (2009): 479–500. doi:10.1123/japa.17.4.479.

McDermott, Orii, Martin Orrell, and Hanne Mette Ridder. "The Importance of Music for People with Dementia: The Perspectives of People with Dementia, Family Carers, Staff and Music Therapists." *Aging & Mental Health* 18, no. 6 (2014): 706–716. doi:10.1080/13607863.2013.875124.

Moody, Elaine, and Alison Phinney. "A Community-Engaged Art Program for Older People: Fostering Social Inclusion." *Canadian Journal on Aging/La Revue Canadienne Du Vieillissement* 31, no. 01 (2012): 55–64. doi:10.1017/s0714980811000596.

National Endowment for the Arts. "The Arts and Aging—Building the Science." February 2013. Accessed August 12, 2014. https://www.arts.gov/publications/arts-and-aging-building-science.

National Endowment for the Arts. "The Summit on Creativity and Aging in America | NEA." Arts.gov. November 2, 2015. Accessed February 2016. https://www.arts.gov/publications/summit-creativity-and-aging-america.

Noice, Helga, and Tony Noice. "An Arts Intervention for Older Adults Living in Subsidized Retirement Homes." *Aging, Neuropsychology, and Cognition* 16, no. 1 (2008): 56–79. doi:10.1080/13825580802233400.

Pargament, Kenneth I. *The Psychology of Religion and Coping: Theory, Research, Practice*. New York: Guilford Press, 2001.

Sixsmith, A., and G. Gibson. "Music and Well-Being for People with Dementia." *Aging and Society* 27, no. 1, 127–145.

Stallings, Jessica Woolhiser. "Collage as a Therapeutic Modality for Reminiscence in Patients With Dementia." *Art Therapy* 27, no. 3 (2010): 136–140. doi:10.1080/07421656.2010.10129667.

Stewart, Ellen Greene. "Art Therapy and Neuroscience Blend: Working with Patients Who Have Dementia." *Art Therapy* 21, no. 3 (2004): 148–155. doi:10.1080/07421656.2004.10129499.

LGBTQ Seniors and Mental Health: Providing Compassionate Care to Age with Dignity

Scott Valentine

This chapter focuses on LGBTQ senior citizens and how to fulfill their mental health needs. Resources and life experiences are not identical for all seniors; thus it is important to note where these differences are and to be willing and able to accommodate them (Baltes and Baltes, 1990; Fredriksen-Goldsen and Muraco, 2010). A chronic history of being told they were immoral or mentally ill has left many LGBT seniors unwilling to seek out institutional help. Because of lifelong discrimination, LGBT elders are at greater risk for isolation or withdrawing from society due to the fear of being discriminated against (Adelman, 2006; Barker, Herdt and de Vries, 2006; Francher and Henkin, 1973). The Institute of Multigenerational Health at the University of Washington conducted a study on LGBT seniors and found that they have higher rates of disability, grief, depression, loneliness, and substance abuse (Fredriksen-Goldsen et al., 2014a). Many of these factors are directly related to the social stressors and extensive discrimination in housing, employment and health care, which were existing while they came of age (Baltes and Baltes, 1990; Bell and Valentine, 1995; Grant, 2010). What complicates matters is their relative invisible status within aging health care. LGBT seniors have only recently been the target of professional care and researchers alike paying attention to their unique needs (Cahill, South, and Spade, 2000).

Dr. Marcy Adelman's pioneering study, Needs Assessment Survey of LGBT Seniors in the San Francisco Area, pointed out that an overwhelming two-thirds of those surveyed lived alone and only 15 percent had biological children; 60 percent of those with children indicated they were unavailable to assist them if not fully abandoning them because of their identity (Adelman, 2006). Not having a biological family in a health care system designed for such a support network to exist is a leading cause for LGBT senior health discrepancies (Adelman, 2006; Fredriksen-Goldsen et al., 2010). Secondarily, Dr. Adelman's and many other studies have also pointed to the lack of financial stability rampant throughout the LGBT senior community too, again due to rampant discrimination through the course of their lives, contributes to poorer health outcomes. However, it is very important to point out that LGBT seniors in general are aging well (Cornwell, Laumann, and Schumm, 2008; D'Augelli and Grossman, 2001). With more social and political support over the last several years, many have stepped out of the closet. Despite progress for younger LGBT individuals, the senior community is still an underserved population whose primary needs require your help to build a safety net of mental health services for those who are most at risk.

I have found through both research and in practice the most useful tool and method has been to use a resilience framework that allows you and the senior client to recognize all contributing factors affecting LGBTQ elders' quality of life and state of mental health. As mentioned earlier, many of these stressors are based in fear and history of being immoral, and the fact that no one able to help take care of their basic needs as they age (Barker et al., 2006; Bell and Valentine, 1995; Fredriksen-Goldsen et al., 2014b). I have always agreed with Dr. Fredriksen-Goldsen's definition on community and individual resilience for the aging as it being, "[the] behavioral, functioning social and cultural resources utilized under adverse circumstances to cultivate successful aging" (Fredriksen-Goldsen, 2014, p. 488). Resilience models are not a fancy tool; if anything, they build upon skills you have already cultivated in your day-to-day lives. By incorporating such a multidimensional framework of social context, life course perspective, personal and social resources, you can do your very best to provide the best and inclusive care not just for LGBTQ seniors, but also for anyone in the aging community (Grant, 2010; Grossman, D'Augelli, and Hersherber, 2000; Hatzenbuehler, Phelan, and Link, 2013).

My own research has focused on the effects of LGBT senior well-being through the lenses of housing, health care, and social activity. LGBT senior community's own resilience has often taken the form of informal networks like chosen family constructions, a matter I will discuss later on and is evident in the attached story of Mitch, an individual I had the pleasure of working with this past year. Mental health has been a secondary focus in my research, but in order to do the work I set out to do, it is an area impossible to avoid. As a young gay man myself, I am watching my own parents age, seeing their physical health's ups and downs; I recognize my sister and I play an essential role in their mental health. Our being able to talk with and advocate for them has been a great relief for them both. Being part of their process made me self-reflect on my own future while I age, questioning not who will advocate for me but who is currently doing this for LGBT elders in my parents' age?

When I came across the seminal report, Healthy People 2020, published by the U.S. Department of Health and Human Services and Institute of Medicine (2010), it identified the needs of LGBT seniors as a top national priority. It stressed how crucial it was to close the vast health disparities among LGBTQ seniors and fellow senior citizens, a relatively large and invisible population whose mental health has not been widely tracked throughout the United States (Fredriksen-Goldsen et al., 2014b). This was my call to action, motivating me to work with and for *my* aging community. Focusing my efforts on the LGBT aging community has shown me that if we can begin to provide care for the most vulnerable of the vulnerable, we can only better understand how to improve the overall quality of life for all senior citizens. We know that adverse mental health is not always a pathology or an illness plaguing particular demographics, but can be a temporary state brought on by social stressors (Fredriksen-Goldsen et al., 2014b). For many LGBT seniors, that temporary state has been aggravated by social stressors for a majority of their lives. My hope with this chapter is to lay to rest any negative stereotypes of LGBTQ seniors, while pointing out their mental health needs, empowering you to do your best work with every and all senior citizens despite their gender identity.

LGBT Seniors: Underserved, Underrepresented, and at Risk

Demographically, LGBT seniors are more likely to suffer from mental illness or have poor mental health than heterosexual seniors where many studies have linked a chronic history of discrimination to these higher levels. Saying this, however, can be misleading and is fully addressed in the preceding section. It is important to realize the LGBT senior population is smaller nationally. No national survey or census data has captured an accurate number, leaving us only able to estimate how many LGBT seniors presently live in the United States. Those estimates hover round 4.1 percent of living senior citizens or roughly 1.5 million seniors 65 and older (U.S. Census Bureau, 2002, 2008).

Being exposed to a lifetime of discrimination and legal prejudice, one would see a higher presence of poorer mental health outcomes. Studies on mental health of LGB seniors estimates one in six for GB men, one in four LB women have poor mental health when compared with similar heterosexual demographics (Barker et al., 2006; Elder, 1998). Research has pointed out these higher levels are because of the continued subjection to chronic stressors related to their experiences of discrimination and violence (Barker et al., 2006; Ilan, 1995; Kelly, 1999). In a recent report by the Transgender Center for Equality, again, based on estimates which I do consider low, one in eight transgender seniors are likely to have poor mental health due to an even greater amount of chronic stressors related to finances, access to compassionate care, increased probability in being a victim of discrimination and violent crimes, and estrangement from biological family members.

LGBTQ elders are faced with many nuanced and unique challenges related to these historically chronic stressors and contributing factors such as financial stress related to job discrimination throughout their lives. While more inclusion for LGBT individuals has provided for more openness among LGBT seniors who are willing to share their life stories, it is estimated that the majority of LGBT seniors are afraid of self-identity, a direct result of homophobic/transphobic climate preexisting during their earlier lives (Barker et al., 2006, Berger, 1980). With new legal protections, a lot of the guesswork and stress have been lifted when planning for their future (Cahill et al., 2000). For those who feel newly liberated to live their own lives, we are starting to see new studies that are identifying the benefiting factors of aging well as an LGBT senior. For example, the ability to be no longer denied access to one's partner despite not being married is one such social stressor many no longer have to fret over (Cahill et al., 2000). This sudden openness and acceptance have not been appreciated by all in the community. A noted trend has been the choice to remain deeply closeted into old age, creating significant effects related to mental health such as substance abuse, depression, isolation, and self-loathing (Kimmel, 2006). Another heartbreaking reality is, despite such progress, it is impossible to account for or socially retrain individuals on staff who continue to believe LGBT is morally wrong. A handful of new studies have pointed to the terrifying reality that because of discrimination in aged care, many LGBT seniors are having to closet themselves, which presents new mental health problems for them (Johnson and Mutchler, 2013; Szymanski and Gupta,

2009). But it is not just nursing homes where this discrimination is felt. Think of the many touch points any senior citizen has on a weekly basis? It could be the receptionist at the dentist, a home-aid worker from Meals on Wheels, their neighbor, or even one of your colleagues who disproves of their identity. With my work on senior housing, though federally mandated, many affordable housing complexes do not heavily enforce anti-discrimination policies. Sure you will get angry from time to time, but keep in mind it is up to you to remain compassionate in the situation and to help mitigate those feelings on their behalf.

LGBT History and Mental Health

History is often the major player in furthering one's understanding of the mental health needs of LGBT seniors. With so many stereotypes about elderly individuals from being forgetful to asexual, in order to provide great care for the LGBT community you must first know how the field of mental health care intersects LGBT seniors' lives, which likely continues to affect their mental health. We live in an age where being proud of your self-identity is more or less normalized. But for LGBT seniors, our rush to identity might be a traumatic experience for them to acknowledge such a personal insight. As a mental health specialist, you are already at an advantage for your inquiry into understanding a wide spectrum of human conditions. It is with great importance one must be aware of the possible anxiety of being LGBT and a senior citizen.

For all LGBT baby boomers, homosexuality was at one point considered a mental illness. The psychiatric field and society went to great lengths to pathologize LGBT individuals. Homosexuality was considered diagnosable and treatable until 1974 when it was removed as a mental disorder from the American Psychological Association's *Diagnostic Statistical Manual of Mental Disorders* but remained categorized as a sexual orientation disturbance until the mid-1980s. Transsexualism was also seen as a mental illness until 1992 when it was declassified as a mental illness and absorbed by a new term and disorder, *gender dysphoria*. Complicating matters because of this pathology, the LGBT identity had several false stereotypes attached such as pedophile, immoral, and a devil worshiper. Homosexuality and presenting as gender nonconforming were and are still criminalized in the United States (Bell and Valentine, 1995). Many non-LGBT individuals do not fully realize how social stigma and the pathology of being homosexual continue to affect the mental health of many LGBT seniors today. Despite the field of psychology and researchers debunking many of these stereotypes, including proving homosexuality as a natural occurrence, many people still refuse to believe otherwise.

LGBT baby boomers came of age at a time when who they were was criminal. Throughout the 1940s to 1950s, if you were out-ed, you could lose your job or end up in prison. One method of self-preservation was to closet oneself, a term given to hiding one's sexual and gender identity by acting heterosexual (Birkholtz and Blair, 1999; Walsh and Crepeau, 1998). Sodomy laws would ruin lives overnight. A simple arrest for attending a gay bar or being caught holding the same sex's hand would become an act of public shaming, printed in the daily newspaper (Walsh and Crepeau, 1998). For some, when you have lived a majority of your life being told you are sick, you tend to believe it. Coming of age during this era is unimaginable for many of us. Hash and Rogers acknowledge that although these difficult experiences can create a host of problems for LGBT individuals, they can also help them develop unique skill sets or strengths that their non-LGBT counterparts do not necessarily benefit from as they age (Hash and Rogers, 2013). As mentioned in the beginning of this chapter, resilience is a major contributor to their daily survival, creating networks of friends to care for each other or, as a negative response, withdrawing as an act of self-reliance (Kertzner et al., 2001). But as the LGBT community ages en masse, many are seeing their life-long networks becoming greatly stressed. While they age, so are their chosen family members, becoming unable to care for not just themselves but each other (Iwasaki and Ristock, 2004). The AIDS epidemic has also left a great amount of grief and health care distrust throughout the LGBT senior community, where many lost their entire chosen family to the virus (Fredriksen-Goldsen, 2014b; Johnson and Mutchler, 2013). Some historians and studies point to AIDS, in addition to a chronic history of mental health professionals pathologizing LGBT individuals, as another attributor for broad distrust of health care professionals among the LGBT senior community.

Open discussion about homosexuality, identifying as a gendered category or a sexual preference, was simply not done on a national scale like it is today (Birkholtz and Blair, 2008; Fredriksen-Goldsen et al., 2014b). Historic prejudice against today's LGBT elders continues to stand in the way of full participation in community for many LGBT seniors. It impedes full access to institutions, programs, and opportunities to age with dignity based on assumed or experienced discrimination related to being LGBT (Meyer, 2001; Szymanski and Gupta, 2009). Perhaps the most pushback I have seen is the lack of interest or fear by seniors to attend community events with peers, who are likely to still see them as immoral. With the first LGBT baby boomers now reaching age 65 as "out" individuals, more visibility raises new questions about inequalities and states of mental health for LGBT aging individuals. Those challenges and inequalities LGBT elders face have rapidly come into more focus since the Marriage Equality Act was passed in 2014 (Meyer, 2001; Pinquart and Sorensen, 2001).

Consider the elder lesbian, Edie Winsor, who could not see her partner of 50 years in her last days due to the federal government not granting chosen family members the right to see their loved ones in the hospital. Her case was upheld by the Supreme court, extending new rights to the LGBT community (Kaplan and Windsor, 2015). Recently, we are becoming more aware of the continued trauma and struggles in the transgender community. It is not just violence toward younger transgender individuals, but also violence toward the senior population. A 60-year-old transgender woman I worked with faced the daily fear of being physically harmed by her neighbors. Running from her car to her apartment had become a daily ritual because she had been threatened multiple times and had been viewed as a monster. Unable to afford a safer residence due to her transitionary health care costs and lack of savings after years of being discriminated against for being her authentic self, her mental health was heavily stressed by this recurring trauma. For her, the act of survival was tied to isolating herself. It is not without saying that non-LGBT individuals may also experience similar moments; for example, single elderly individuals whose care has been provided by neighbors who move or get too busy often run into the same problem.

LGBT Senior Care: Providing Compassionate Care, It Is Not Rocket Science

On several occasions I have been asked how come no standard of care exists for LGBTQ seniors' mental health needs? Simply put, their needs are no different than yours, mine, or our grandparents; they are just more concentrated. Health care has been modeled after the family unit where aged individuals tend to be ignored. As mentioned earlier, LGBT seniors are less likely to have a biological family to rely on while they age (Adelman, 2006; Cahill et al., 2000).

The first studies on sexual minority research were done in the 1960s. These were often conducted as a means to dispel the myth that homosexual individuals were "unhappy" and leading unfulfilled lives (Fredriksen-Goldsen and Muraco, 2010). Though we have seen the aging field better understand healthy aging and well-being for both individuals and communities, LGBT senior citizens have largely been ignored throughout the research process (Grossman et al., 2000; Orel, 2004). This major gap in research has been attributed to several factors, the two most prominent being all national censuses do not include questions on gender and sexual identity, and a lifetime of victimization, discrimination, and clinical opinion of LGBT individuals has caused many to avoid medical care altogether (Wang, 2017). Another dilemma often cited has been the broad range of cultural identities, social affiliations, and intersecting identities, ethnically and culturally, within the LGBT community. Therefore, an omission of LGBT elders in gerontological research, along these lines, has left professional counselors without a substantive bridge to connect resources or create treatment plans measuring successful outcomes (Mabey, 2011; Wallace et al., 2011). Despite considerable research surveying the aging community, you will find fewer that tackle intersectional relationships relating individuals to mental health outcomes. While some do exist, this is an area of study severely lacking and could benefit from more research.

Singular identity is not a mutually exclusive means to understand the lived experiences of an LGBT elder. It has been noted that, when assumptions are used to generalize about LGBT seniors or seniors with many group affiliations, this can cause more stress and a feeling as though we, the provider, are raking their identities on their behalf (Boyle and Paniagua, 2008; Lewis and Marshall, 2012). One must realize that intersecting identities of sexuality, gender, race, and ethnicity are geometric rather than additive (Pinquart and Sorensen, 2001; Walsh and Crepeau, 1998). When beginning to work with a client who identifies as LGBT, you may need to consider or recommend multiple services he or she will need but also in the back of your mind ask, are these services LGBT inclusive? Many senior programs fail to acknowledge or support LGBT seniors (Fredriksen-Goldsen et al., 2010, 2014b). I have worked with several seniors who refuse to attend social gathers or events hosted by organizations only because "no one like me is there" or "they don't want someone like me there." This kind of thinking complicates their sense of self-worth, again connected to the enduring legacy of chronic discrimination against LGBT individuals.

Social Support as a Means to Improve Mental Health for LGBT Seniors

It is difficult for anyone to age well with great mental health without some kind of social support. Though a majority of LGBT seniors have proven it is their own will and resilience that keep them going, it is not always the case, so do be aware of the constellation of issues out there (Kimmel, 2006). In this chapter, you have been shown how a chronic history of discrimination has led to poorer mental health outcomes; why LGBT elders rely less on children, siblings, parents, and in-laws simply; and how many constructing a chosen family they trust and rely has been instrumental to their success (Coleman and Pandya, 2002).

When we do not find support networks, this can exacerbate our own mental health and feeling of loneliness. It is then no different for an LGBT senior. Those who self-isolate do it as an act of self-preservation, and some are able to structure a vibrant life full of social outings where they do not have to discuss their gender and sexual identity (closeting). One experience I observed was when working with an older man who did not identify as gay. A Vietnam veteran, he showed up one day to a weekly LGBTQ luncheon we held in downtown Boston. Claiming he was there against his will but on his way to the Veterans Affairs Hospital, his VA bus driver dropped him off to get lunch before his appointment. At first, he presented as a tough and prickly character, who distrusted everyone. Sitting alone, and ignoring others, his first visit was assumed to be his last. However, he began showing up weekly, saying he was only there for the cheap food. As time passed, we slowly saw him join another table. He began to make friends. Though he did not self-identify as gay, over the course of several weeks, he told me his personal history, which included his 30-year romance with his male partner, who had died 3 years prior. Disabled, he had relied on his partner to take care of him and be his social companion. His partner's sudden death left him depressed, angry, and isolated. For a year, he tried to get by, but he only saw his health decline and withdrew from community. Though, he still did not identify as gay, he found a safe space in our weekly luncheon. We saw how much more relaxed and gregarious he had become over four months. By sharing in a laugh or two weekly, his arguably poor mental health showed a vast improvement.

To some, the unbearable feelings of being chronically told you are ill or not an equal can compound their sense of self-worth, producing poorer mental health outcomes (University of Chicago, 2009). Studies in both San Francisco and Los Angeles have found roughly 75 percent of aging LGBT individuals live alone when compared to 30 percent of single heterosexual senior citizens. A significant lack of access to inclusive community programs only complicates and compounds LGBT seniors' isolation because they may have to closet themselves for the sake of being among peers and staff who do not accept LGBT individuals. Reassurance and providing an accepting atmosphere were perhaps the best tools when working with LGBT seniors like our vet above.

Your role will soon become much more complex as the list of services and providers offering care to vulnerable communities will hopefully also include guidelines and best practices for LGBT citizens (Lewis and Marshall, 2012; Szymanski and Gupta, 2009). It would be great to all stories ended as happily as above, but keep in mind the fear many LGBT seniors internalize runs deep. I have heard time and time again where LGBT senior clients have been called "your kind," an unpleasant way to dissuade and defame an LGBT individual in a provider's office. When this has occurred, merely sticking up for your client can mean asking for their manager or asking them to clarify what they meant. In both cases, de-escalation happens relatively quickly since you have given them a singular moment to recognize what they have done tends to not align with their mission. Your goal should be to prove your client with tolerant wrap around care when it comes to their mental health needs. The best way to avoid any stress traps at all is to do your research in advance, finding supportive groups, inclusive programs, and LGBT-friendly providers that will benefit LGBT seniors. The best way to combat loneliness for LGBT seniors is to show them they are supported by not just you, but also multiple resources.

The only way to really understand how to support the mental health needs of any LGBT senior is to work with one. Each one is case by case. Some have felt the impact of life-long discrimination, others have glided through life unscathed, while some have found in their later years it was the time to begin the fight for LGBT equality. Regardless, I have found, LGBT seniors are perhaps the liveliest characters I have met with some of the most loving and long-term relationships I have been privileged to watch.

I wanted to end with the story of Mitch, a 68-year-old transgender man, I worked with while doing research on transgender aging and well-being. As I have time and time again mentioned, the mental health needs of LGBT seniors are unique in that they have managed to construct their own course and matrix to fulfill their needs; what you must do is be willing and able to look for the signs of depression, substance abuse, and loneliness and to connect them with identity reaffirming services needed for them to age with dignity.

Mitch at 68 Years Old

I am retired due to a head-on collision. [My] back is metal. I am 68 years old, and I am a co-founder of a transgender health and education alliance. We want to help transpeople with the aging process.

A close friend died. He had ovarian cancer [but because he was a transgender man] no one would treat him. We take guys [to doctors who will treat transmen] every year. [The exams are] for free. The doctors [make it more comfortable by having us come] to their private offices, not an Ob-Gyn clinic. Transmen—in an Ob-Gyn clinics—[they] have been treated like crap. It's like, the minute they get you up there and start it, they act like something is wrong with you.

I once had a nurse, she looked at [my chest scars] and she said, "What happened to you? I've never seen scars like that before," and I said, "I got three stories for you: Shark attack, Vietnam, and I used to be a woman and I cut my boobs off."

"Well that's not it," she looked at me, paused and then said, "It could have been a shark attack, I don't know how the shark could have bit you around here and couldn't bit the back. How long were you in Vietnam?"

I said, "I've never been in Vietnam a day in my life."

She looked at me kind of funny and she said, "Well how did a shark bite you?" I said the shark didn't bite me either, so see you later. And out that door I walked.

I [was once] run out of an Ob-Gyn office. I was sitting there inside the office, and she comes into the exam room. I'm sitting there, she comes in and she goes, "Where is your wife?" I said, "I don't have a wife." She goes, "Where is the patient?" I say, "That would be me," She responded, "Not in this office you are not, I don't see your kind here."

I knew I was in trouble when I saw those little footprints things on the wall, you know the, Jesus-was-carrying-him image and when I was seeing that up there I thought, "I don't think this is going well." Because I know Jesus was carrying me and he's carried me for many years—God love me because he's had to, or I wouldn't be here. I had a feeling he was going to have to carry me right out that door.

She [called security] giving them directions, "Escort Miss so and so right on out of this front door." Out the front door I went. As I was leaving she yelled out, "Don't come back here and be sure to tell your friends, if you have any, not to come into this office because we do not see your kind here." Everybody in the office, of course, heard and saw.

I have to give credit to another organization for making me believe in myself. I wouldn't speak in front of people; I would just stay in a corner and really wouldn't say very much. One of the organizers, who later became my mentor, came over and said, "You are with me now, come here and we would go into a room." The next year, I will never forget what happened, that changed my life. I was going along with her and she says, "I want you to see what happens when you go into the hotel and you have to go in and talk to the people about how to receive a transperson when they [arrive] because they need to know how to treat transpeople. They've never had a group of transpeople; this is our first year here and we need them to understand [who] transpeople are and how they should treat us." She said, "How would you like to be treated . . . we want them to understand just that." Of course I agreed. Afterward she came back over and said, "I want you to see this, I want you to hear it. You'll sit in the front with me. Want you to seat up here." So I am sitting in the first row corner, in a dirty t-shirt and blue jeans. Right then, here come the leaders of the hotel staff, where we are having [this particular] event.

She begins speaking, goes on about this, that, and the other thing. Then she surprised me [by putting me on the spot], "Okay we are going to be hearing from Mitch. [He] is going to tell you [about addressing] trans-people visiting here."

I could have crawled under a rock. I could have slithered like a snake away because I had never really stood up in front of any group of people and told them how I felt [as a transman]. I thought, "I think I will kill her. When this is over, I . . . Will . . . Kill . . . Her."

Thinking to myself, "Look at me, I'm filthy," and at that moment she introduces me, "He's been unloading supplies in back and he's been working with me all this time, but I want you to really meet this guy because he's got potential, he's going somewhere." I got up as she begins directing me, "tell them how do you [want] to be treated when you [enter a new place]."

"Transpeople, we are just like you." I said, "You may see somebody walk up to your desk, and [they might have a] wig on, or they could look like a quarterback from Notre Dame with a dress on [but regardless], address them as ma'am. If you see somebody walk up, and they wear their hair really short, but then they've got a chest like Dolly Patton pretending like their chest is a built, muscle chest—that's a sir." I [went on and on] and finally said, "but if you are not really sure, ask them. It never hurts to ask. We are just people, everyday people, just like you. Do yourself a favor, give us a chance, you really will like us. We are really a fun group."

I just stood there and talked and talked away. At the end, I turn[ed] around, and started walking down the aisle, but this one guy was sitting on the aisle's edge. He sat there with a sour face on. I stopped. I backed up. "Excuse me, you cannot catch it," I said, "You cannot catch it, and if you could, you might like it."

My friend on the stage burst out laughing. She came up to me later and said, "You're going to be just fine." She always told me, "When you go into a meeting, present yourself well. Dress well, because people are never going to forget what you look like. Walk with your head up. Draw attention to yourself. Make people understand you. Make people notice you." She really made me understand speaking [up] for the community, being a voice for the community. For that, I will forever be thankful.

What's keeping me going now is to feel like I am helping others. We are not like the other transalliances around town, we do more with health care. Honestly, without those people in my life, I would not have a life. I would be sitting at home deteriorating. I don't go around telling everybody that because I don't want everybody to know my personal business.

The house that I had for 38 years burned to the ground, because I let a couple of friends come stay there, [after they] lost their home. They had a very small child. Well—me being Mitch—I told them to come stay with me. At that point in time, my mother was seriously ill, she was dying of cancer. I was back and forth from my home to hers. My mother's needs were first. I was still the other person (female), at that point in my life. I was basically stationed at my mother's house since it was across town.

One day, my neighbor called when I was sitting there with my mum. [She had to break some bad news] saying "I just don't know how to tell you this, but your house is on fire." It was that winter, we had huge ice storm. I called my mom's next door neighbor to watch her while I slid across town [in my truck]. So I slip and slide all the way over to where my home was, and as I arrived, all I see was flames coming out of my house. I got out of my pickup truck, and my knees collapsed and I just fall to the ground. I just lost it. Thirty-eight years of my life is gone. Everything I owned was gone. The only thing they were concerned about was themselves. The girl [was just excited she got her school books out]. The neighbors had to hold me back, I almost killed her.

Later, I found out they took the hot ashes out of the fireplace and put them in a cardboard box on my wooden porch. My neighbors called the fire department, but there was nothing left. Those two morons didn't burn though. I lost my home and ended up moving back in to my parents' home; my mother then passed away. I didn't want to be living in [that house] at all because I knew if I went back to that house, I would die in that house. I am still there now. My mom died there. My dad was in a coma there before they took him out to go to the hospital. My childhood life was there, of which I remember nothing about my childhood, from the point after I came out of elementary school.

My whole life is just shut off, it's like it's a blur. My therapist and I have begun to uncover the terribly god awful [things that] happened to me when I was really small. But from what I've been figuring out, I'm like, "If I've got it shut off that bad, I don't want to know what it is, okay? Don't bring that skeleton out of the closet."

Last year I had to quit doing all my lawn work, that I was doing to make a little extra money off of my SSI. Last month I lost my pickup truck, so I could pay the tax on my home. Being on Medicare, yet still paying for my medical bills is heavier still. And being in my mom and dad's house—which is not my own—and having no memories of living with them now, and drawing SSI—which is a drop in the bucket—for shit. Having no money in the bank. I know, don't even have my own vehicle now. I have a motorcycle in my garage, of which now I'm just about half-chicken to ride because I'm afraid somebody's going to knock me off with my humpty dumpty back.

When I had to call [friends and ask], "you want to buy my truck so I could pay my taxes?" I lost myself. I almost lost my mind. I am not the only one in this town living this kind of life. What happens to trans-people like me? We can't go to assisted living because my God Almighty, damn! Look what that costs? What happens when I end up back [there]? I was in a wheelchair [after the accident], because they didn't think my back was going to ever heal. If it weren't for my last doctor, I wouldn't be walking today.

But what happens when I have to permanently go back to [assisted living]? My doctors talk about another surgery [to correct my back]. Because the bottom is so sturdy with all that metal, the top of my back is beginning to sway. I said, "Oh no, no, no, no. Not until it sways so badly that I cannot even stand anymore." [It's like] I have to go and have shocks put in to my back, to keep me stable now. What happens when I can't hold this anymore, and I have to go be put in that wheelchair. I can't even get myself, hardly, into my bathroom in the house I'm living in, because when I sit on the toilet, my knees touch the tub. I had to literally lift up my dad, to get him on and off the toilet. Same with my mother. When she took care of me after the accident, you [could not even] get a chair in there. She had to lift me up. It's only me. How am I going to take care of myself when it's just me? What if something happens and I am alone?

After my parents passed, I moved in to that house. I fully transitioned too. The neighborhood is—and I'm not lying—straight out of *Gone with the Wind.* Confederate flags. Hallelujah praise God! So, here I am, moving back on the same street that I grew up on, in this little town [I tried to forget].

I had just finished my chest surgery, and did not tell anything to anybody. People never paid much attention because I have always looked very masculine. One day, I went [down to the] mailbox. I did not have my shirt on. Driving down the road, here comes one of my neighbors. She goes on by, but all of a sudden the car stops. She reverses back up the street, [and stops right in front of me]. She'd been on the street longer than anybody else, and I was like, "Oh my God, what is going on?"

She calls me by my other name. I slowly turn around. I walk over [to her] and she looks up. She looks down. [She pauses and then suddenly says], "Thank God, you finally done it!" she said, "About damn time! About damn time! You scared the shit out of me. I thought you were your [dad's ghost] standing at the mailbox. You look just like him!" She kept repeating, "So glad you done it. I'm so glad you done it. You really look good. You look happy now." [Meanwhile] I'm standing there in shock. She's freaking me out. "You look really great," and she said, "but I want you to know I'm proud of you."

I said, "Excuse me?"

She said, "You took care of your parents. You waited till your parents passed away so wouldn't embarrass them. And now you're living *your* life. I'm proud of you." Before she leaves, she asked, "How's everybody treating you on the street? Do I have to straighten them out?"

I looked at her and I said, "No, they're doing pretty good so far."

She said, "You call me if you have a problem. You have any problem, you call me. I'll straighten them out." She said, "By the way, everything in my house is still where it always has been. The candy bowl is still on the sitting on the table. Come see me anytime."

And I'm like, "Oh, wow." When you got her approval, you got just everybody's approval. I went on back in the house, and I thought, "Well, this may not be as bad as I thought it [could] be."

I really see [myself] staying there in that house, and trying to fix the house to work for me. I will be there until the house—or I—fall apart, and they carry me away. At least my parents left me the home I was raised in. The home I will probably croak in. And I thank them for it.

I'm just the type of person that if someone came over and said, "Mitch I need a place to stay," I'd say, "yes, you have a room for as long as you need it." My doors are open to this community and that's the way it is. Because I was raised that way and I will die that way, because I believe in taking care of everybody. If the good Lord graces me with money in any state, form, or fashion, there are 2 or 3 houses that are empty in the neighborhood and available for purchase. I would love to buy those homes and turn them into [LGBT-friendly] residences. I would like to make it an LGBT community for people who are older because the houses are solid. They are very solid. I would like to turn it into a place where people are older and they could take care of one another.

When my mother died, I became male. Everybody backed up and said, "Oh shit, no. I'm not messing with that." I went and told my brother, I went and sat down in front of him, he and I [were not] talk[ing]. I sit down at his house, [looked right at him, and said], "I got something to tell you."

Do you know what he said? "Do you have cancer?" I said no. He said, "Then nothing's worse than that."

I thought, "You better sit down and listen" and said, "Well, it's time for me to start living my life, and this is what I'm going to do . . ."

He looked at me and he said, "Did you read that shit in a book somewhere? Or you picked something out of a book? Do you know what the hell you're fixing to do? Why in the hell are you going to do that shit?"

"Cause of the one word that you will never understand in your life," [I said. "Because you've never walked in these shoes. Respect. I've never had it, and I want it, and I want it bad, and I am going get it [by being me]. I've lived for everybody else in this world—all my life, for 56 years, by God— I am going to live my life for me. I want respect, I want something you've had all of your life. You've never had people treat you [the way I have been treated]. [I've put up with] people, and you, treating me like shit. People beat my ass in school." I said, "Here, put on [my shoes]. Walk in them [for] 24 hours in my life. Just 24 hours is all I ask you to do. And then you come talk to me."

I gave him an ultimatum, "I'm fixing to walk down these stairs right now" and I said, "You can either walk with me [be part of] this journey, or [I will disappear,] and we will never have to speak again. The choice is yours."

Silence, but then my sister in-law interrupted, "Well, you just let us know what you need. Isn't that right?"

References

Adelman, Marcy. "Introduction." In *Lesbian, Gay Bisexual and Transgender Aging: Research and Clinical Perspectives*, edited by Marcy Adelman, 1–19. New York: Columbia University Press, 2006.

Baltes, P. B., and M. M. Baltes. "Psychological Perspectives on Successful Aging: The Model of Selective Optimization with Compensation." In *Successful Aging: Perspectives from the Behavioral Sciences*, edited by P. B. Baltes and M. M. Baltes, 1–34. Cambridge, MA: Cambridge University Press, 1990.

Barker, Judith, Gilbert Herdt, and Brian de Vries, "Social Support in the Lives of Lesbian and Gay Men at Midlife and Later," *Sexuality Research and Social Policy: Journal of NSRC* 3, no. 2 (2006): 65–72.

Bell, D., and G. Valentine. "Introduction." In *Mapping Desire: Geographies of Sexualities*, 1–23. New York: Routledge, 1995.

Berger, R. M. "Psychological Adaptation of Older Homosexual Males." *Journal of Homosexuality* 5 (1980): 161–175.

Birkholtz, M. and S. Blair. "'Coming Out' and Its Impact on Women's Occupational Behavior." A Discussion Paper. *Journal of Occupational Science* 62 (September 1999): 68–74.

Boyle, Michael, and Paniagua, Freddy A. Comprehensively Assessing Cognitive and Behavioral Risks for HIV Infection among Middle-Aged and Older Adults. *Journal on Educational Gerontology* 34, no. 4 (2008): 267–281.

Cahill, Sean, Ken South, and Jane Spade. *Outing Age*. Boston: Policy Institute of the National Gay and Lesbian Taskforce, 2000: 1–72.

Coleman, B., and S. M. Pandya. "Family Caregiving and Long-Term Care." AARP Public Policy Institute, 2002. http://assets.aarp.org/rgcenter/il/fs91_ltc.pdf.

Cornwell, B., E. O. Laumann, and L. P. Schumm. "The Social Connectedness of Older Adults: A National Study." *American Sociological Review* 73 (2008): 185–203.

D'Augelli, A. R., and A. H. Grossman "Closure of Sexual Orientation, Victimization, and Mental Health among Lesbian, Gay, and Bisexual Older Adults." *Journal of Interpersonal Violence* 16 (2000): 1008–1027.

Elder G. H. "The Life Course as Developmental Theory." *Child Development* 69 (1998): 1–12.

Francher, J. S., and J. Henkin. "The Menopausal Queen: Adjustment to Aging and the Male Homosexual." *American Journal of Orthopsychiatry* 43 (1973): 670–674.

Fredriksen-Goldsen, K. I., L. Cook-Daniels, H. J. Kim, E. A. Eroshem, C. A. Emlet, C. P. Hollis-Ellis, and A. Muraco. "Physical and Mental Health of Transgender Older Adults: An At-Risk and Underserved Population." *The Gerontologist* 54 (2014a): 488–500.

Fredriksen-Goldsen, K. I., Charles P. Hoy-Ellis, Jayn Goldsen, Charles A. Emlet, and Nancy R. Hooyman. "Creating a Vision for the Future: Key Competencies and Strategies for Cultural Competent Practice with Lesbian, Gay, Bisexual and Transgender Older Adults in the Health and Human Services." *Journal of Gerontological Social Work* 57 (2014b): 80–107.

Fredriksen-Goldsen, K. I., and A. Muraco. "Aging and Sexual Orientation: A 25-Year Review of the Literature." *Journal for Research on Aging* 32 (2010): 372–413.

Grant, J. M. "Outing Age 2010: Public Policy Issues Affecting Lesbian, Gay, Bisexual, and Transgender Elders." National Gay and Lesbian Task Force Policy Institute (2010). www.thetaskforce.org/reports and research/outing age.

Grossman, A. H., A. R. D. D'Augelli, and S. L. Hersherber. "Social Support Networks of Lesbian, Gay, and Bisexual Adults 60 Years of Age and Older." *The Journals of Gerontology* 55B, no. 3 (2000): 171–179.

Hash, Kristina M., and Rogers, Anissa. "Clinical Practice with Older LGBT Clients: Overcoming Lifelong Stigma through Strength and Resilience." *Clinical Social Work Journal* 41, no. 3 (2013): 249–257.

Hatzenbuehler, M. L., J. C. Phelan, and B. G. Link. "Stigma as a Fundamental Cause of Population Health Inequalities." *American Journal of Public Health* 103 (2001): 813–821.

Ilan, Meyer H. "Minority Stress and Mental Health in Gay Men." *Journal of Health and Social Behavior* 36 (1995): 38–55.

Iwasaki, Y., and J. Ristock. "Coping with Stress among Gays and Lesbians: Implications for Human Development over the Lifespan." *World Leisure Journal* 46 (2004): 26–37.

Johnson, K. J., and J. E. Mutchler. "The Emergence of a Positive Gerontology: From Disengagement to Social Involvement." *The Gerontologist* 54 (2013): 93–100.

Kaplan, Roberta, and Edie Windsor. "Equal Dignity." In *Then Comes Marriage: United States vs. Edie Windsor and the Defeat of DoMA*. New York: W. W. Norton & Company, 2015: 289–314.

Kelly, J. "The Aging Male Homosexual: Myth and Reality." *The Gerontologist* 17 (1999): 328–332.

Kertzner, Robert M., Mary E. Barber, and Alan Schwartz. "Mental Health Issues in LGBT Seniors." *Journal of Gay and Lesbian Mental Health* 15 (2001): 335–338.

Kimmel, Douglas. *Lesbian, Gay Bisexual and Transgender Aging: Research and Clinical Perspectives*, 6th ed. New York: Columbia University Press, 2006: 1–13, 23–44, 98, 111, 234–254.

Lewis, Michele K., and Isiah Marshall. *LGBT Psychology*. New York: Springer, 2012: 113–165.

Mabey, John. E. "Counseling Older Adults in LGBT Communities." *The Professional Counselor: Research and Practice* 1, no. 1 (2011): 57–62.

Meyer, I. H. "Prejudice, Social Stress, and Mental Health in Lesbian, Gay, and Bisexual Populations: Conceptual Issues and Research Evidence." *Psychological Bulletin* 129 (2001): 674–697.

Orel, N. A. "Gay, Lesbian, and Bisexual Elders." *Journal of Gerontological Social Work* 43, no. 2 (2004): 57–77.

Pinquart, M., and S. Sorensen. "Gender Differences in Self-Concept and Psychological Well-Being in Old Age: A Meta-Analysis." *Journals of Gerontology Series B—Psychological Sciences & Social Sciences* 56 (2001): 195–213.

Szymanski, Dawn, and Arpana Gupta. "Examining the Relationship between Multiple Internalized Oppressions and African American Lesbian, Gay, Bisexual and Questioning Persons Self-Esteem and Psychological Distress." *Journal of Counseling Psychology* 56, no. 1 (2009): 110–118.

University of Chicago. "Few Friends Combined with Loneliness Linked to Poor Mental Health and Physical Health for Elderly." *Science Daily*, March 19, 2009. www.sciencedaily.com/relseases/2009/03/09038113616.htm.

U.S. Census Bureau. "Demographic Trends in the 20th Century, Census 2000 Special Reports." CENSR-4, Table 5, November 2002.

U.S. Census Bureau. "Projection of Population by Age and Sex for the United States: 2010 to 2050." NP2008-t12, August 14, 2008.

U.S. Department of Health and Human Services et al. "Healthy people 2020." (2010): 1–5, 8–23.

Wallace, S. P., S. D. Cochran, E. M. Durazo, and C. L. Ford. "The Health of Aging Lesbian, Gay, and Bisexual Adults in California." Health Policy Research Brief, UCLA Center for Health Policy Research (March 2011): 1–5, 23–40. www.healthpolicy.ucla.edu/pubs/Publication.aspx?pubID= 495#download.

Walsh, A., and E. Crepeau. "'My Secret Life': The Emergence of One Gay Man's Authentic Identity." *American Journal of Occupational Therapy* 52 (1998): 563–569.

Wang, H. L. "Census Bureau Caught In Political Mess Over LGBT Data." National Public Radio. http://www.npr.org/2017/07/18/536484467/census-bureau-found-no-need-for-lgbt-data-despite-4-agencies-requesting-it.

CHAPTER SIX

Invisible and Overlooked: Substance Use Disorders in Aging Adults

Annie Fahy

America is in the midst of social and cultural reboot. The way that we receive and process information (including the acceptance of "fake news") has expanded through technology. Social media have instigated changes that increase inclusion and offer opportunities to combat oppressive policies as well as create space for oppressive voices to gather. Changes in the social contracts that address criminalization of substances, legalization of illicit substances, and health care parity for addiction care have happened at a momentous rate during the Obama administration, culminating in the Surgeon General's groundbreaking report at the end of 2016 (Drug Policy Alliance, 2016; Office of the Surgeon General, 2016). This report ends the notion that substance use disorders (SUDs) arise from a moral weakness and places SUDs in the realm of a brain-based bio-behavioral illness. This shift to a public health model for SUDs, along with the passage of the Mental Health and Addiction Parity Act (MHPAEA) in 2008, protects persons who are diagnosed with SUDs, and offers multiple pathways for definition and treatment of SUDs (SAMHSA, 2016). The republican plans to repeal and disrupt the Affordable Care Act (ACA) among other potential changes make health care an uncertain landscape into the next decade (Kapur, 2016). While uncertain, the Surgeon General's report formalizes a long-needed redefinition of SUDs that will guide professionals in the care of aging adults struggling with substances (Office of the Surgeon General, 2016). This is the good news in the field of bio-behavioral illness that includes a spectrum of SUD conditions. Research with SUD has prioritized younger users for effective interventions despite many studies noting the expansion of an older population (Dowling, Weiss, and Condon, 2008; Moos et al., 1994; Patterson and Jeste, 1999). Community health workers are on the frontline of this opportunity for expanded practice since demographic projections agree that there is a rapidly growing population of seniors whose substance use has expanded as they age (Gfroerer et al., 2003).

SUDs combined with other aspects of aging hold a unique and uncharted space in our culture (SAMHSA, 1998). Problems with substances in seniors are often difficult to detect because of other chronic conditions and assumptions that aberrant behaviors may be caused by dementias, depressions, or simply because *someone is old* (Benshoff and Harrawood, 2003; Bodiger, 2008; Barrett and Chang, 2016; Patterson and Jeste, 1999; SAMHSA, 1998).

Current community mental health workers need expertise with SUDs and seniors and will surely become innovators and leaders in best practices as they do. Hopefully this will spark more research in this under-investigated need. The issues that intersect with elders struggling with SUDs touch on all the elements at the core of meaning-making in the human experience. Care providers, families, and policy makers are challenged with ethical concerns for end of life and its quality, as well addressing the biases and fears that accompany aging diverse changes that happen as we age.

In this chapter, the terms *elders*, *older adults*, *aging adults*, and *seniors* are used interchangeably. A caveat is inserted to accommodate the fact that aging is a dynamic process that is constantly receiving new members to its ranks. A note about other terms: this article uses substance use disorders (SUDs) to describe situations that have some spectrum of risk and harm and may also be applied to process disorders with food, sex, and gambling (Office of the Surgeon General, 2016). As typical in behavioral health, one size does not fit all, so care providers are advised to discern *recreational use* (the objective is fun) from *self-medicating* or *prescription use* (the objective is comfort or relief from habitual use) or *dependence*. Care providers must be careful not to superimpose their own preferences and biases for abstinence-only solution as they address SUDs with clients. Addiction as a brain disease is the old disease jargon prevalent in the last part of the 20th century (Office of the Surgeon General, 2016). Language matters, and mindfully we seek to find language that works for and with clients. Self-medication theory and harm reduction paradigms offer terms that may better fit when addressing substance use with clients (Denning and

Little, 2012; Peele, 1989, 1995). Today's elders are matchless compared to other generations in both longevity, disability, and a wealth of home-grown expertise in self-medications and experimenting with substances throughout their life span for recreation and relief (Benshoff and Harrawood, 2003; Dowling et al., 2008; Gfroerer et al., 2003; Patterson and Jeste, 1999). Nonjudgmental curiosity and active neutrality still remain the best assessment tools for any potential SUD (Denning and Little, 2012, 296; Miller and Rollnick, 2012).

Since the policy of best practices with all care is based within the context of the therapeutic rapport, primary care and community mental health workers must address their own biases about aging and care. A discussion of attitudes regarding challenging societal situations and difficult individual presentation requires a brave introspection and a supervisor who is knowledgeable when it comes to elders whose needs may be hidden, marginalized, or unorthodox (Denning and Little, 2012, 237–330). I encourage the reader to question the perspectives of the author and others for ageism and challenge what doesn't serve in this ill-defined terrain (Achenbaum, 2015).

Introduction

The U.S. population of persons 65 and over is expected to double from 35 million in 2002, according to census and other projections, to 70 million by 2050 (Vincent and Velkoff, 2010; Waysay et al., 2016). The United States is not alone in these population shifts, according to worldwide assessments that estimate by the year 2047 people over 65 will outnumber the world's children (Suzman and Beard, 2011, 1–2). This means that as we near 2025, 80 percent of the world's aging population is likely to struggle with some disability (Waysay, 2016, 1008). According to the Global Burden of Disease Study, in 2010, mental health and SUD conditions account for 7.4 percent of the global disease burden worldwide and expected to rise. Neuropsychiatric disorders (including SUDs) will comprise five of the top ten causes of disability worldwide (Whiteford et al., 2013). This increase in longevity means innovating, as this expanding population is likely need supportive resources that don't yet exist (Suzman and Beard, 2011, 12). Seniors living with additional mental health diagnosis, chronic pain, and other medical or cognitive conditions make assessing for SUDs more difficult (Barrett and Chang, 2016, 345). Gfroerer's widely accepted model predicts an expansion from 1.7 million of elders with SUDs currently to 4.4 million in 2020 (Gfroerer et al. 2003, 131). The World Health Organization estimates that currently 10–20 percent of the world's elder population is living with Alzheimer's, Parkinson's, or stroke, with these numbers also growing (Waysay 2016, 1008). Dementias and disorders that affect judgment, self-medication and other cognitive functions may also increase the risk for SUDs, especially prescription misuse (Dowling et al., 2008, 210). Research is focused on solving SUDs in youth while older people present differently and have increased vulnerability due to unique needs that are certainly of grave concern to a health care system looking at population health needs (Dowling et al., 2008, 210; Patterson and Jeste, 1999, 9–10). We also know little about the effects of drug use on aging brains and the residual effects of SUD as someone ages. The current research into SUD as a brain disorder is beginning to delineate brain changes with SUD that persist long after use stops (Office of the Surgeon General 2016, 2). There is some investigation linking past substance use that disrupts dopamine systems to disorders like Parkinson's disease, predicting more cases as cocaine users age (St. Jude's Research Hospital, 2005). While alcohol has a relationship to some dementias, more studies clarifying these relationships are needed (Tyas, 2001, 30). Since many SUDs in seniors go undetected, providers may mistake SUD symptoms for Alzheimer's disease or other dementias or just normal symptoms and miss the opportunity for correct diagnosis and improvement (Dowling et al., 2008, 213).

These numbers are a taste of a bigger equation that puts complex management of elders with bio-behavioral illness, SUDs, and a wide continuum of chronic care needs squarely on the shoulders of primary care and community mental health workers in the coming years. We must factor in economic disparities that affect resources, outcomes, and plan, for support to elders and their caregivers (Dowling et al., 2008; Patterson and Jeste, 1999; Whiteford et al., 2013).

SUDs and Elders: An Underserved Population

Care for aging adults historically resides with families, and complicated issues stay in the shadows of family secrets. American health care has not prepared for the unique problem of SUDs in seniors and tends to give preference to younger users (Vestal, 2016). The need for comprehensive and integrated services for the nation's elders will drive changes in all areas of care, and we must start with stigma as the biggest barrier to helpful solutions and adequate care (Gfroerer et al., 2003; SAMHSA, 1998; Whiteford et al., 2013).

SUDs in older populations may come from a life of moderate or problematic user or may arise in one's sixties from situations related to aging (Benshoff and Harrawood, 2003). There may be a lack of understanding about treatment, drug interactions, and complications associated with SUDs that may be missed by providers and caregivers (Dowling et al., 2008). Additionally, ageism and stigma influence systems addressing the needs of elders. Many providers avoid exploring SUDs and other concerns and may assume that any physical and mental deterioration are signs of normal aging, dementia, or other conditions. Workers may not have skills in caring for the aging populations and may avoid gaining skills with these clients because of a tacit permission fueled by unconscious ageism. Robert N. Butler MD, who first identified ageism in 1969, is more resonant and relevant with today's demographics, according to Achenbaum; in his history of ageism, Butler states:

> A systematic stereotyping of and discrimination against people because they are old, just as racism and sexism accomplish this with skin color and gender. . . . I see ageism manifested in a wide range of phenomena, on both individual and institutional levels—stereotypes and myths, outright disdain and dislike, simple subtle avoidance of contact, and discriminatory practices in housing, employment, and services of all kinds. (Achenbaum, 2015, 1)

Ageism may be the most challenging frontier of marginalization. However, the emerging generation of today's older substance users will have a variety of values, aspirations as well as past substance experience that needs attention individually as well as holistically. There may be a lack of understanding about treatment, drug interactions, and complications associated with SUDs that may be missed by providers and caregivers. The abundance of aging seniors, along with those tasked with care, must advocate and give voice to the particular, diverse, and special needs of seniors who have more agendas about recreational use than past generations. As a society, how we treat our elders will convey our deeper values for respect and dignity across the age span (Achenbaum, 2015; SAMHSA, 1998). It is ironic that all of us *are* headed to our own inevitable membership as seniors, and our potential struggles may also be rendered invisible by a society that devalues the end of a life (Morissette, 1996).

SUDs and Elders: The Political Context

SUD care is affected by domestic drug policies that are tinged with political agendas with some users and substances stigmatized by disparities in criminalization and incarceration. Systemic incarceration of minority users fuels more stigma and stereotypes and impacts care seeking on all levels.

Macro changes within our system that address systemic racism and all the "isms" provide the context for shifts in how we view problematic SUDs (Chin, 2002). This current generation of seniors, who came of age in the 1960s, is the first to arrive with their own expertise of recreational substances as well as alcohol and prescriptions (Dowling et al., 2008; Gfroerer et al. 2003; Patterson and Jeste, 1999). Cultural differences may also affect how people seek and engage with help for SUDs. There are some small studies with African Americans and transgendered adults identifying hesitance to seek professional help for depression and related concerns (Fredrickson-Goldsen et al., 2014; O'Connor et al., 2010). Seniors may also have sensory or cognitively deficits. Gender differences are also significant since many homebound clients are women (SAMHSA, 1998). Older adults who worry about their own autonomy and loss may be more sensitive to visible and invisible stigma and avoid seeking treatment (Fredrickson-Goldsen et al., 2014; O'Connor et al., 2010). Caregivers and health care workers must be rigorous with assessing their own feelings of helplessness when working with aging clients as they travel the certain passage toward death.

Discussion about aging employs dramatic language like *floods of seniors and gray tsunamis* that may add to the stigma that is already embedded in health care systems. Workers must practice mindfulness with language and attitudes that feed bias and affect care (Gordon, 2014). Older people grow more invisible as they disappear out of the flow of the world. Aging brings progression of losses in a youth-, beauty-, and achievement-oriented culture. Current seniors live longer with more sickness and disability (Bodiger, 2008; Whiteford et al., 2013). Seniors must adapt to loss of partners and community, loss of choices and abilities, sensory and pleasure, roles, and resources as well as increased dependence on others (Grant, 2014; SAMHSA, 1998). The current cohort of seniors may suffer from complicating chronic conditions; diabetes, heart and lung conditions, and chronic pain. Their issues with substances get lost in a plethora of other challenges in a society that devalues their contributions and is overburdened by their care (O'Connor et al., 2010; Patterson and Jeste 1999; Samet, Friedmann, and Saltz, 2001; SAMHSA 1998;). Providers need a crash course in normal aging and also how to assess for depressive symptoms, past trauma history, cognitive and sensory losses, and SUD. Caregivers and the patients themselves may not identify or understand the risks of substance use in its subtler forms and in the context of other complex needs (Benshoff and Harrawood, 2003; SAMHSA, 1998).

Trauma exposure is a well-known risk factor in relapsing SUDs (Denning and Little, 2012). Less well known is the role that adverse childhood experience (ACE) plays. ACE research by Felitti and others marries statistical connections of disruptive experiences of childhood to later life health problems. Researchers investigated four categories of childhood experiences that may affect neurodevelopment and ineffective coping and lifelong health outcomes including SUDs, mental health, lifestyle, and chronic diseases. These analyses measure specific types of childhood conditions with emotional, physical abuse, neglect, and also the presence of chaotic parenting due to family situations like SUDs, mental health, and incarceration. The ACE study is notable for the size of its cohort (13,494 adults), and the correlation of ten elements of ACE exposure and their relationship to chronic conditions later in life (Felitti et al., 1998). Participants of this research were employees of the Kaiser Health system and were functioning well in their lives. Multiple health risk effects were correlated with the presence of one or more types of ACE exposures, with severity of health consequences intensifying based on the number of total ACE items. Briefly, there was a significant statistical link to the presence of one or more categories of adverse childhood experiences and the development of chronic conditions, both physical and behavioral disorders later in life. ACE authors hypothesize that ACE exposure creates disruptions in neurodevelopment and emotional and cognitive impairment, leading to disruptions in physiologic processes, and high-risk behavioral coping that results in later expressions of bio-behavioral illness (Felitti et al., 1998; Fuller-Thomson et al., 2014). Although much of this research is being utilized in prevention work with at-risk children, primary health care is beginning to activate education about ACE vulnerabilities in older populations and the lifelong effects of trauma. Trauma history as well as early onset SUD is known to be a high-risk factor for relapsing SUDs (Denning, Little, and Glickman, 2004, 77, 205–207; Office of the Surgeon General, 2016, 2–21). Discerning differences in age and types of trauma show a significant connection between physical and sexual abuse and SUDs (Fuller-Thomson et al., 2016, 1458–1459). Assessment of these factors and symptom management for self-medicating factors like pain, insomnias, and anxiety is an important adjunct to SUD interventions (Barrett and Chang, 2016; Fuller-Thomson et al., 2016, 1454).

SUDs and Elders: The Context and the Substances

SUDs and the culture of substance use are shifting with the addition of acceptance of medication-assisted treatments combined with other evidence-based interventions (Botticelli, 2016). The opioid epidemic and reforms have stimulated a national conversation based in science and compassion, and facilitates inclusion of SUDs into primary care settings

(Munoz, 2016). The potential repeal of ACA without a replacement looms; however, the opiate crises have created one of the few issues with bipartisan support, although not necessarily bipartisan funding (Cherkis, 2016). Health care workers, especially those working with seniors and SUDs, must develop vigilance about advocacy for this underserved group (SAMHSA, 1998). Narratives about *what is fun, what is acceptable, what is criminal,* and *what kind of suffering becomes an unintended consequence of SUD* impact our care of them. Priorities that surround users are also undergoing rapid redefinition as grandma and grandpa enter the cohort that has very little research to address and design care (Vestal, 2016).

The modern disease concept of addiction treatment has unfurled and unraveled through the 20th century married to Alcoholics Anonymous, and an abstinence-only modality. Treatment is shifting away from criminal justice venues that targeted minority users to health settings (Chin, 2002). Drug courts as a main purveyor of treatment for younger users who cross legal lines are not applicable to most seniors with SUDs who are unlikely to enter through a criminal justice pathway. Instead, they may hide in plain sight masking as aging, depression, or eccentricity. Seniors with SUDs may go unnoticed or excused by tolerant family or a fragmented care delivery system (Benshoff and Harrawood, 2003, 43–44). Linked primary care and behavioral health services, along with other settings catering to seniors, need updated knowledge of differential assessment treatment options that reduce harms and strive for improvement of functionality and quality of life (Dowling et al., 2008, 245; Samet et al., 2001, 86–87).

Today's seniors came of age in the psychedelic 60s with fewer inhibitions about substances than the generations before them and multifaceted experiences with substances. Providers must sort chronic conditions from situational ones (Dowling et al., 2008, 211; Patterson and Jeste, 1999, 1184). Brain research on the effects of substances and seniors has not been a priority because of an urgent focus on adolescent effects and a belief that older users mature out as they age (Dowling et al., 2008, 211; Patterson and Jeste, 1999, 1184; Sabet, 2016). In addition to vast experiences with recreational substances, this cohort of elders has grown up through decades of rampant advertising for unhealthy lifestyle choices like nicotine.

SUDs and Elders: Substances

Current legal changes in marijuana law are also conducting the largest social experiment of sorts since prohibition, with expanding medical use legal in 25 states and recreational adult use legal in 5, with several more states expected to expand (Drug Policy Alliance 2016; Sabet, 2016). The

Tax Foundation estimates the marijuana industry as a $45 billion industry with the same need to convert new users as the alcohol and tobacco business (Berke and Verrill, 2016; Sabet, 2016). Regulating the marijuana industry will focus on young users and public safety similar to the alcohol industry (Pacula, Wagenaar, and Caulkins, 2014; Sabet, 2016). One difference with marijuana is the length of time it remains in the body after use (Sabet, 2016). Legalized marijuana conveys safety to seniors who rolled their first joint while the Grateful Dead were singing "Truckin.' " Proponents highlight its natural qualities; however, a visit to the pot shops in Denver demonstrates that legal marijuana is also a big business (Sabet, 2016). Seniors who are expecting the marijuana of their youth may experience a shock with the intensity and variety of today's product and may not perceive risks (Pacula et al., 2014; Sabet 2016). According to estimates, since 2002, marijuana use has increased from 10.4 percent to 13.3 percent with daily use increasing from 1.9 percent to 3.5 percent (Compton et al., 2016; Lubin, 2016). Although this study saw no increase in marijuana use disorders, another study reports a 2.9 percent increase in disorders during 2002–2012 (Lubin, 2016). Marijuana's effects on cognitive function are not well defined. One hypothesis is that some older users may have more vulnerability to Marijuana because of current health status and/or predispositions to neurological impairments that may increase risk for more toxic effects (Pope et al., 2003). Seniors users may see medical uses for marijuana that can medicate pain and are expended into many cancer treatments as a sign that they are safe for them to use for their own palliative purposes (Drug Policy Alliance, 2016; Sabet, 2016). As many states shift to legal distribution and many seniors have access through friends and families in other states, mental health and other care workers need to explore marijuana use with their clients (Pope et al., 2003; Sabet, 2016; SAMHSA, 1998). While marijuana use may seem harmless, Dowling notes increases in emergency visits resulting in admission in the ages of 60–64 for illicit substances such as cocaine, marijuana, and stimulants use (Bogunovic, 2012; Dowling et al., 2008).

Following a trend in popular culture promoting medical and mental health benefits of illicit substances, seniors are more likely to explore effects of illicit substances like mushrooms, mescaline, and other hallucinogens. News of research exploring medical benefits of many illicit substances travels as fast as the Internet announcing the exploration. Ayahusca (a traditional Amazonian brew) has shown beneficial effects on PTSD, while MDMA (3,4-methylendioxymethamphetamine, also known as *ecstasy*) shows usefulness with trauma and anxiety (Escobedo, 2014; Mithoefer et al., 2011). A business weekly notes that Burning Man is attracting more older attendees, and many informal groups are forming to organize visioning experiences with hallucinogens (Kircher, 2015). A new study in participants who have intractable depression has shown a significant effect from guided psilocybin mushroom trips (Escobedo, 2014; Khazan, 2016). These two double-blinded studies from John's Hopkins and New York University have reported sustained improvement in conditions after treatment. Although small studies, both studies involved utilizing clinical guides during the experience and/or follow-up processing adjunct talk therapy to process the mushroom experience (Khazan, 2016). These promising results may open a new wave of self-medication in seniors without previous inhibitions toward illicit substance or others who are frustrated with traditional pharmacology. Doctors are beginning to explore the use of stimulants in elders to increase motivation, cognition, apathy, and fatigue. While these treatments may be attractive to seniors, care must be taken with regard to fragile mental health and also medical conditions like heart disease that might not tolerate these substances' other effects.

Health care changes often arrive after epidemics like HIV and catalyze paradigm shifts (Armstrong, 2007). The opiate epidemic, for these times, is likely to redefine much about our understanding of SUD as a brain disease and expand treatments and compassion (Office of the Surgeon General, 2016). Rampant opiate misuse and overdose crosses all socioeconomic populations, ages, and cultures. Medical providers have not been effective guides or managers of pain, leaving people to create their own solutions. Opiates have predictable risks because of their biochemical characteristics, tolerance, and an increasing need for more drug to get the same effect, overdose potential, and the way the brain changes with SUD may continue long after the drug is stopped (Denning and Little 2012; Office of the Surgeon General, 2016). Unbounded prescribing by physicians has created unprecedented use and overdose across all socioeconomic populations. Regulatory changes to manage overprescribing have abruptly cut off patients from drugs that require a transition to other coping skills and can force a choice into the illicit drugs market (Bodiger, 2008; Botticelli, 2016; Patterson and Jeste, 1999). Young users often take up treatment beds, and interventions are not designed for older patients (Kindy and Keating, 2016).

For most seniors, alcohol is still king, but the current epidemic of opiate dependence is likely the event that is most driving attention to elders and SUDs (Vestal, 2016). Dr. Nora Volkow estimates 2.1 million people might be abusing opiates with an estimated 467,000 addicted to heroin (Volkow, 2014). Regulatory changes by most states to address the problem create other challenges for medical providers and patients, as they force a suspension of opiates without adequate plans for detox and pain management. Lack of understanding about SUD and complex detox needs push many toward *doctor-shopping* heroin and illicit drugs (Vestal, 2016). As a result, many are also combining substances. Regional differences in prescribing and use are also notable with pockets of the epidemic in the south and in depressed socioeconomic parts of the country (Esposito, 2015). Gender is also significant, as death rates for older white women have risen significantly related to substance combinations (Kindy and Keating, 2016). There is no doubt that combinations of alcohol and prescriptions used separately and together are significant risks to this generation of seniors (Dowling et al., 2008).

Most prescriptions are synthetic opioids like OxyContin, Percocet, and Fentanyl patches. These medications, which were formulated for acute pain caused by cancer and other serious injury, are prescribed more liberally to elders for chronic pain conditions like arthritis and fibromyalgia (Esposito, 2015; Manchikanti et al., 2012). Between 2006 and 2012, 78 percent of ER visits involved misuse of regular prescriptions and 11 percent of these involved opioids (Esposito, 2015). Complications from even small doses of opioids are increasing in Americans over 45 (Esposito, 2015). Out of every 1,000 persons on Medicare, 6 have a diagnosis that utilizes opioids (Vestal, 2016). The media research and prevention have focused on younger users and the high risk of accidental overdose and taken steps to limit prescribing and educate physicians, although this action alone has not reduced overdose deaths (Vestal, 2016). Cutting off one supply of these medications to someone who is addicted creates another problem as the user looks to the illicit substance market (Manchikanti, 2012). Seniors who have become dependent are more likely to combine or add in other prescriptions or turn more to alcohol. Poor pain management increases isolation and hopelessness, and so sufferers are more likely to self-medicate. While deaths are prevalent with synthetic opioids due to mixing substances or overdose, senior deaths may be under-reported or attributed to other causes (Esposito, 2015). Cognitive changes and confusion both from aging, medical conditions, and the opioids can cause another layer of confusion, overdose, and other injuries from falls and misuse, both inadvertent and intentional (Esposito, 2016).

Past and present injection drug use (IDU) is a risk factor for many health problems, and seniors account for 10 percent of new HIV cases in the United States (Armstrong, 2007). Seniors with IDU may choose to substitute street heroin for prescription medications that they are no longer able to obtain (Armstrong, 2007). One effective avenue of treatment for opiate dependence is medication-assisted treatment with buprenorphine and other drugs. Utilization of these methods for older users deserves more investigation (Botticelli, 2016; Dowling et al., 2008; Vestal, 2016; Volkow, 2014).

SUDs and Elders: Assessment and Treatment

Identifying SUDs and misuse in aging users is difficult because symptoms may be shrouded by other chronic disease and cognitive symptoms. Assessment of illicit drug use is a difficult needle to thread since estimates from National Household survey data about illicit drug use among seniors are underrepresented (Dowling et al., 2008; SAMHSA, 1998, 2009). SUDs in seniors can be divided into early onset users (prior to age 65) and *late onset users* (with an issue that develops after 65) (Benshoff et al., 2003). Another way is to frame SUDs as chronic or situational (Benshoff and Harrawood, 2003, 44–46). Elders who have a past SUD, described as early onset before age 65, should be evaluated for recurrence of past problems or erosion of coping skills and may present with more complexity of both medical and behavioral health conditions. Late onset SUD tends to come more out of a situational condition such as loss of a partner or other stressors (Bogunovic, 2012). Late onset SUD may be difficult to spot since symptoms may not meet thresholds for SUD, according to established guidelines for amounts, frequencies, tolerance, or adverse consequences (Dowling et al., 2008; Patterson and Jeste, 1999). In fact, elders may not experience negative effects of substance intoxication but may instead become sleepier and less trouble. Other conditions or medications may complicate the effect of the substance or the problem may stem from purposeful or inadvertent misuse. Seniors may have an outwardly stable looking life (APA, 2013; Dowling et al., 2008). They may also actively try and hide their use out of fear of judgments or being forced into abstinence treatment (Denning and Little, 2012; DiClemente, 2003; SAMHSA, 1998). Many seniors only see medical providers who rely on assessment tools like the G-MAST and are too time-pressured for skilled assessment conversations (Naegle, 2012; Samet et al., 2001; SAMHSA, 1998). While tools are helpful, the doctor is likely to miss SUD diagnosis in favor of medical conditions. According to a study by the Council on Alcohol and Substance Abuse (CASA), physicians were asked to diagnose a case of a 60-year-old woman with prescription drug and alcohol abuse symptoms, and only 1 percent of the MDs correctly diagnosed the patients primary presenting SUD (Bodiger, 2008).

Assessment of SUD utilizes widely accepted diagnostic criteria updated in 2013 in the *Diagnostic Statistical Manual of Mental Disorders, Fifth Edition* (*DSM-5*), and there are no specific identifiers for differences in older adults

(APA, 2013; Benshoff, 2003). Updates in the *DSM-5* offer a broader public health view of SUD, utilizing three modifiers: mild, moderate, and severe. The current criteria include 11 items:

- Using in larger amounts or for longer than intended
- Wanting to cut down or stop using, but not managing to
- Spending a lot of time to get, use, or recover from use
- Craving
- Inability to manage commitments due to use
- Continuing to use, even when it causes problems in relationships
- Giving up important activities because of use
- Continuing to use, even when it puts you in danger
- Continuing to use, even when physical or psychological problems may be made worse by use
- Increasing tolerance
- Withdrawal symptoms

Under 2 symptoms = no disorder; 2–3 = mild disorder; 4–5 = moderate disorder; 6 or more = severe disorder. While these criteria may be helpful in organizing assessments, these items may not be relevant to older users (APA, 2013; Office of the Surgeon General, 2016; Patterson and Jeste, 1999, 1184–1185).

Adjusting assessment for seniors means assessing details including physical, mental, and situational vulnerabilities; risk of harms including misuse and overdose; and functional assessment of coping and activities of daily living (Patterson and Jeste, 1999, 1184–1185). SAMHSA has provided physicians with pocket tools validated for older patients but these only target alcohol and are not a substitute for a good relational assessment (SAMHSA, 1998).

Depression may activate SUDs in seniors who have lived the bulk of their lives with an expectation of comfortable retirement, which may be limited by chronic disease, losses, and hopelessness. American culture is not senior-friendly. Many face years without meaningful activity, connected communities, and accommodations for their needs, as well as fear of dependence, isolation, and suffering (O'Connor, 2008). Chronic disability, ineffective coping, pain, boredom, social isolation, cognitive deficits, and unresolved emotional dynamics set the stage for SUDs (Dowling et al., 2008; SAMHSA, 1998). While younger adults value healthier lifestyles, many seniors are ill-equipped for complex disability (Armstrong, 2007; Patterson and Jeste, 1999).

SUDs and Elders: Functional Assessments

Assessment begins with establishing a baseline of functioning. Collaboration between the patient, supports, and other providers will yield a more cohesive picture of functioning and plan for normal aging. Plan should include assessments and interventions to reevaluate with changes. Assess motivations and expectations for misuse like cost, depression, frailty, passive suicidality, cognitive impairments, financial difficulties, and/or visual impairments that cause misadministration.

Assessment should also include mobility, social needs, sensory, and cognitive and other age-related changes with individualized specifics. For example, an older person may not have adequate hearing for a group intervention or may have visual changes that affect reading and mobility. Not only the persons themselves and their families but also many younger professionals are not aware of normal age-related sensory and cognitive changes. Seniors with mental and physical health compromises have higher overall use of treatment and crises services and intensive case management (Moos et al., 1994).

The expansion of prescription medications marketed directly to patients rather than MDshas created an era of super-consumer. Older adults grew up expecting medication to fix all their ills. The fix-it paradigm for seniors means many medications and different SUD presentations of misuse. Seniors may intentionally become their own pharmacist with prescriptions, herbal remedies. and recreational drugs (Dowling et al., 2008). Experts warn that underuse or erratic use, either prescribed or over-the-counter drugs in its extreme, may go from misuse to abuse (Dowling, 2008). Supplements also create interaction problems with other prescriptions. A good SUD assessment needs to factor in health conditions and stressors that may induce medication misuse like financial gaps as well as a comprehensive assessment of what medications that the person is taking and how. Assessing medications using *explore—provide—explore* conversation common in motivational interviewing is a good method for assessing and providing information about resources, finances, ability to problem-solve, and motivations for misuse (Miller and Rollnick, 2012). Asking and understanding what the person wants the drug to do and if it is working is a good place to start (Denning and Little, 2012).

One invaluable resource is the American Geriatrics Society Beers Criteria, a chart addressing medication complications. Its purpose is to improve the care of older adults by reducing their exposure to potentially inappropriate medications. This information should be used in collaboration with medical team members and is not a recommendation of clinical practice, but only a guide (American Geriatric Society, 2012). Many communities are looking holistically at SUDs but may not be focused on seniors. Some progressive communities are beginning planning for more residents with dementias (Dobner, 2014). Two prevention studies with seniors noted in the Surgeon General's report address drinking and involve brief feedback sessions that have been effective at changing misuse and reducing amounts of use (Office of the Surgeon General, 2016). Brief feedback sessions are also effective with college students, so may be expanded into primary care and other settings with skillfulness.

Aging itself presents a puzzle of what to focus on when physical, cognitive, and emotional changes are unique aspects of the person's end-of-life story. Agency, autonomy, comfort, and meaning-making get lost in medical management and crises-oriented management. Untrained workers may hold one extreme presentation of older substance users: an uncle or a homeless man who waits for the liquor store to open and miss a grandpa who followed the Grateful Dead around the country. Although older people do present for treatment, many are extreme presentations for detox needs (Kindy and Keating, 2016). Many treatment professionals may have outdated views of SUD or be unaware of special needs around aging clients. The ACE literature gives credence to the idea that ineffective coping continues unless replaced by better skills (Fuller-Thomson et al., 2016). Quite simply, the belief that many people move from the tumult of youth and into their adult roles and spontaneously recover, while true enough when it fits, should not eliminate accurate assessment for later onset SUD. Long-term users, who have organized their whole lives around chronic chaotic SUD, tend to represent, to untrained workers, a gestalt of the problem rather than a small slice of it.

SUDs and Elders: Brain Science

All thoughts and perceptions are controlled by a cascade of chemistry and electricity in the brain. The Surgeon General's report links SUD with brain changes and vulnerabilities (Office of the Surgeon General, 2016). Substances act on neurotransmitter systems both in the amounts of activated neurotransmitters and also on receptor-bonding abilities that can disrupt a multitude of functions (Dowling et al., 2008). In addition to the effects of the substance, which acts on the chemical reward systems of the brain, its effects and disruption cause discomfort as the drug wears off. This creates a preoccupation and also obsessive drug seeking to ward off the negative effects of withdrawal. As we begin to better understand the adaptive capacity of the brain, we also understand that SUD can leave long-term chemical and structural changes and impairment that take time to reverse (Office of the Surgeon General, 2016). Aging creates both natural diminishment in neurotransmitters and structural changes that affect these processes. SUD also creates gaps in these areas that may be more severe in elders. More investigation of SUD and aging brains is needed for better interventions (Dowling et al., 2008). Interesting research notes the intersection of neurobiology processes with chronic pain, depression, and SUD and adapts mindfulness oriented recovery enhancement, acceptance and commitment therapy, interpersonal psychotherapy, and cognitive-behavioral therapy, with promising results in a small nursing study (Barrett and Chang, 2016).

SUDs and Elders: What Works

Lack of confidence in assessment, misapplication, or premature diagnosis is likely to create discord within the client. Providers need SUD education and training in empathic listening and readiness assessment, collaborative planning, and also time management abilities to have these rapport-oriented and empathic assessment skills (Denning and Little, 2012; Miller and Rollnick, 2012; Tatarsky, 2003). Accurate understanding requires relational and technical skills and a willingness to listen without judgment (Denning and Little, 2012; DiClemente, 2003; Miller and Rollnick, 2012). The future management of these issues will likely create new clinical collaborations originating in primary care settings with all biobehavioral team members (Samet et al., 2001). Just as medical personnel must become knowledgeable with behavioral situations, behavioral professionals must become aware of chronic disease presentations.

SUDs and Elders: Conversation Is the New Medicine

Care of elders incorporates biological, emotional, and cultural meanings as well as end-of-life concerns. How do we begin? This is the conversation about the conversation. The key is shared meaning-making involving caregivers and providers during a profound element of life. Relational modes of working with SUDs like motivational interviewing and motivational enhancement therapy, which deals with readiness, confidence, and motivation for change; harm reduction, which addresses safety, comfort, and quality-of-life concerns looking for incremental safety–focused behavior change; and trauma informed care, which incorporates the potential that past trauma may be a complicating factor in the case presentation, are all useful methods because they share power with the client. These methods also rely on hope and mindful presence that may be challenging when dealing with end of life. It requires a new, shared language that the worker and the client find together. These three modalities represent a paradigm shift from an authoritative medical model of care to a collaborative power-sharing way of being (Elliott et al., 2005; Fallot and Harris, 2009; Denning and Little, 2012; Grant, 2014; Miller and Rollnick, 2012; Tatarsky, 2003). A good explanation of these is available in many arenas and should be a part of every community mental health worker's training and supervision (Fahy, 2013). All three of these related modalities facilitate assessment and interventions in conversations about well-being, cost/benefits, and change.

It's important to understand what is optimal functioning and possible improvements while also addressing the passage to increasing change and inevitable death. Consider losses and stressors and useful coping strategies. Harm reduction and motivational interviewing join with trauma informed care as a complement to each other in handling most conversation about change. They are based in rapport and mutual explorations, expanding and deepening meaning and values. They invite the patient and/or the team of caregivers to formulate a plan that fits and is workable. Adopting these to comfort care and end-of-life tasks takes practice and support.

Since adults may present with varying disability and age-related situations, providers need to assess assumptions with clients and their caregivers about hopes and expectations. Community health workers learn on the job and develop wisdom from mistakes and missed details as well as successes. Curiosity is indispensable, since your client can be the expert in his or her own needs for healthy aging. Exploring versions of what is hoped for and preserving values and function and also attending to comfort makes a hierarchy of aging needs when addressing SUD. Assessing whether loss of function is a natural part of this individual's aging or a target for improvement is the challenge. So, your instructions: Pay attention, be curious (really curious), and become partners with your client.

Conclusion

Seismic shifts in language, policy, and meta-narratives are drivers to mobilize innovations needed to address SUD and misuse in the aging population. Social redefinitions utilizing public health and harm reduction frameworks are preferable when looking at SUDs in general and with the special population of elders, since they embrace a client-centered philosophy and much of this will happen in primary care settings that are overwhelmed by time pressure and an uncertain health care future. More research in specialty aging populations and cost benefits that surround SUDs and seniors is needed. Most care providers need specific training in aging issues as well as basics of SUDs and use increased training in relational interventions.

Healthy aging also includes visioning for unplanned health changes and other losses that are inevitable in some form but also cannot always be anticipated because everyone has their own mysterious appointment with illness, disability, loss, and death. Working with seniors who struggle with SUDs more than anything means creating the listening space to find the solution in collaboration with the clients and their family. Workers must sort through aging concerns and end-of-life issues and ignore the chaos that surrounds the current health care delivery system. True client-centered interventions and evidence-based cohesion combined with compassion will be the guiding forces for the future of this issue.

References

Achenbaum, W. Andrew. "Ageism: A History since 1969." *Generations Journal of the American Society on Aging* 39, no. 3 (2015): 10. Published electronically October 19, 2015. http://asaging.org/blog/history-ageism-1969.

American Geriatric Society. *AGS Beers Criteria for Potentially Inappropriate Medication Use in Older Adults.* New York: American Geriatric Society, 2012.

American Psychiatric Association. *Diagnostic and Statistical Manual of Mental Disorders.* 5th ed. Arlington, VA: American Psychiatric Publishing, 2013.

Armstrong, Gregory, L. "Injection Drug Users in the United States, 1979–2002: An Ageing Population." *JAMA Internal Medicine* (2007). doi:10.1001/archinte.167.2.166. http://jamanetwork.com/journals/jamainternalmedicine/fullarticle/411538.

Barrett, Kathleen, and Yu-Ping Chang. "Behavioral Interventions Targeting Chronic Pain, Depression and Substance Use Disorder in Primary Care." *Journal of Nursing Scholarship* 48, no. 4 (2016): 8.

Benshoff, John, J., and Laura, K. Harrawood. "Substance Abuse and the Elderly: Unique Issues and Concerns." *Journal of Rehabilitation* 69, no. 2 (June 2003): 7.

Berke, Jeremy, and Courtney Verrill. "We Went to One of the Largest Marijuana Business Conferences in the World. Here's What It Was Like." *Business Insider* (2016). Published electronically June 19, 2016. http://www.business insider.com/cannabis-business-conference-2016-6/#because-recre ational-marijuana-remains-illegal-in-new-york-state-none-of-the-prod ucts-on-the-expo-floor-contained-thc-a-psychoactive-ingredient-in-the- plant-instead-products-were-made-from-other-chemical-extracts-like-can nabidiol-also-known-as-cbd-its-often-used-for-both-therapeutic-and-medi cinal-purposes-but-doesnt-actually-get-people-high-under-certain- restrictions-cbd-is-legal-in-all-50-states-3.

Bodiger, David. "Drug Abuse in Older US Adults Worries Experts." *The Lancet* 372 (November 8, 2008): 1.

Bogunovic, Olivera. "Substance Abuse in Aging and Elderly Adults." *Psychiatric Times* (2012). http://www.psychiatrictimes.com/geriatric-psychiatry/substance-abuse-aging-and-elderly-adults.

Botticelli, Michael. "Michael Botticelli Discusses Addiction and Rehabilitation in America." *Media Planet* (June 2016): 3.

Cherkis, Jason. "Congress Finally Passes Bipartisan Legislation to Address the Opioid Epidemic." *Huffington Post,* July 6, 2016.

Chin, Gabriel, J. "Race, the War on Drugs, and the Collateral Consequences of Criminal Conviction." *The Journal of Gender, Race & Justice* (2002): 23. Published electronically November 12, 2002. http://poseidon01.ssrn.com/delivery.php?ID=061081024013113026079022117009099014000053053031010004101021101001122011102061042029058044015080116093 1110170.

Compton, Wilson, M., Beth Han, Christopher M. Jones, Carlos Blanco, and Arthur Hughes. "Marijuana Use Disorders in Adults in the USA 2002–2014: Analysis of Cross Sectional Surveys." *The Lancet Psychiatry* 3, no. 10 (2016): 10.

Denning, P., and J. Little. *Practicing Harm Reduction Psychotherapy: An Alternative Approach to Addictions.* 2nd ed. New York: Guilford, 2012.

Denning, Patt, Jeannie Little, and Adina Glickman. *Over the Influence: The Harm Reduction Guide for Managing Drugs and Alcohol.* New York: Guilford, 2004.

DiClemente, Carlo, C. *Addiction and Change: How Addictions Develop and Addicted People Recover.* New York: Guilford, 2003.

Dobner, Susan. "Bruges: A Dementia-Friendly City." The protocity.com, 2014.

Dowling, Gayathri, J., Susan, B. Weiss, and Timothy, P. Condon. "Drugs of Abuse and the Aging Brain." *Neuropsychopharmacology* 33 (2008): 9.

Drug Policy Alliance. "Marijuana Legalization and Regulation." 4, 2016. http://www.drugpolicy.org/marijuana-legalization-and-regulation.

Elliott, Denise, Paula Bjelajac, Roger Fallot, and Beth, G. Reed. "Trauma-Informed or Trauma-Denied: Principals and Implementation of Trauma-Informed Services for Women." *Journal of Community Psychology* (July 2005): 16.

Escobedo, Tricia. "Could This Be the Next Medical Marijuana?" In *This Is Life with Lisa Ling,* edited by Lisa Ling. CNN, 2014.

Esposito, Lisa. "Silent Epidemic: Seniors and Addiction." U.S. News and World Report (2015). Published electronically December 15, 2015. http://health.usnews.com/health-news/patient-advice/articles/2015/12/02/silent-epidemic-seniors-and-addiction.

Fahy, Annie. "We Are All Addiction Counselors Now: Strategies with Problem Substance Use." In *Community Mental Health Practice: Diverse Populations and Challenges,* edited by D. Maller and K. Langham, Vol. 2, 27–44. Santa Barbara, CA: Praeger, 2013.

Fallot, Roger D., and Maxine Harris. "Creating Cultures of Trauma Informed Care (CCTIC): A Self-Assessment and Planning Protocol." Community Connections, Version 2 (February 7, 2009): 18. Published electronically July 2009. https://www.healthcare.uiowa.edu/icmh/documents/CCTIC Self-AssessmentandPlanningProtocol0709.pdf.

Felitti, Vincent J., Robert F. Anda, Dale Nordenberg, David F. Williamson, Alison M. Spitz, Valerie Edwards, Mary P. Koss, and James S. Marks. "Relationship of Childhood Abuse and Household Dysfunction to Many of the Leading Causes of Death in Adults. The Adverse Childhood Experiences (Ace) Study." *American Journal of Preventative Medicine* 14, no. 4 (1998): 13.

Fredrickson-Goldsen, Karen I., Loree Cook-Daniels, Hyun-Jun Kim, Elena A. Erosheva, Charles A. Emlet, Charles P. Hoy-Ellis, Jayn Goldsen, and Anna Muraco. "Physical and Mental Health of Transgender Older Adults: An at Risk Population." *The Gerontologist* 54, no. 3 (2014): 12.

Fuller-Thomson, Esme, Jessica L. Roane, and Sarah Brennenstuhl. "Three Types of Adverse Childhood Experiences, and Alcohol and Drug Dependence among Adults: An Investigation Using Population-Based Data." *Substance Use Misuse* 51, no. 11 (September 18, 2016): 10.

Gfroerer, Joeseph, Michael Penne, Michael Pemberton, and Ralph Folsom. "Substance Abuse Treatment Needed among Older Adults in 2020: The Impact of the Aging Baby-Boom Cohort." *Drug and Alcohol Dependence* 69 (2003): 8.

Gordon, Michael. "Gray Tsunami: A Dangerous Metaphor in Aging Discourse." HMC Communications, 2014. http://www.managedhealthcareconnect .com/blog/gray-tsunami-dangerous-metaphor-aging-discourse.

Grant, Gabriella. "Working with Elders Who Have Trauma Histories." California Center of Excellence for Trauma Informed Care, 2014.

Kapur, Sahil. "GOP Readies Swift Obamacare Repeal with No Replacement Ready." In *Bloomberg Politics*. New York: Bloomberg.com, 2016.

Khazan, Olga. "The Life-Changing Magic of Mushrooms." *The Atlantic* (2016). http://www.theatlantic.com/health/archive/2016/12/the-life-changing-magic-of-mushrooms/509246/.

Kindy, Kimberly, and Dan Keating. "Risky Alone, Deadly Together: Overdoses on Combined Prescriptions Plague White Women." *Washington Post*, August 31, 2016. https://www.washingtonpost.com/classic-apps/helpful-alone-deadly-together-overdoses-on-combined-prescriptions-plague-white-women/2016/08/31/877428f0–5e68–11e6–8c8b-bf430a787cff_story .html#comments.

Kircher, Madison, M. "What It's Like to Go to Burning Man with Your 60-Year-Old Dad." *Business Insider* (2015). Published electronically September 11, 2015. http://www.businessinsider.com/go-to-burning-man-with-parents-2015–9/#everyone-at-burning-man-goes-by-a-playa-name-a-nickname-or-alternate-persona-to-be-used-throughout-the-festival-in-the-desert-my-fri end-was-known-as-artichoke-a-vegetable-she-identifies-with-for-its-loving-nerdy-literary-erotic-and-architectural-qualities-1.

Lubin, Gus. "Americans Have Radically Changed Their Views on Weed over 25 Years." *Business Insider*, September 2, 2016. Published electronically September 2, 2016. http://www.businessinsider.com/americans-changing-views-on-weed-over-25-years-2016–9.

Manchikanti, Laxmaiah, Standiford Helm, Bert Fellows, Jeffrey W. Janata, Vidyasgar Pampati, Jay S. Grider, and Mark V. Boswell. "Opioid Epidemic in the United States." *Pain Physician* 15 (2012): ES9–ES38, Opioid Special Issue. http://www.painphysicianjournal.com/current/pdf?article=MTcwNA%3D %3D&journal=68.

Miller, William R., and Stephen Rollnick. *Motivational Interviewing.* 3rd ed. New York: Guilford, 2012.

Mithoefer, Michael, Mark, T. Wagner, Ann T. Mithoefer, Lisa Jerome, and Rick Doblin. "The Safety and Efficacy of ±3,4-Methylenedioxymethamphetamine-Assisted Psychotherapy in Subjects with Chronic, Treatment-Resistant Posttraumatic Stress Disorder: The First Randomized Controlled Pilot Study." *Journal of Psychopharmacology* 25, no. 4 (October 3, 2011): 14.

Moos, Rudolph H., Jennifer, R. Mertens, and Penny L. Brennen. "Rates and Predictors of Four-Year Readmission Rates among Late Middle-Aged and Older Substance Abuse Patients." *Journal of Studies on Alcohol* 55, no. 5 (1994): 9.

Morissette, Alanis. "Ironic." Burbank, CA: Warner Brothers, 1996.

Munoz, Cecilia. "Making Mental Health and Substance Use Disorder Parity Work." In *The White House Barak Obama.* Washington, DC: The President of the United States, 2016.

Naegle, Madeline, A., "Alcohol Screening and Assessment for Older Adults." *Try This: Best Practices in Nursing Care to Older Adults,* no. 17 (2012): 2. https://consultgeri.org/try-this/general-assessment/issue-17.pdf.

O'Connor, K. *Mental Health Treatment Seeking among Older Adults with Depression.* Pittsburg, PA: University of Pittsburg, 2008.

O'Connor, Kayien, Valire, C. Copeland, Nancy K. Grote, Gary Koeske, D. Rosen, Charles F. Reynolds, and Charlotte Brown. "Mental Health Treatment Seeking among Older Adults with Depression: The Impact of Stigma and Race." *American Journal of Geriatric Psychiatry* 18, no. 6 (2010): 12.

Office of the Surgeon General. "Facing Addiction in America the Surgeon General's Report on Alcohol, Drugs and Health." Washington, DC: Health and Human Services, 2016.

Pacula, Rosalie L., Alexander C. Wagenaar, and Jonathan P. Caulkins. "Developing Public Health Regulations for Marijuana: Lessons from Alcohol and Tobacco." *Journal of Public Health* 104, no. 6 (2014): 7.

Patterson, Thomas L., and Dilip V. Jeste. "The Potential Impact of the Baby Boom Generation on Substance Abuse among Elderly Persons." *Psychiatric Services* 50, no. 9 (1999): 5.

Peele, Stanton. "What Is Addiction and How Do People Get It? Values, Intentions, Self-Restraint and Environments." In *The Diseasing of America.* Lexington, MA/San Francisco: Jossey-Bass, 1995.

Pope, Harrison G., Jr., Amanda J. Gruber, James I. Hudson, Geoffrey Cohane, Marilyn A. Huestis, and Deborah Yurgelun-Todd. "Early-Onset Cannabis Use and Cognitive Deficits: What Is the Nature of the Association?" *Drug and Alcohol Dependence* 69 (2003): 7.

Sabet, Kevin. "Smart Approaches to Marijuana." Speech, National Conference on Addiction Disorders, Sheraton Hotel, Denver, August 19, 2016.

Samet, Jeffrey, Peter Friedmann, and Richard Saltz. "Benefits of Linking Primary Medical Care and Substance Abuse Services: Patient, Provider and Societal Perspectives." *Archives of Internal Medicine* 161, no. 1 (2001): 14.

St. Jude's Research Hospital. "Evidence Links Cocaine Abuse and Parkinson's Disease." *Science Daily* (2005). www.sciencedaily.com/releases/2005/12/051214084800.htm.

Substance Abuse and Mental Health Service Administration (SAMHSA). "Implementation of the Mental Health Parity and Addiction Equity Act (MHPAEA)." Rockville, MD: U.S. Department of Health and Human Services, Substance Abuse Administration, 2016.

Substance Abuse and Mental Health Service Administration (SAMHSA). "Substance Abuse among Older Adults Treatment Improvement Protocol." In *Series 26*, 204. Rockville, MD: U.S. Department of Health and Human Services, Substance Abuse Administration, 1998.

Suzman, Richard, and John Beard. "Global Health and Aging." National Institute on Aging. Bethesda, MD: National Institute of Health, 2011.

Tatarsky, Andrew. "Harm Reduction Psychotherapy: Extending the Reach of Traditional Substance Use Treatment." *Journal of Substance Abuse Treatment* 25, (2003): 7.

Tyas, Suzanne, L. "Alcohol Use and the Risk of Developing Alzheimer's Disease." *Alcohol Research and Health* 25, no. 4 (2001): 8.

Vestal, C. "Older Addicts Squeezed by Opioid Epidemic." *Stateline* (2016). Published electronically July 26, 2016. http://www.pewtrusts.org/en/research-and-analysis/blogs/stateline/2016/07/26/older-addicts-squeezed-by-opioid-epidemic.

Vincent, Grayson, and Victoria A. Velkoff. "The Next Four Decades the Older Population in the United States: 2010 to 2050 Population Estimates and Projections." Washington, DC: U.S. Census Bureau, 2010.

Volkow, Nora D. "Addiction to Opioids: Heroin and Prescription Drug Abuse." Senate Caucus on International Narcotics Control: U.S. Senate, 2014.

Waysay, Mohammed, Wolfgang Grisold, William Carroll, and Raad Shakir. "World Brain Day: Celebrating Brain Health in the World's Population." *The Lancet/Neurology* 15, no. 10 (September 12, 2016): 1008.

Whiteford, Harvey A., Louisa Degenhardt, Jurgen Rehm, Amanda J. Baxter, Alise J. Ferrari, Holly E. Erkine, Fiona J. Charlson, Rosana E. Norman, Abraham D. Flaxman, Nicole Johns, Roy Burstein, Christopher J. L. Murray, and Theo Vos. "Global Burden of Disease Attributable to Mental and Substance Use Disorders: Findings from the Global Burden of Disease Study 2010." *The Lancet* 382, no. 9904 (November 2013): 9.

CHAPTER SEVEN

Supporting Our Elders on Their Sexual Journey

Melissa Fritchle

Maturity is the ability to live fully and equally in multiple contexts; most especially, the ability, despite our grief and losses, to courageously inhabit the past the present and the future all at once. (Whyte, 2015, p. 139)

Of all the changes that we go through if we are lucky enough to reach old age, the changes to our sexual self are probably the least discussed. As a culture, we tend to pretend that we sexually come "of age" around puberty, learn everything we need to know, and then things stay static until we are old and gray and unable to be sexual anymore. Nothing could be further from the truth.

In actuality, our sexuality begins the moment we are born and is shaped throughout our entire life. Most of our learning about sex is indirect and so most of us reach well into adulthood sexual experiences without ever getting accurate and helpful sexual information. And yet, nothing about our sexuality stays static, giving us an opportunity to relearn and rediscover our self in subtle and not so subtle ways. Once we come to understand that sexuality is much more than a group of body functions or behaviors that we may or may not choose to engage in, we see that there is never a time when we are unable to be sexual.

Our sexual self encompasses so much more than our physical self. Sexuality is deeply relational, being driven and influenced by whom we are drawn to and whom we love. It is also internal and private, with some parts of our sexuality staying within the realm of thought, fantasy, and unnamed yearning forever. Sexuality is social and political with aspects of identity, personal safety, affiliations, rights, hopes, and dreams as powerful motivators. Sexuality is cultural, with shared ideas, images, archetypes, blind spots, myths, and communal wounds. Sexuality is something that evolves with us through life transitions, changing as we step into different roles and phases. It is colored by all of our experiences, our past, and our present and our expectations of the future. Sexuality can be spiritual and is a focus and fascination for many religions and so is entwined with our transpersonal self, including our sense of awe, connection, discipline, sin, goodness, and the sacred. Sexuality calls on our body, that part of us that others immediately see and respond to, a body that ages without our consent, that teaches us about limits as well as pleasures.

And yet, the social construct we live in depicts sex as something belonging to the young, extending into childbearing years, and then? It disappears. Or it is ridiculed. Jokes depicting dirty old men or pathetic women trying to hang on to their sexuality are sadly common. Healthy, happy sexual expression for elders is rarely portrayed—except behind closed doors. This is damaging for many reasons. Most broadly, it perpetuates the myth that sexuality only fits in a narrow framework, which then keeps us silent about our own diverse experiences. For people who are aging, there will be changes and challenges related to sexuality that deserve support and accurate information. This support is denied if elder sexuality is ignored. Also for many people, the elder years are rich in personal growth and reflection. Elders are able to invest time in self and relationships in ways they may not have been able to in previous life phases. Repair, reevaluation, and reconciliation regarding past experiences can be a crucial part of late life. The opportunity for healing is potent.

Our current generation "coming of age" now, the boomers, have had a more liberal perspective on sexuality than previous generations. They have grown older in a society that was much more open about sex than ever before, and they are speaking up more. We, as mental health practitioners, must be ready to listen. We need to have resources and education to help and advocate for vibrant sexual elders. And we need to ready ourselves, for our own elder years, making room for the full expression of sexuality throughout a lifetime.

Start the Conversation

As sex therapist, I have many clients who come to me very motivated to get more enjoyment out of their later years. They often tell me that their relationship and their sexual exploration had to take a backseat for many years while they focused on career and/or family. They had well-crafted fantasies in mind about retirement and time for themselves. They may feel a sense of freedom, of having less to lose, less people to impress or placate, and they want to finally please themselves. As they enter into this later phase of life, when they can potentially pull back from other responsibilities and obligations, they find that there are now sexual challenges they had not envisioned in their late life fantasies. They may find that years of benign neglect have affected their intimacy and bond more than they anticipated, or that new insights are allowing them to see that they want something different from their sexuality than they have had before.

Here are some foundational recommendations for talking about sex with elder clients:

Initiate the topic. Any group whose sexuality has been made invisible or the target of jokes is likely to feel vulnerable. You should take the lead by showing that the topic is open and comfortable for you. You can simply ask, "How are you feeling about your sexuality lately?" You may get a dismissive response, such as "Ach, I am an old lady, that is no longer an issue for me." Or "You don't want to hear about that. It's depressing." Or "Nothing to talk about there." I encourage you to gently lean in, just a bit, by responding with "Tell me about that" or "How do you feel about that?" If they really seem uncomfortable, of course let it go. But by compassionately and steadily inviting the topic, you are validating their sexuality and sexual concerns as a meaningful topic to explore.

Don't assume you know what it is like for them. The sex-for-18-year-olds model that we were taught may not apply (it may never have applied, but that is a different chapter in a different book) and can effectively shut down communication if it appears that is all you can relate to. Even if you are also 70, you don't know what being 70 entails for them. Ask what it is like for them. Don't assume. Also don't make guesses about what problems they may be having. While erectile difficulties may be common, they are not a given. Neither is low desire nor painful sex. The client in front of you has his or her unique experience; be ready to honor that without taking shortcuts like generalizations.

Remember sexual diversity applies for all of us. Yes, the abuela sitting in front of you may enjoy being flogged and tied up. Aging does not diminish the vastness of our sexual desires. After the death of a longtime partner, family members may find out about grandpa's bisexuality for the first time. The old stereotype of sexually conservative old people no longer applies. Educate yourself on the spectrum of human sexuality so that you are aware and support all clients.

Process an entire life of sexuality. It is never too late to heal or better understand what came before. It is never too late to find new answers or change one's mind. The elderly clients coming to see you are not just concerned with the sex that is happening now; they may be grappling with sex that happened when they were teenagers. Be careful that you are not quietly shutting down therapeutic work because of a conscious or unconscious belief like, "What does that matter now?" I have had a client at age 65 talk for the first time about abuse that happened when she was 11, begin exploring masturbation from a self-loving perspective and experienced her first orgasm.

Being sex positive can include abstinence as a valid choice. For some clients, choosing to end the physically active aspect of their sex life is the sound decision. Sometimes physical pain or fatigue simply outweighs the pleasures. Sometimes, the risks of a new relationship are not appealing. Sometimes sex is just an element of life that they feel ready to let go. Conscious abstinence can be positive. Supporting clients in considering their options, grieving and addressing the losses involved, and finding new outlets for sensate pleasure, touch, intimacy, and other needs is key.

Be mindful of your own countertransference. Sexuality can be triggering and we all grow up with myths and biases and, indeed, wounds. Be compassionate and also honest with yourself about your limitations and triggers. Know that you can seek support. As an experienced sex therapist, I frequently offer consultations for therapists who are struggling with their clients' sexual content. Reach out to a clinician you trust. And also know that you can refer out if it feels outside of your scope or comfort level.

Changing Relationships

> *I love Sir and I love being out there in my sexuality. And that's it. My children have got their own lives now.* (Peaches, quoted in White, 2010)

Romantic love is not just for the young (or the young looking). We can continue to be invigorated and nourished and challenged by it throughout our lives. We can inspire love and lust and butterfly-in-the-stomach excitement even when we are frail, bald, and age-spotted. We as therapists, and as members of a diverse community and world, need to open our eyes to these late-life love stories. We need to invite people to tell them, to give people a place to process them, to learn from them, and to honor them.

Many of these relationships are sexual. A 2005 AARP study showed that 62 percent of men and 51 percent of women aged 65–69 said that sexuality is still an important component of relationship (AARP, 2005; Bradford and Meston, 2007). Research for the American Association of Retired Persons (AARP, 2005) found that approximately one-third of survey respondents reported having intercourse once a week or more, and more than half of the respondents said they engaged in sexual caressing on a regular basis.

Our elderly clients will be engaged and activated in their relationships. Some may be deeply aligned in love relationships that have lasted more than half of their life. Some will be in new relationships, perhaps experiencing the rush of new love for the first time in years. Some may be grieving lost love, some seeking simplicity of friendly companionship, and some hoping for a final passion unlike any other that has come before. Whether facing challenging such as the frustrating familiar arguments of a 20-year marriage or the doubts and missteps of dating as a new divorcee, it is never too late to learn new relationship skills.

Aging Together—Couple's Work

Aging together can feel like new territory with no map. Couples have lots of choices to navigate as to how they envision and craft their life now. Attitudes and perspectives about what is possible and what is important can be in conflict in ways that are painful. When I work with couples, I often initiate a discussion about their sexual hopes and the gifts they see their shared sexuality offering them. For elderly couples, these discussions are extremely valuable, and often complex. They may start a process of unfolding questions about their sexual viability, self-esteem, intimacy and connection, fears, new limitations and frustrations, and desires long held back.

I have met many couples who are inspired by retirement and a sense that there is no time to waste. They seek sex therapy to overcome old patterns together and open themselves to experimentation and new ways to conceive of their shared sex life. Often times, the work we do goes back to difficult years in their relationship, processing past infidelity, struggles with infertility or unplanned pregnancies, times of low desire, or long-held secrets. It is different working with couple's issues that have been 20 years in the making. The depths of resentment and doubt that things will never change are foundational to address. But it is deeply inspiring to see the transformation that can happen and to realize that we always have the potential to see each other anew, and to love more deeply.

As the ability to have vigorously physical sex may wane, elders may find that sex becomes more focused on mental or emotional excitement. Fantasy and sex talk may be a new arena to explore. Fetishes, gender play, and other sexual variety may take on more importance as penetrative sex becomes less the norm. Ideas of what a sexual encounter will be can expand, now including gentle tickling of the skin, holding one another, kissing for hours, sharing sexual memories, or watching porn. The couple may need to take some risks to learn new ways to relate sexually and to communicate about what is exciting and satisfying now.

Caregiving can, of course, impact desire and sexual dynamics in many ways. If one partner takes on the active caregiving role, those tasks may interfere with seeing their partner sexually. Old roles and rules can change dramatically, leading to new power dynamics. Giving couples permission to talk about both the past and favorite memories, as well as what has changed now, is very helpful.

One partner may be at peace with his or her active sex life is coming to an end and may have even looked forward to letting go of the experiences of obligations or pressures around sex. While for the other partner continued sexual interaction is vital to that partner's happiness and sense of connection. I think many of us resist starting conversations about sex because we are afraid of facing the conflicting desires of two people who very much want to stay committed to one another but also want to be true to themselves. It can feel devastating to dig into the disappointments and grief over sexual yearnings that are not available in the relationship one has chosen to remain in. However, I believe it is valuable to have the discussions and to bring decisions into the open so that clients can understand their own motivations and their partners. And hopefully be able to find an agreement that is acceptable for both of them.

Divorce and New Dating

And, of course, many people are starting new relationships in their senior years, either after divorce or after the death of a spouse. Based on U.S. Census data from 2000, looking at people 65 and older, approximately 58 percent of women and of 26 percent men were single, divorced, widowed, or never married (Tamborini, 2007). Navigating the dating scene after years away from it can be intimidating. The new realities of sex and communication can bring up a lot of questions, and therapy can be a great place for a client to explore this aspect of his or her life.

Dissatisfaction in relationship doesn't get easier as we age, and many of our elders are choosing to end long-term commitments. In 2010,

25 percent of U.S. divorces involved someone over 50 years old. One in twenty of the people seeking divorce were over 65 (Maggio, 2016). Many of these people never thought they would be starting over in the later years of their life. Some may be seeking solitude or increased commitment to family, but many are seeking fresh passion with someone new.

Clients who are new to dating after many years often benefit from talking though their fears, expectations, and questions about the process. Helping them to rediscover their own intuitions, values, desires, and options is a goal. New sexual relationships may bring up concerns about sexual performance or frustrations about newly discovered limitations of their body. While it is always important to be comfortable communicating about sex, elderly clients in particular need to be able to talk explicitly about potential pain, positions that work, pacing, and what their body needs. New relationships also can uncover sexual identity and desires that were previously private. When dad starts dating again and the how-they-met story included finding his new partner on FetLife, a social network for the BDSM, fetish, and kink community, this can bring new issues to the family conversation. Clients may need to balance advocating for independence and personal privacy with pride and hope in expressing important aspects of who they are now—a tricky balance at any age.

Some clients may worry about being targeted or projected on because of their age. Internalized ageism may make it difficult for them to see themselves as viable, desirable partners, especially if their date is younger. Stereotypes and cultural mythologies about "sugar daddies," "cougars," or the exploited senior citizen may complicate judgment and increase reactivity in friends or family members. Helping clients get more confident in their ability to assess a date's genuine interest, their own safety, and their unique appeal and charisma is key.

Single elders may have difficulty finding community to meet people for dating or sex. They may feel they have to choose between dating scenes geared toward the elderly or scenes that they find exciting but in which they may stand out as one of few older people. Online dating has opened new doors and the Internet exposes people to options they may have not even been aware of before. As sex educator Carol Queen points out, "I think it's easier for younger people, in general, to go out and look for partners. The Internet levels the playing field and allows older people to seek partners, making it easier to find new romance—or, for that matter, a tryst with a sex worker. It also brings the sexual world to a generation of people who may not have had as much access to explicit materials earlier in their lives, so I think for some, it sparks or gives permission for new erotic interests" (White, 2010).

Relationships and Residential Care

For many of our elderly, there may come a time when they need more care than they can get in their home. Some may move to residential facilities when their needs for care are minimal, and they simply wish to simplify their life and prepare for the future. Some may require skilled nursing care or dementia care that family cannot provide. Sometimes clients will be moving with a spouse or partner and can continue sharing a bedroom. In other situations, only one person in a partnership may be leaving the home and now living separately with only visits from their loved ones. In any case, moving into these new living environments mean new relationships and new patterns, sometimes inspiring exciting changes, sometimes fearful dislocations and losses.

Because the topic of elder sexuality has been ignored, there is little consensus or regulation regarding how to address sexuality of patients in residential care facilities. It may surprise you, or not, to know that most facilities have no stated policy in regard to residents' sexuality. They may reference dignity and privacy, which are relevant, but not specifics related to sexual activity. Trainings to staff at care facilities are clearly needed.

One problem with lack of direct guidelines, as expressed by Alison Rahn, whose PhD thesis is focused on aged care home residents and intimacy, is that "As a result, residents are subject to the whims, personal values and knee-jerk reactions of the staff members who care for them, many of whom are often young and without much training" (Selinger-Morris, 2016). Studies from Georgia State University and University of Maryland both found that staff at care facilities frequently admitted to discouraging or directly interfering with romantic or sexual relationships developing between residents (Feller, 2016). And staff can have quite a lot of impact on residents' relationships, deciding on allowance for overnight guests or privacy during visits, reporting to family members on what they witness, making condoms or lube available, helping move patients from wheelchairs to beds or otherwise prepare them for dates, and encouraging socializing and friendships or not.

Lesbian, gay, bisexual, and transgender clients have reason to be especially concerned about how they will be received in residential settings. Many revisit the painful choice of hiding their sexuality or gender for fear of coming up against discrimination, harassment, or ignorance. A study by the Milwaukee County Department on Aging found that for fear of not being welcome, gay seniors were five times less likely to visit an aging care facility (Bennett, 2008). Some facilities may require that clients be married to share a bed, something that was not available to gay people until recently, and so many elderly clients living in committed relationships may not have taken that legal step. For those not seeking to share a room with an established partner or able to afford a private room, they may be placed according to binary gender rules that do not apply to them. Or they may be seen as a problem roommate for patients or staff who have biases about homosexuality or gender variations.

The good news is that change seems to be happening. More often, there are stories of care facilities like the Hebrew Home in the Bronx that have developed clear sexual expression policies for residents, are hosting proms, providing Do Not Disturb signs for doors, and even dating services (Hu, 2016). As rights and equality grows for gay, lesbian, bisexual, and transgender people, so will awareness and education for staff and caregivers. It is not acceptable for people to be afraid that seeking the support they need means having to forgo their own sexual decision -making, rights, or freedoms.

Changing Bodies and Health Concerns

Despite limitations in sexual functioning and altered repertoires of sexual behavior . . . everyone can function sexually in some satisfying ways— even though one may be required to differentiate from cultural norms about sexuality in order to embrace this viewpoint. (Gill and Hough, 2007, p. 223)

It is difficult for many of us to talk to doctors about something as sensitive as sexuality. For the elderly, it is made especially difficult by the invisibility of their sexuality. It may be common for a doctor to assume their 20-year-old patient is actively sexual but less so when the patient looks like her grandmother. When concerns about reproductive care are no longer relevant, routine STD screens and conversation about sexual health can unfortunately get skipped as well.

In a 2007 study of sexually active women, 57 to 85 years old, only 22 percent said they had discussed sexual concerns with their doctors since turning 50 (Lindau et al., 2007). This is not surprising. But it is unfortunate. Encouraging your clients to search out doctors whom they can talk to comfortably becomes increasingly important as clients age and are more likely to deal with medical conditions that can affect sexual function and pleasure. Also myths and fears about common changes due to aging are important to address and often can be relieved or adjusted to such that sex is still easy and enjoyable.

It is true that aging introduces changes to our bodies that can feel un-welcome. They certainly happen without our consent! And many of these changes directly relate to the ways we see ourselves sexually. Issues of self-esteem, body image, gender presentation and expectations, strength, and more may cause clients to have to reevaluate—what is sexy? Many of the secondary sex characteristics that our culture so admires fade. Many people find these changes disorienting and may need to grieve the old ver-sion of themselves.

Many of the sexual changes in female bodies happen well before old age and are related to menopause, usually occurring around age 50. The hormonal changes during this time can introduce symptoms such as thin-ning and reduced flexibility in vaginal tissue, reduced lubrication, and sometimes less intense arousal responses and sensation. There is no one way that all female bodies respond to these changes.

Male bodies also experience a decline in their androgen hormones around age 50. It is more gradual but can introduce sexual changes such as needing more time and more stimulation to get an erection, less rigid erections, and less sensitivity in the penis. Orgasm can feel less intense with less ejaculation and the refectory period gets longer, and the body needs more time between erections.

For many of my clients, their physical changes due to aging are made increasingly painful because they are ashamed to talk to their partner or partners about what is happening. I have met many people who have suf-fered sexual pain for years silently or who have denied sex because they were humiliated about losing their erection. Supporting clients in talking about these changes, helping them to normalize and depersonalize sex-ual performance concerns, and ideally inviting them to shift their sexual paradigm from one that perhaps featured more vigorous orgasm and/or penetration-focused sex to one that is more fluid, with multiple possibili-ties for sexual pleasuring that do not require one's body to perform on command. Many clients find a slower, more full body style of sexuality opens up very welcome new sensual discoveries at this time in their life. Being able to securely communicate about what feels good and what doesn't is a skill that safe, nonshaming discussions in therapy can help develop.

Sexual Implications of Illness and Pain

Of course when we don't feel good or are in pain, being actively sex-ual seems less appealing. Studies indicate that many elderly couples stop being sexual together because of an illness (Leiblum and Segraves, 1989. However, pleasure and physical closeness can be a comfort during times of stress. Orgasm has been found to release a hormone that reduces pain sensitivity (Whipple and Komisaruk, 1985). The benefits of touch and emotional closeness are becoming more and more acknowledged. Arthritis and other chronic pain conditions frequently affect sexual activity.

Other conditions interfere with sex in various ways and should always be considered. Cardiopulmonary illnesses can affect functioning but may also create fears about exertion or excitement in the client or for their partner. The risks of cardiac death from sexual activity are actually quite low, with sex generally expending the cardio energy it takes to climb two flights of stairs (Gill and Hough, 2007). Reassurance and approval from their doctor is key. Cancer diagnosis and treatments can directly impact sexual response and functioning and also affect body image and self-esteem. Complications due to diabetes and degenerative neurological disorders, such as Parkinson's, are associated with sexual concerns (Bradford and Meston, 2007). Ongoing gynecological problems such as uterine fibroids and endometriosis can have severe impacts on sexuality, and hysterectomy can result in changes in sensation, orgasm, and desire.

Help clients to recognize their own resilience. It is true that being able to get back to the functioning and sex life they had before may not be a reasonable goal. However, there is a new sexuality that can be found through a focus on what a client CAN still do and enjoy. Encouraging a client to reduce goal-oriented sexual mindsets (must have intercourse, must orgasm) and instead to get curious about sensation, impulse, and possibility is helpful. The more a client explores, the more potential they will find for themselves.

Be ready to problem solve. There are enough messages out there telling elderly clients to give up on their sex life. Don't be a part of that. As a sex therapist, I talk explicitly to my clients about sexual positions, masturbation habits, and other details. I know that for some clients a tip about how to support their hips with a cushion or using a sex toy that doesn't require them to grip it with painful arthritis can open up pleasure again. You don't have to be that explicit to be helpful. Just be aware that those options do exist out there for people, be encouraging, and have solid referrals and resources for clients to get sexual health support.

Medications and Sexual Side Effects

American elderly are commonly prescribed multiple medications. And many of the medications prescribed have sexual side effects, such as increased erection difficulties, reduced sensation and delayed or absent orgasm, and reduced libido. As mental health practitioners, we should of course know that most classes of antidepressants (SSRIs, tricyclics, and monoamine oxidase inhibitors), antianxiety medications (benzodiazepines), and older antipsychotic medication (phenothiazines) all have been linked to sexual side effects. We should also be aware of commonly prescribed drugs such as anti-hypertensives, alpha blockers, beta blockers, diuretics, cholesterol-lowering medications, heartburn medications, and antiandrogens often used in cancer treatment all can have significant and often surprising sexual consequences (Finger, 2007, pp. 48–52).

Keeping an open dialogue with clients about their sexual health and satisfaction will put you in a position to help them assess the effects of their medications and the benefits and costs. You can encourage them to bring direct questions to their doctors. Sometimes reducing the dosage can eliminate negative effects. Their doctor, if it is considered safe, could possibly approve drug holidays. However, with elderly clients, you will want to stay aware of their ability to handle complex drug schedules and variations to routines. Stay in consultation with clients' prescribing doctors and alert them if you have concerns. For many clients, the need to take the medication takes priority, and so your work with them may be grief work about the sexual losses and frustrations they may be experiencing.

Sexually Transmitted Diseases

As our elderly stay healthier and actively sexual, they have more of a chance of being exposed to sexually transmitted diseases (STDs). The vitality of this new generation of seniors who plan to keep dating and engaging with new sexual partners, enhanced by the availability of Sildenafil drugs making penetrative sexual play more possible, has created a rise in new STD cases. The Centers for Disease Control cites HIV and other STD rates for seniors are increasing faster than for the general population, with reported incidences doubling between 2000 and 2010 (Savastio, 2016).

It is important to remember that this generation did not receive sex education about STD prevention when they were coming of age sexually. Many seniors still think of condoms only in the context of pregnancy prevention, so assume condom use doesn't apply to them. Old misunderstandings and prejudices about the "kind of people who get STDs" can get in the way of adequate STD prevention practices. A 2010 National Survey of Sexual Heath and Behavior found that only 6 percent of people aged 61 and older reported using condoms, as compared to 40 percent of college-aged participants (Emanuel, 2014). A study from the Annals of Internal Medicine found that older men using Viagra actually were six times less likely to use a condom than men in their twenties (Emanuel, 2014).

When talking to seniors about sexuality, it is critical that we talk about STD prevention. Advocate for STD testing, both with your clients directly and within the agencies. Programs designed to educate and provide screenings to seniors are needed and will continue to be. In 2014, the Department of Health and Human Services released a report on Medicare use that showed that between 2011 and 2012, 2.2 million Medicare recipients received free STD testing and counseling (Emanuel, 2014). And there is still an unmet need.

Cognitive Decline and Dementia

It is helpful . . . to be reminded that intimacy is a need and improves well-being, that capacity needs to be assessed and its lack not assumed, that it is fundamental to allow free expression and that our own pre-determined perceptions may need to be addressed. (International Longevity Centre, 2011, p. 2)

The fact that we have so little literature or open discussion about how we conceive of consent and sexual rights for a person who has dementia reflects the social stance that we do not see sexuality as a need for the elderly or the disabled, that it is more comfortable to deny that sexuality can survive well into old age, much less that it can still be a potent factor even as our cognitive abilities decline.

Clients with developing dementia may display various changes in regard to their sexual behaviors. Decreased sexual interest and initiation are common, but not true for everyone. They may show changes to preferences or requests for new sexual behaviors. The partner with dementia may become less aware and attentive to their partner's feelings or boundaries. They may develop some awkwardness in sexual interactions, particularly in regard to the flow of behavior (International Longevity Center, 2011.) When sex is a source of comfort, increased requests for sex make sense and may challenge a partner's ability to respond. Some new sexual disinhibition may result in inappropriate comments or advances, public masturbation, or nudity, but research suggests this is not that common, with rates of this type behavior estimated at 2–17 percent for men and women (Series et al., 2005, as cited in International Longevity Center, 2011).

Issues of Consent

How do we decide if a person with signs of dementia is able to consent to sexual activity? Global determinations of competence are unlikely to work, since mental state and ability to be cognizant can vary greatly from day to day or moment to moment. An elder who may on one day remember his or her spouse and their faith may the next day have no recognition of either a person or a personal value system, however deeply held throughout his or her life. What rights does the person have to make choices in those moments? As noted by Kuhn, "A resident may perform poorly on a mental status test but his or her preference for a special friend or lover be quite evident" (as cited in the International Longevity Centre, 2011).

The deep changes a person can go through when in dementia really call in to question aspects of personality and self that we normally take for granted. Who are we if we no longer remember who we were? Do we need to be able to comprehend the big picture view of our life to make decisions for ourselves in the moment? To what extent does the past matter if we no longer remember it? The dislocation of relational bonds can be most painful, when years of love and commitment are simply no longer shared by one partner.

Take a moment to note your initial thoughts and feelings related to this case: Evelyn has had a 25-year marriage to Ted. For most of her life, she openly identified proudly with her role as loving wife and had always shown deep affection for Ted. Now Evelyn has been experiencing probable Alzheimer's and was moved to a residential care facility two years ago. At first she was withdrawn and sometimes frightened of this transition. This past year she has developed a friendship with another resident, Saul, and this has brought Evelyn out of her shell. Even as she becomes less and less likely to remember her family members, she is laughing and engaging more when with her new friend. They are frequently seen now holding hands and kissing, and seek time alone together in their rooms. It is clear to her friends and family that Evelyn would not have wanted to cause Ted pain, and it is very painful for him to witness this new relationship progressing. However, it is also clear that Evelyn currently does not recognize Ted as her husband and has been made happier by being able to connect to Saul. If it was decided to separate Evelyn from Saul, she would not understand the reasons for this and would be heartbroken.

Would it change the way you thought about this case if Saul was aware of Evelyn's marriage and approached Ted for his blessing? Why or why not? What about if Evelyn and Saul were unable to remember to use lubricant and Evelyn is having some abrasions and discomfort after sex?

It is not necessarily clear cut to decide if a person is competent to consent to sexual behavior. There are some foundational questions to address. For example: Does the person recognize their partner and is not mistaking them for someone else? Is the person capable of expressing themselves, verbally and/or physically? Is the person capable to take into consideration the rights of other people, understanding the need for privacy, not exposing others to unwanted sexual behavior or nudity, able to stop and respect a "No"? How is privacy, or lack thereof, affecting sexual expression? Is sexual activity safe for this person physically?

Family Support

Because there are no established protocols for decision making regarding sex and dementia, often family members and caregivers are forced to respond and decide how to handle the situation. As mental health practitioners, we may be in the role of assessing competence and comfort with a client with dementia. Perhaps more commonly, we will be working with and supporting family members who will need to be involved in the process. In assessing a client's current sexual behaviors, it will be helpful to get a sexual history, which may give clues to certain motivations or behaviors. This information may need to come from a family member, with the understanding that there may be a lot that they do not know. Even with this background, we will be faced with many difficult questions about how to integrate the past and the present. Do we have an obligation to protect continuity of the person, their past expressions of self, values, and commitments? Does this obligation weigh heavier than an obligation to protect the rights of the person as they experience themselves now?

The happiness of the client is of utmost importance. That is easy to say. But often we are asked to balance the needs of family members as well. This is especially hard when a person with dementia is developing a new relationship and the spouse or family is witness to this. Part of an assessment regarding sexual behavior should certainly be, how damaging or stressful might it be to forcibly end an old or a newly developing sexual relationship for the person with dementia? Will the client understand why they are being denied contact with a partner? Also we must consider how painful this is for their family. How do we balance the benefits of a current emotional and/or sexual connection with the pain it might cause their family or legal spouse?

Understand that family members are processing their grief and loss of their loved one as they knew them. Honoring the emotions and desires of the person in the now can be much more fraught for family members with faiths that include concepts of sin and punishments for behaviors in this lifetime. They are facing tough decisions with almost no cultural modeling to refer to, so family sessions to process can be invaluable. Recognizing that unfamiliar or inappropriate sexual behavior can feel scary or threatening to others, it can be helpful to remind family members that the person with dementia is not trying to make them uncomfortable but is currently unaware that their behavior is problematic. Also including caregivers can be valuable so everyone can be aligned in supporting one another. Advocating for trainings for family members and caregivers that include issues of sex and touch will help create a more supportive environment for everyone. Multidisciplinary and multi-person teams of care allow for broader input and better ability to assess competing needs and interests.

As stated in *The Last Taboo* (International Longevity Centre, 2011), "There are no set rules on dementia in this area and there are certainly no set answers. As you know, each situation and resident is unique" (p. 4). Working with clients facing dementia requires us to face very challenging questions. Honoring each client's dignity and self-expression, as well as their need for human contact and connection, is a significant task. One well worth our attention.

Sexual Abuse and the Elderly

Adult Protective Services (APS) is a critical system in protecting our elderly for various forms of abuse, in investigation, in interventions, and in collecting data. Currently the APS has no federal oversight, and so procedures and practices and even definitions of abuse vary state by state and sometimes within states. Marriage and family therapists, social workers, and professional counselors are all mandated reporters for elder abuse. As always, it is your obligation as a mental health practitioner to know the legal definitions of elder abuse and the mandated reporting laws in your area and to follow them.

Attempting to gather statistics on rates of abuse can be frustrating, and I found that often sexual and physical abuse numbers are combined, making it difficult to assess how much sexual abuse is being reported. A thorough study on the rates of elder abuse in New York state in 2011 differentiated between documented cases of abuse, those reported to an authority, APS, police, and the like, and self-reported cases through private interviews. Note this study combined physical and sexual abuse into one category. It found a rate of documented reports at 1.13 for every 1,000 elders.

However, it found self-reported cases at 22.4 per 1,000 (Lifespan of Greater Rochester, 2011). Clearly the important implications being that there is a lot of abuse going unreported and, therefore, unaddressed.

It is a sad reality that the more vulnerable people in our communities are also more likely to face abuse. One in three U.S. adults 65 or older is living with a disability, making them more vulnerable to abuse (National Center on Elder Abuse, 2016). As elders may need more help with daily living, they may need to seek out support people to come to their homes, giving access to their personal space, private information, and their body. Residential care requires many new interactions with strangers and the hope that the people you meet are deserving of trust.

Dependency and a New Vulnerability

The necessity of help for intimate personal care creates a new vulnerability. Being in residential care and medical care facilities and/or having new people coming in to the home to care for them increases the risk of sexual abuse. Since practices vary greatly on how care workers are screened in these different environments, responsibility falls on the family to investigate what those screening procedures might be and who will be caring for their relative.

Independent living may also cause someone to be targeted as vulnerable and without resources to protect themselves. Sexual abuse by a family member or caregiver in the home may be very difficult for the elder to report, as this may be a very important relationship for them and also they may be afraid that ending that relationship will also end their ability to live at home.

Signs and symptoms of sexual abuse can be misinterpreted as signs of dementia, and vice versa. We may find a sudden unwillingness to get undressed or shower, unexplained fear of a particular person, agitation and distress, and discomfort being touched or cared for in ways that were fine yesterday. These new behaviors can, appropriately, bring up questions of abuse. Because people experiencing dementia may not be able to articulate their feelings or even recall what inspired their current feelings, it can be difficult to get clarity on what is causing distress, even for the most vigilant caregivers.

Basic care, such as helping someone with toilet hygiene or changing clothes, can feel violating and frightening to a client who is experiencing dementia, making these necessary acts feel like abuse. The fear and humiliation that a client can feel when receiving appropriate care can be heartbreaking to witness and very confusing to navigate. It is critical to give clients as much agency, patience, and explanation of what is needed to be done as possible.

We support our elder clients by asking them about their relationships with their caregivers and talking about their discomfort and the challenges of navigating new boundaries. Careful, considered assessment of abuse should always be on our minds. Tracking signs of dementia and ability to consent to sexual interactions is complicated, and it can be helpful to have a treatment team familiar with the client to consult.

Fighting for Visibility and Respect

My experience was that interactions with these patients did more to change negative stereotypes about aging in these health professionals in training than any other training experiences they had. As interns frequently commented, "You just never think the same about your older clients (or your grandparents) after you have an 80 year old woman telling you how much she enjoys oral sex." (American Psychological Association Committee on Aging member, Antoinette M. Zeiss, PhD, cited in APA, n.d.)

We as mental health professionals have to be careful to not let our vision and understanding of sexuality get compressed into the tiny box that society tends to privilege. This is important as we relate to all of our clients, and particularly true as we engage with our elderly clients. We are in a position to advocate for their sexual viability and rights. The way that we openly and actively invite sexual issues into our work with elder clients is, in itself, sending the message that their sexuality is not invisible to us, and is not ignored or dismissed. That is, in fact, an aspect of mental health.

In referencing the many people who find sex just as satisfying in their old age as in their youth, clinical psychologists Bradford and Meston write, "Their 'secret' seems to lie not in the pursuit of a sexuality left behind in early adulthood, but in a positive, adaptive attitude towards aging that includes entitlement to sexual well-being" (p. 43). We can support that entitlement by envisioning and inviting continued curiosity, exploration, pleasure, and growth.

The primary thing we must know and acknowledge about elder sexuality is that it exists and is important. It is an aspect of self that remains, tender and exciting, into our latest years.

References

AARP, TNS NFO Atlanta, AARP Research, May 2005. "Sexuality at Midlife and Beyond—AARP." 2005. Accessed February 3, 2016. http://assets.aarp.org/rgcenter/general/2004_sexuality.pdf.

Bennett, J. "Invisible and Overlooked." Newsweek.com. 2008. https://www.news week.com/id/159509/output/print+.

Bradford, A., and C. Meston. "Senior Sexual Health: The Effects of Aging on Sexuality." In *Focus on Sexual Health*, edited by Leon VandeCreek, Frederick L. Peterson, and Jill W. Bley, 35–46. Sarasota, FL: Professional Resource Press, 2007.

Emanuel, E. "Sex and the Single Senior." *New York Times*, January 18, 2014. http://mobile.nytimes.com/2014/01/19/opinion/sunday/emanuel-sex-and-the-single-senior.html.

Feller, Stephen. "Assisted-living Facilities Limit Sexual Freedom among Older Adults, Study Says." UPI. August 8, 2016. Accessed October 30, 2016. http://www.upi.com/Health_News/2016/08/08/Assisted-living-facilities-limit-sexual-freedom-among-older-adults-study-says/3071470673981/?spt=sec&or=hn.

Finger, W. "Medications and Sexual Health" In *Innovations in Clinical Practice: Focus on Sexual Health*, edited by Leon VandeCreek, Frederick L. Peterson, and Jill W. Bley, 47–62. Sarasota, FL: Professional Resource Press, 2007.

Gill, K., and S. Hough. "Sexual Health of People with Chronic Illness and Disability." In *Focus on Sexual Health*, edited by Leon VandeCreek, Frederick L. Peterson, and Jill W. Bley, 223–243. Sarasota, FL: Professional Resource Press, 2007.

Hu, W. "Too Old for Sex? Not in This Nursing Home." *New York Times*, July 13, 2106. http://www.nytimes.com/2016/07/13/nyregion/too-old-for-sex-not-at-this-nursing-home.html?emc=edit_th_20160713&nl=todaysheadlines&nlid=25521003&_r=1.

International Longevity Centre. "The Last Taboo: A Guide to Dementia, Sexuality, Intimacy, and Sexual Behavior in Care Homes." 2011. Accessed October 30, 2016. http://www.ilcuk.org.uk/.

Leiblum, S. R., and R. Segraves. "Sex Therapy with Aging Adults." In *Principles and Practice of Sex Therapy*, edited by S. R. Leiblum and R. C. Rosen, 352–381. New York: Guilford Press, 1989.

Lifespan of Greater Rochester. *Under the Radar: New York State Elder Abuse Prevalence Study—Self-reported Prevalence and Documented Case Surveys, Final Report*. 2011. Accessed October 30, 2016. http://ocfs.ny.gov/main/reports/Under%20the%20Radar%2005%2012%2011%20final%20report.pdf.

Lindau, S., L. Schumm, E. Lauman, W. Levinson, C. O'Muircheartaigh, and L. Waite. "A Study of Sexuality and Health among Older Adults in the United States." *New England Journal of Medicine* 18 (2007): 461–468.

Maggio, Esq. By Gerald A. "The Divorce Rate for Seniors Is Rising." California Divorce Mediators RSS. April 7, 2016. Accessed October 30, 2016. http://www.cadivorcemediators.com/2015/12/the-divorce-rate-for-seniors-is-rising/.

National Center on Elder Abuse, "Abuse of Adults with a Disability." Accessed on October 13, 2016. https://ncea.acl.gov/resources/docs/Abuse-Adults-Disabilities-2012.pdf.

Savastio, Rebecca. "Senior Citizens Spreading STDs Like Wildfire." *Guardian Liberty Voice*, August 23, 2016. Accessed October 30, 2016. http://guardianlv.com/2014/01/senior-citizens-spreading-stds-like-wildfire/.

Selinger-Morris, S. "Seniors Leading Australia's Latest Sexual Revolution." ABC News. August 1, 2016. Accessed October 30, 2016. http://www.abc.net.au/news/2016–08–02/seniors-leading-australias-sexual-revolution/7681008.

Tamborini, C. "The Never-Married in Old Age: Projections and Concerns for the Near Future." *Social Security Bulletin* 67, no. 2 (2007). Accessed December 4, 2016. https://www.ssa.gov/policy/docs/ssb/v67n2/v67n2p25.html.

Whipple, Beverly, and Barry R. Komisaruk. "Elevation of Pain Threshold by Vaginal Stimulation in Women." *Pain* 21, no. 4 (1985): 357–367. doi:10.1016/0304-3959(85)90164-2.

White, R. "The Old Masters: BDSM's Popularity Grows among Senior Citizens." Gapersblock.com. 2010. http://www.thecsph.org/the-csph-resources/web-resources/sex-and/sex-and-aging/web-resources/.

Whyte, D. *Consolations—The Solace, Nourishment, and Underlying Meaning of Everyday Words.* Langley, WA: Many Rivers Press, 2015.

Zeiss, A. "Introduction to Aging and Human Sexuality Resource Guide" *American Psychological Association* (n.d.). Accessed December 4, 2016. http://www.apa.org/pi/aging/resources/guides/sexuality.aspx.

CHAPTER EIGHT

Dignity and Companionship at the End of Life: Two Contemplations on Hope, Fear, and Human Flourishing

John Eric Baugher

I was 24 years old and in my second year of graduate school when I signed up to become a caregiver at Community Hospice in New Orleans. It was spring 1993. At Community Hospice, I received no formal training, only an interview with the hospice social worker who enquired about my motivations to volunteer and offered me a brief history of the modern hospice movement. And then I was set loose to care for dying patients in the Crescent City. When I rang the doorbell that first afternoon, Jerome, a thin gay man in his forties, greeted me in his underwear and nightshirt. Speaking across the threshold of his French Quarter apartment, he asked, "How do we do this?" "I don't know," I replied, "I've never done this before." "Me either," he responded, "I've never died before." And then he invited me in. With that invitation began my journey accompanying those who are grieving and dying, embracing not-knowing with a heart receptive to whatever may arise in the face of what at times has presented as seemingly unbearable suffering.

This chapter approaches community mental health from the perspective of contemplative end-of-life care. I begin with this opening encounter with Jerome as a reminder that there are two journeys taking place in the context of community mental health—that of those called consumers, clients, users, or survivors of mental health services and that of the mental health practitioner. Each brings his or her own hopes, fears, vulnerabilities, and strengths to this encounter, and under the right conditions, each can be engaged in the process of becoming, be it healthier, wiser, more confident, more skillful, more experienced, more compassionate, or more whole. This recognition that care in the context of community first and foremost involves *journeying with*, rather than *providing a service to*, is foundational to the perspective on community health practice outlined in this chapter.

This chapter unfolds in three parts. First, I outline how the holistic approach of hospice seeks to affirm the dignity of dying and grieving persons through providing care attuned to the physical, emotional, social, and spiritual dimensions of individuals' lives. Through supporting health and well-being, rather than solely attending to illness and dysfunction, hospice as an institution resonates with the "companionship" perspective of community mental health (Maller, 2013, pp. 8–9) and aligns with developments in related fields that affirm the value of creating positive social environments that support the dignity and well-being of all (see, e.g., Johnson et al. 2016; Ronel, Frid, and Timor, 2011). Supporting dignity at end-of-life cannot be reduced to a set of techniques, but instead, professional expertise must be complemented by a sense of inner peace and journeying with one's own fears and anxieties concerning death, suffering, and embodiment.

Second, based on the understanding that mental health is not just the absence of illness, but the presence of well-being (Keyes and Michalec, 2010), I pose questions regarding what "flourishing" might look like in the context of end-of-life care. I draw specifically on Thomas Kitwood's (1997) concepts of "positive person work" and "malignant social psychology" to invite reflection on the possibilities and limitations of person-centered care in a context where existing concepts and measures of emotional well-being may not apply. Third, I offer two vignettes from my own experience as a hospice caregiver to illustrate tensions and possibilities for providing loving care at the bedside of those who are dying. Each vignette offers a contemplation on hope and fear in the face of death and is followed by reflective questions to support integration of conceptual learning with embodied experience.

Dignity and Companionship in End-of-Life Care

Dying is not inherently undignified, it is simply part of being human.
—Ira Byock (1999, p. 72)

The modern hospice movement is premised on the radical principle that all persons deserve dignified care regardless of who one is or the circumstances of one's life. This principle and its related practices have profound implications for our survival and flourishing as a species (Baugher, forthcoming). But what might it mean to provide "dignified care"?

At mid-20th century, Dame Cicely Saunders, Elisabeth Kübler-Ross, and other visionary women sought to revolutionize the culture of dying and standards of care in modern medical institutions in England and the United States (Kastenbaum, 2009). As medical professionals themselves, these pioneers of the modern hospice movement witnessed firsthand the immense suffering of dying persons that arose, not solely as a *natural* progression of cancer or other terminal illnesses, but from *social* conditions that inhibited medical staff from attending to dying persons in the fullness of their needs and experience (see Kübler-Ross, 1969; Saunders and Clark, 2006). Under the medical model established in the late 19th and early 20th centuries, illness became understood as resulting from "localized pathologies of the body," with death viewed as "no more than an extreme example of disease" (Seale, 1998, p. 77). Through this medical gaze, death became an enemy to be fought with medical technologies and pharmacological interventions that *attacked the disease*, but did not *care for the person*. As historian Emily Abel (2013) explains, doctors "began to view death less as a human norm and more of a medical defeat" such that the "imperative to avert death increasingly took priority over the demand to relieve pain and suffering at the end of life" (p. 2). For the male-dominated medical establishment, death represented failure, and in such a context, death was managed with silence, hidden away in hospitals (Howarth, 2007; Walter, 1991), leading to what sociologist Norbert Elias (1985/2001) diagnosed as the "loneliness of the dying" in modern societies. The hospice founders sought to offer "a better way of caring for the dying" (Stoddard, 1978) based on two foundational guidelines: (1) "patients, family, and staff all have legitimate needs and interests" and (2) "the terminally ill person's own preferences and life-style must be taken into account in all decision making" (Kastenbaum, 2009, p. 152).

Hospice seeks to care for the whole person recognizing that dying persons not only suffer from physical pain, but have social, psychological, and spiritual needs as well. The holistic approach of hospice is extended to the family and wider support network of the patient in the understanding that the needs of the family might at times be just as great or greater than the needs of the patient. Hospice care is provided by an interdisciplinary team of professionals comprised of physicians, nurses, social workers, chaplains, and therapists as well as lay volunteers who work collaboratively to meet the various needs of dying persons and their families on their own terms (Connor, 1998). If the individual wants to die at home, then hospice sends care into the home to make this possible. In any case, hospice seeks to provide care wherever the person may be, at home, in a hospital, in a nursing home or assisted living facility, and where such programs exists, even in prisons. Hospice care includes controlling physical pain through the use of morphine and other opioids, but not in isolation of other interventions to address the "total pain" of dying persons. Cicely Saunders introduced this radical new concept in 1964, illustrated through the narrative of Mrs. Hinson, a patient in her care at the time:

> One person gave me more or less the following answer when I asked her a question about her pain, and in her answer, she brings out the four main needs that we are trying to care for in this situation. She said, "Well doctor, the pain began in my back, but now it seems that all of me is wrong." She gave a description of various symptoms and ills and then went on to say, "My husband and son were marvelous but they were at work and they would have had to stay off and lose their money. I could have cried for the pills and injections although I knew I shouldn't. Everything seemed to be against me and nobody seemed to understand." And then she paused before she said, "But it's so wonderful to begin to feel safe again." Without any further questioning, she had talked of her mental as well as physical distress, of her social problems and of her spiritual need for security. (Clark, 2014)

Today hospice is often associated with "palliative care," a recently recognized specialization in medicine, nursing, and social work aimed at optimizing the quality of life for patients and their family members through addressing their "physical, intellectual, emotional, social, and spiritual needs" and through maximizing "patient autonomy, access to information and choice" (NHPCO, n.d.). Central to palliative care are "therapeutic relationships" in which an interdisciplinary team of professionals and voluntary caregivers provides *individualized* care attuned to specific needs and cultural contexts of patients and their family members (Baldwin, 2011). Palliative care and hospice care are seen as virtually synonymous in terms of guiding values and practices, with the primary differences being eligibility and location of care. To be eligible for hospice programs, a patient must have a terminal diagnosis with a life expectancy of six months or less and must no longer be seeking curative medical interventions. Palliative care has no such restrictions; it is comfort care that can be combined with curative medical interventions at any stage of illness. Under hospice programs, patients may receive care in their homes, hospitals, nursing homes, or residential hospices, whereas palliative care is most often administered in a medical institution that has a specialized palliative care team (Villet-Lagomarsino, 2016).

Some social scientists have interpreted the rise of palliative care as a move away from the founding ideals of the hospice movement, a turn back into the medical model that the hospice founders sought to critique (Clark and Seymour, 1999; James and Field, 1992). To outline this critique, I surface here a paradox in hospice care that predates the rise of palliative care and has direct bearing on community mental health practice: the tension between the *autonomy* of the client and the *expertise* of the professional. This tension can be seen in specific notions of a "good death" among hospice practitioners that involve dying persons approaching death with conscious awareness, acceptance, and a willingness to process one's feelings, which may not align with the wishes of dying persons or their family members (Abel, 1986; Clark and Seymour, 1999; Walter, 1994). Despite the ideal of patient autonomy, non-acceptance or "denial" of death may be seen as problematic by hospice workers "who see it as their role to facilitate acceptance and eventual surrender to death" (McNamara, Waddell, and Colvin, 1994, p. 1505; see also Baugher, 2009). The tension between these competing motivations is heightened with the shift away from the generalist hospice worker toward greater specialization under palliative care, leading to the possibility of staff "doing too much *to* the patient, not *for* the patient" (McNamara, et al., 1994, p. 1505; *italics added*) and the increasing "predominance of physical over social, psychological and spiritual care" (James and Field, 1992, p. 1373). In the words of one observer, "the relationship of genuine 'real care' gives way to the application of 'palliative care' techniques," such that "death is no longer a truth to be confronted but a process to be managed" (Bradshaw, 1996, p. 418).

My intention in sketching these historical shifts in end-of-life care in the modern era is to highlight the centrality of *dignity* in the holistic, relational work of community health practitioners and to invite contemplation about its meaning at the level of practice. In the contemporary United States, aging, illness, and dying are often experienced as an affront to one's dignity as one loses the capacity to do for oneself even the most basic activities of daily living (Byock, 1999). In such a cultural context, it is particularly crucial that health care practitioners cultivate the capacity to distinguish between the *actual needs of another* for help with certain tasks and *one's own urge* to do something simply to avoid being in the presence of suffering. In caring for a 93-year-old man over the course of the final year and a half of his life, for example, I witnessed how getting up from his living room chair turned from a routine and relatively effortless action for him to a formidable physical and emotional challenge, which in the final weeks of his life often took well over a minute and carried deep significance for his identity as a hard worker and capable human being. Good care in this context meant recognizing that the process of standing up without assistance was for him a primary intention of his standing up.

Sociologist Lynn May Rivas (2004) suggests that "the most caring part of care" for workers who care for dependent adults is helping to sustain the fiction that the person in their care is "independent" (p. 79). In other words, human services workers help protect the "dignity" of care recipients by pretending that a hierarchical relationship is, in fact, one of equality. I offer here an alternative view of dignity drawing on the work of Donna Hicks (2013), a scholar-practitioner in the field of international conflict resolution. For Hicks, dignity is as "an *internal state of peace* that comes with the recognition and acceptance of the value and vulnerability of *all* living things" (p. 1; *italics added*). Rather than acting on the pretense that recipients of one's care are independent, providing dignified care at end of life involves breaking down the alternative fiction that caregivers *themselves* are independent, invulnerable, and categorically separate from those who are dying. Anthropologist Renée Rose Shield (1988) documents, for example, how nursing home workers are often unable to offer companionship to residents out of the fear of recognizing their own "potentiality as old" (p. 16). Truly accompanying another at end of life involves recognizing that there is no dying "other" apart from "us"; we are like those in our care—dying (although not labeled as such)—and they are like us—living (although not always recognized as such). As Sandol Stoddard (1978) expresses in her classic statement on the hospice movement:

> Participation in this work is apt to produce exhilaration because of the changes we experience in our perception of such crucial matters as love and time, sickness and health, birth and death, and journeying, and the meaning of life itself. In receiving the dying as significant and fully conscious members of the hospice community we are at the same time reincorporating the awareness of death into our own lives, and this is a liberating form of illumination. (p. 145)

Good care for those who are dying requires health care practitioners to contemplate one's own mortality and cultivate "an internal state of peace" in the face of one's own fears and anxieties regarding death, dying, and embodiment. Such is the cost and the gift of journeying with others at end of life.

Personhood, Care, and Human Flourishing

Community health practitioners do more than treat illness; they promote well-being. This understanding that health is not simply the absence of illness, but the presence of well-being is expressed in the World Health Organization definition of mental health as "a state of well-being in which an individual realizes his or her own abilities, can cope with the normal stresses of life, can work productively and is able to make a contribution to his or her community" (WHO, 2016). Decades of research have identified several dimensions of human flourishing including positive affect, avowed quality of life, self-acceptance, personal growth, purpose in life, environmental mastery, autonomy, positive relations with others, social acceptance, social actualization, social contribution, social coherence, and social integration (Keyes and Michalec, 2010, p. 127). What are the possibilities and limitations for applying such understandings and concepts to the context of end-of-life care? Do the notions of working "productively" and making "a contribution" to the community reveal a bias against those who are dying? Do concepts such as social contribution, social actualization, and environmental mastery preclude the experience of particular forms of aging and dying that threaten taken-for-granted understanding of dignity and personhood?

Sociologist Clive Seale (1998) argues that the suffering associated with certain forms of dying, such as those involving dementia, simply cannot be "overcome" even by the best human care (p. 190). Of course, the validity of such a view is premised upon what is meant by "overcoming" suffering and how one understands "the best" care we can offer each other. Elsewhere I have written of the capacity of those providing spiritual care to individuals with dementia to "see more than diminishment," the possibility for loving connection and "beholding the fullness of life" even in the face of declining cognitive capacities (Baugher, 2012, pp. 226–227). Such a view resonates with psycho-gerontologist Thomas Kitwood's (1997) path-breaking work on "positive person work," in which he identifies 12 processes that affirm the dignity and well-being of individuals living with dementia, including *recognizing* the individual's unique thoughts, feelings, and preferences, *validating* his or her lived experience even if it contradicts one's own perceptions of reality, and providing a *holding* environment or safe psychological space for the individual to express freely his or her experiences and concerns. Kitwood contrasts such person-centered care with "malignant social psychology," a range of actions that undermine personhood and well-being, even if not maliciously intended by caregivers. These 17 behaviors include treating the individual like a child (*infantilization*), talking about the individual in the third person in his or her presence (*ignoring*), not acknowledging the reality of the person (*invalidation*), and not attending to an obvious need (*withholding*). Kitwood's work forms the foundation for various person-centered models of care for individuals living with dementia (Mitchell and Agnelli, 2015). More broadly, the processes of positive person work and malignant social psychology provide powerful lenses for thinking through the nature of good care and human flourishing in the context of various forms of aging and dying, not just dementia.

Some scholars have raised concerns that Kitwood's model may not be attainable in all circumstances, and may inadvertently burden caregivers with a sense of "guilt and despair" when they "cannot achieve the ideal of maintaining personhood" of those in their care (Innes, 2009, p. 16). To explore the possibilities and limitations of person-centered care at end of life, I offer here two vignettes from my own experiences at the bedside of those who are dying. In reading these vignettes, I invite you to bring attention and curiosity to whatever thoughts and embodied sensations arise in response to the dynamics I describe. Such an awareness can support you in compassionately living into your own deepest intentions for your work as a community health practitioner. Following each vignette, I offer reflective questions to support exploration of your own sense of what human flourishing could mean when one is near death, as well as the skills, capacities, and inner resources you would need to provide skillful care as a community health practitioner in such an encounter.

Two Contemplations on Hope and Fear

Central to hospice care is honoring the wishes of dying persons and supporting their agency in all matters pertaining to their care. Yet what does human flourishing and person-centered care look like when those desires are frustrated or, due to bio-medical realities, are simply unable to be met? The first vignette concerns a woman who expresses what may seem an unusual fear as she turns toward death. The second vignette offers a more detailed story of a woman who hopes for what her body will soon no longer allow. Susan and Lisa[1] both died the week following these encounters. While the contexts of their lives and the content of their hopes and fears are quite different, the experiences of both women invite community health practitioners to reflect on how we can best support well-being when the health of the body can no longer be sustained.

"Am I Going to Die?"

Susan, a 68-year-old women suffering from chronic kidney disease, had a matter-of-fact air about her. We had just one brief encounter during her time at the hospice. I knocked on her door, entered, and introduced myself and asked if I could visit with her. She seemed reserved, but said yes, her face devoid of emotion when she spoke. I pulled up a chair and took a seat on the right side of her bed. I had only been in Susan's room for a few minutes when Carla, the nurse, entered and asked me to help move Susan up in the bed. Carla reclined the head of Susan's bed and elevated the foot end to make it easier for us to lift Susan with the draw sheet. While Susan was reclined, legs elevated, she asked, "Am I going to die?" Without pause, Carla leaned over Susan and her voice took on a patronizing tone of concern as if talking down to a child: "Oh, well, that's not for us to know, sometimes people come in here and get better, but only God can answer a question like that. Susan, do you want to see a chaplain?" Susan immediately turned away from Carla and looked up at the ceiling in a stare and firmly said, "Just sit me back up." After we had gotten Susan sitting up, Carla said, "Just let me know if you want to see a chaplain" and then she left. This interaction took place in just a few seconds, and then it was gone. Here was an opening, swiftly followed by a closing. The moment was particularly poignant for me because this was my first shift back at the hospice following a week-long retreat on spiritual care during which we focused explicitly on listening deeply to the meaning of questions dying persons pose, particularly the question "Am I dying?"[2]

I moved around to the other side of Susan's bed. Susan continued to stare at the ceiling. After a few minutes of sitting quietly, I asked, "Do you feel you are dying?" Susan made and held eye contact with me. "I want to die," she said. After a pause, she continued, "But I don't know if I will be able to." Hearing her fear, I responded, "We don't know exactly when, but I have confidence you will be able to die quite peacefully when it's time." She closed her eyes. I sat quietly with her for another few minutes. My shift was at an end, and so I told her that I was going to go. I reached out to hold her hand briefly before I left. She tried to lift her hand and apologized for having limited movement in her arm. I reached down, and we held hands for a moment. We looked each other in the eye. I thanked her for allowing me to meet with her and said I would be back at the hospice in a couple of days. "I would be happy to see you again," I said, "and I would be happy if when I came in again, you were no longer here." We held eye contact. I thanked Susan for allowing me to see her good heart. She thanked me in return.

Before I went home for the night, I wrote in her chart that Susan had asked if she was dying and indicated that she appreciates honest communication about her condition and reassurance that she will be able to die peacefully. When I returned to the hospice four days later, Susan was gone. I was told that she had died peacefully that morning. I expressed to the nurse who told me this that I was happy for Susan that she was able to go. "Yes," she said, "Susan had wanted to die for a long time."

CONTEMPLATION

Take a few minutes to sit quietly and just notice what, if anything, arises for you as you reflect on this brief vignette. Allow yourself to register if any thoughts might be running through your mind or any emotional reactions or sensations in your body. If you find it helpful, you might jot down a few notes before reflecting on the following questions either alone or in discussion with a partner or in a small group.

  1) Imagine if Susan had posed her question to you: *Am I going to die?* How confident would you feel in responding? What, in your mind, would have been the most compassionate response to her question?
  2) Reflecting on what was presented in this brief vignette, including the concern Susan expressed, consider what "human flourishing" might look like for her at this point in her life? What elements of care could you imagine offering that would best support such flourishing?

Once you have completed your initial exploration of these questions, you may wish to take a short break before moving on to the next vignette. Feel free to turn back to these reflective questions at a later point.

"I Want to Live, I Want to Live, I Want to Live, I Want to Live"

I arrived at the hospice on Saturday evening for my 5:00–8:00 p.m. shift. The house was "full," as they say, with 14 patients. I ran into Terry, a fellow volunteer I had met before but hadn't seen in a while. We had a friendly exchange, and among other things, she handed me an order from Lisa, the patient in room 109, for an ice cream with chocolate sauce, watermelon, and cantaloupe, "like a sundae." She told me she had just taken down some beans to Lisa, and that in a little while, I should bring her the sundae. She explained that Lisa would need help eating the sundae. "She doesn't have the strength to lift the spoon to her mouth?" I asked. She nodded. Terry had dinner orders for patients in rooms 202 and 206, and I said I could take care of those, so she could go home.

I prepared and delivered the meals to the patients in rooms 202 and 206, and then headed down to see Lisa in room 109. I noticed a sign on the door that read "per request of the family, visitors restricted to only family members." I knocked gently on the door that was just slightly ajar, and a voice said, "come in." Upon entering the room, I noticed that the bed had been inclined and turned sideways up against the wall, and that Lisa was sitting in an upholstered reclining chair in the corner of the room with the wheeled tray table in front of her. As I walked toward her, it hit me immediately, viscerally, that something about Lisa's physical appearance seemed not quite right. My eyes glance quickly to her left arm and the back up to her face, just long enough to take in that her arms were somehow too large in proportion to the rest of her body, particularly her face which seemed dwarfed in comparison. I sat in the chair on the other side of the tray table, slightly to her left. The TV was playing on the wall above and behind me, and as I made eye contact with Lisa, my peripheral vision took in her surrounding body, which seemed almost like a caricature framing her beautiful, relaxed face. Her glasses stylish, rectangular, gold-framed. Her hair straight, once apparently light brown, now mostly gray, pulled back off the left side of her face and pinned up with a barrette highlighting the soft, kind features of her face. Like her naturally graying hair, her face radiated a natural beauty, lips red, unadulterated by make-up.

I introduced myself and indicated that I had been given her request for some ice cream. Her eyes widened, and she said, "Yes, a sundae." But first she would like some of the beans. I noticed a small cup of beans and a spoon on the tray in front of her. The beans had not been touched, so I asked if she would like me to feed her. Yes, she would. She opened her eyes just long enough to receive the spoon of beans in her mouth, and then closed them as she gently shook her head in pleasure whispering lightly, "that's sooo delicious." She made eye contact with me between bites and we repeated this process four or five times, each bite with the same grateful, expressive response. After she finished the fifth bite, she looked me in the eyes and gently stated, "Now that's a beautiful face looking at me," to which I responded "that's just what *I* was thinking."

Between bites, Lisa explained what had made her arms become swollen. As she spoke, I felt no pity or aversion, just a draw to a fellow human who, like me, has a body that isn't completely under her command, and who, like me, takes pleasures in the delights of simple food, and who, like me, enjoys the warmth of loving, undivided attention. After a few more bites, she thanked me and indicated she was done with the beans. I asked if she would like the sundae now. Yes, she would, "vanilla, like a sundae, a banana split," short pauses between each utterance.

As I left her room for the kitchen, I noticed again the "no visitors, except for family members" sign on the door, so I decided to talk first with the nursing staff before bringing Lisa her sundae. There were two CNAs at the front desk. I explained that I had just been in Lisa's room and was about to make a sundae for her, but noticed the sign on her door. Before I could finish, I was cut off, "She does make you feel guilty when you try to leave her room." I began speaking again, only to be cut off by the other CNA with a similar statement expressing how "needy" Lisa can be. I gently continued that I had just been in Lisa's room for about 15 minutes and felt that it was right that I was with her, but given the sign, I just wanted to speak with staff before returning with her sundae. Now able to hear what I was saying, they indicated that, of course, as a volunteer, I could visit with Lisa if I want to, "I am sure she would like the company."

I went to the kitchen to prepare Lisa's sundae. I found a half gallon of vanilla ice cream in the freezer, and at first placed one scoop in a cup with the intention of arranging a few pieces of fruit on top, what I imagined would be just enough for her to eat (she ate no more than half of the small cup of beans), but once I picked up the banana, I realized that I would respond to her request for a "banana split." I found a long, flat, ceramic bowl about the length of a banana, dumped the scoop of vanilla ice cream from the cup into the center of it, and then flanked each side with a half of the banana. There was a squeeze bottle of chocolate fudge sauce in the fridge, which I microwaved briefly before drizzling a bit over the ice cream, and then placed a few pieces of watermelon and cantaloupe on either side of the single scoop.

I returned to Lisa's room and placed the sundae on the tray table with the assumption that I would feed her as I had done with the beans, but when Lisa saw it, her eyes widened, "Wow!" as she reached for the spoon with her right hand. "Do you want to feed yourself?" Lisa nodded yes as she gingerly dug into the ice cream and chocolate sauce. Lisa's right hand was not as swollen as her left, but both were large, puffed thick and hard. Her fingers were as thick as hot dogs with just the tips by the fingernails the size they must have been before she had gotten sick. She raised the first bite of ice cream to her mouth, but had to bend her head down to allow the spoon to reach her tongue. She slurped the ice cream and chocolate sauce, commenting with eyes closed on how delicious it was. She cut through one side of the banana with the spoon and attempted to raise it to her mouth. The banana fell off the spoon and onto a small towel that was draped across her lap. She scooped up the banana, and this time I gently pressed upward on her wrist helping her to comfortably bring the spoon to her mouth. She ate about half the sundae this way, closing her eyes and moaning with pleasure with each bite.

At one point, while she was eating her sundae the nurse came in with some pills that she handed to Lisa in a small cup. Lisa managed to raise the cup to her mouth and, leaning back, was able to shake them into her mouth. I raised a plastic tumbler of ginger ale to her mouth and she took a few sips through the straw and swallowed the pills. While Lisa was working on getting the pills in her mouth, I asked the nurse if there was a small table we could place her left arm on so it would not just hang down to the side. She responded that there were no small tables at the hospice and that she just uses pillows. I wasn't sure how to make sense of her response, since there was no surface on which to place the pillows to elevate her arms. After the comment about the pillows, she then added, "This is her bed, she sleeps in this chair." I wondered what it was like for Lisa to hear herself talked about in the third person, especially about such intimate matters like where she sleeps.

Lisa had a sheet wrapped around her sides, draping down covering her legs, stomach, and groin. Up top, all she was wearing was a large bandage of gauze and tape in the shape of a dickey around her neck and down her shoulders, back, and chest. Out the top of the bandage on the left side of her neck, a small section of the skin cancer was visible. The section of her torso from just below the chest down to the navel was exposed, as were both her arms. The only other covering she had was a pink bathrobe draped across her lap and a small white towel on top of that that had caught the piece of falling banana. She ate about a third of the sundae, and then said she had had enough. She closed her eyes and appeared to be resting. I asked if she would like me to stay or go. "Please don't go," she said, explaining how "embarrassing" it was to be talking to someone and then open your eyes and realize the person was gone. She talked often with her eyes closed. There was an IV port in her right arm, and she indicated that the drugs made her a bit "loopy." Lisa appeared to be heavily drugged, but quite lucid, nonetheless.

She asked if I had any children. "Yes," I responded, "two daughters, one 5 and one 18." She explained that she had three adult children who couldn't agree on how she should be taken care of, and that their arguing over her care was really difficult for her. "I just want everyone to be at peace." She expressed that she wished she could make them stop arguing, and then acknowledged that it was beyond her control. "I know I have to let go," she said, "and as you know, not letting go makes my sadness and pain worse."

I reached out and held Lisa's left hand, lifting up her arm and placing it on the arm of the chair. Her hand was quite cold and felt like dead weight. Almost immediately after me taking her hand, she responded, "that's warm." I asked if she would like me to rub her hand with some cream, and she eagerly said, yes, and opened the drawer to the table indicating that there was lotion in there. As we talked, I massaged her left hand and arm, and then her right hand noticing that the temperature of her hand warmed in response to the massage. Her eyes were closed for most of the time I massaged her arms.

While I was massaging her arms, Lisa explained that she had had breast and skin cancer for 12 years, although it had gone into remission 6 years earlier. The doctors, she said, were wrong in the past about how long she had to live, and she suggested that they would be wrong again this time. "The doctors say that this time I will not make it through this, the cancer is too far advanced. But no one can tell me there is no hope. No one can tell me there's no hope." "There's always hope," I offered, "it just depends on what you are hoping for." She opened her eyes, and with a deep yearning, she quietly stated over and over, "I want to live, I want to live, I want to live, I want to live." In her yearning, I could hear the resisting letting go that she had mentioned a few minutes before, and I gently, but directly, asked, "Are you hoping to live forever?" I paused and then continued, "At some point these bodies of ours give out and we just can't live in them anymore." In saying this, I didn't understand myself as engaging in truth telling or of cutting through denial. I didn't feel myself on a high horse, and I realized as I sat with her that what I was saying applied as much to me, my wife, and my children, as it did to her.

I continued massaging, and after a pause, I asked, "What's the hardest part about dying?" Opening her eyes, she immediately responded, "The people you leave behind." "Your children?" I asked. She nodded, and then her head dropped down slightly to the left and she began panting in shallow exhalations, what seemed like deep, despairing tears. The expression of pain on her face touched me deeply, and I felt an impulse to reach out to her in her grief. I stopped massaging her left hand and allowed it to rest on my right knee, and trusting my impulse to hold her in her suffering, I began gently stroking the left side of her forehead and head, sometimes with the front of my hand, sometimes with the back of my fingers. The features of her face softened to my touch. She continued sighing deeply. I trusted my impulse to kiss her forehead.

A few minutes later, the CNA entered the room and nervously tried to help me peel myself away from Lisa with phrases like, "Oh, you know how it is with so many dishes to do, and with other patients buzzing and needing help." She then stood behind me assuming I would immediately get up and leave with her. "I'll be there in a few minutes," I said. A bit surprised, the CNA left. I sat with Lisa for another ten minutes or so, stroking her head until her breaths had softened into a rhythmic sleep.

CONTEMPLATION

Take a few minutes to sit quietly and allow yourself to register any thoughts that might be running through your mind or any emotional reactions or sensations you may be experiencing in your body in response to what you have just read. If you find it helpful, you might jot down a few notes before reflecting on the following questions either alone or in discussion with a partner or in a small group.

1) From your perspective, do you see ways that I or the other members of the hospice team acted that may have threatened Lisa's dignity or well-being? Alternatively, do you recognize elements of person-centered care in this encounter? Overall, what registers in your body when you try to imagine Lisa's experience, and reflect on the quality of care she received at this hospice?

2) Why might you imagine Lisa's family had placed the sign on Lisa's door, "Per request of the family, visitors restricted to only family members"? Do you think Lisa was aware that the sign was there? Why or why not? How might the sign point to underlying tensions in the principles of hospice and the ideal of person-centered care?

3) Drawing on Cicely Saunders' concept of "total pain," what needs and forms of suffering did Lisa present in this vignette? As a community health practitioner, what capacities or inner resources do you believe you would need to care for Lisa or someone in a similar situation?

Once you have completed your initial exploration of these questions, allow yourself to let go of the specifics of the encounter and take a minute or two to reflect more spaciously on your own experience as a reader. You might notice the quality of lighting or the temperature of the space you are in, or how your body feels supported by the chair or sofa you may be sitting on or the earth or floor beneath your feet. If you would like, you might take two or three deep breaths, and perhaps close this contemplation by sending out wishes for comfort and well-being to all with hopes and fears in the face of declining health. If you are so inclined, you might extend those well wishes out to all in your field, fellow community health practitioners, colleagues, or fellow students, being sure to include yourself in that loving embrace.

Concluding Remarks

This chapter invites community health practitioners to reflect on the caring practices and inner resources that support dignity at end of life. While individual members of a caregiving team will bring different forms of expertise depending on their training and professional role, supporting dignity at end of life requires that all health care practitioners cultivate an internal sense of peace through journeying with one's own hopes and fears regarding death, suffering, and embodiment. When our own unattended fears shield us from the sorrow we encounter in our work, we may see ourselves as charitably helping *those others* who are dying, expressed as pity for those unfortunate ones who must endure such suffering. Yet as Cicely Saunders (1965, 2003), the visionary founder of the modern hospice movement, reminded us many decades ago, dying persons are "not going through a strange, dramatic or just unlucky experience, to be written up as such with sentimentality or sensationalism, but an all-too-common experience such as ordinary people have always faced and somehow managed to come through" (p. 3). Only when we learn to rest in our own dignity and authentic presence, accepting all that we are—our living and our dying, our power and our impotence, our knowing and our not-knowing—are we then able to lovingly accompany those nearing the end of life. In the words of the Christian theologian, Henri Nouwen (1974/2004), "The friend who can be silent with us in a moment of despair or confusion, who can stay with us in an hour of grief and bereavement, who can tolerate not knowing, not curing, not healing and face with us the reality of our powerlessness, that is a friend who cares" (p. 38). Such spiritual friendship is foundational to skillful community mental health practice.

Person-centered care is crucial to supporting the dignity of those who are dying. In turn, the realities of dying bring into relief the limits of our care. Humbly accepting these limitations, that even under the best conditions our care will be imperfect, is crucial for sustaining ourselves in our own journeys as health care practitioners. Guilt, despair, burnout, these are the fruits of our own arrogant grasping to position ourselves as the one who heals, the one who serves, the one who makes things happen. But we cannot secure the good death of another; we cannot ensure another's dignity at end of life. We can only help create a web of loving interconnections that invite *each of us* from our own agency and genius to peacefully rest in the inherent goodness of our being. Our care will always be imperfect, for we are just one part of a whole. And it is through embracing such imperfection that the ideal of person-centered care can guide us as an inspiring *intention* for our practice, an intention that affirms our own basic dignity, without burdening us as a *goal*, some*thing* external to us, that may or may not be attainable. Dignity and companionship at end of life, at *any point in life*, cannot be attained, only lived. Such is the nature of human flourishing.

Notes

1. All names used are pseudonyms. Some minor details of the cases have been changed to protect anonymity.

2. The retreat was part of a certificate program in contemplative end-of-life care I completed in 2011. For more information on the program, see http://www .spcare.org/en/ceolc/main.

References

Abel, Emily K. "The Hospice Movement: Institutionalizing Innovation." *International Journal of Health Services* 16, no. 1 (1986): 71–85. doi:10.2190/ rqbv-j2pg-vfnm-1h97.

Abel, Emily K. *Inevitable Hour: A History of Caring for Dying Patients in America.* Baltimore, MD: Johns Hopkins University Press, 2013.

Baldwin, Moyra A. "Attributes of Palliative Caring." In *Key Concepts in Palliative Care,* edited by Moyra A. Baldwin and Jan Woodhouse, 7–11. Thousand Oaks, CA: Sage, 2011.

Baugher, John Eric. *Compassion Unbound: Prisons, Hospice, and the Pedagogy of Contemplative Care. Palgrave Series on Altruism, Morality, and Social Solidarity.* London: Palgrave Macmillan, Forthcoming.

Baugher, John Eric. "The Behaviorist Turn in Hospice Care." In *The Many Ways We Talk about Death in Contemporary Society: Interdisciplinary Studies in Portrayal and Classification,* edited by Margaret Souza and Christina Staudt, 331–335. Lewiston, NY: Edwin Mellen Press, 2009.

Baugher, John Eric. "The 'Quiet Revolution' in Care for the Dying." In *Inner Peace—Global Impact Tibetan Buddhism, Leadership, and Work,* edited by Kathryn Goldman Schuyler, 211–238. Charlotte, NC: IAP—Information Age Publishing, 2012.

Bradshaw, Ann. "The Spiritual Dimension of Hospice: The Secularization of an Ideal." *Social Science & Medicine* 43, no. 3 (1996): 409–419. doi:10.1016/0277-9536(95)00406-8.

Byock, Ira. *Dying Well: Peace and Possibilities at the End of Life.* New York: Riverhead Books, 1999.

Clark, David. "Total Pain': The Work of Cicely Saunders and the Maturing of a Concept." *University of Glasgow, End of Life Studies,* September 25, 2014. Accessed February 21, 2017. http://endoflifestudies.academicblogs.co.uk/ total-pain-the-work-of-cicely-saunders-and-the-maturing-of-a-concept/.

Clark, David, and Jane Seymour. *Reflections on Palliative Care.* Buckingham, UK: Open University Press, 1999.

Connor, Stephen R. *Hospice: Practice, Pitfalls, and Promise.* Washington, DC: Taylor & Francis, 1998.

Elias, Norbert. *The Loneliness of the Dying.* New York: Continuum, 1985/2001.

Hicks, Donna. *Dignity: Its Essential Role in Resolving Conflict.* New Haven, CT: Yale University Press, 2013.

Howarth, Glennys. *Death and Dying: A Sociological Introduction.* Cambridge, UK: Polity Press, 2007.

Innes, Anthea. *Dementia Studies: A Social Science Perspective.* Los Angeles: Sage, 2009.

James, Nicky, and David Field. "The Routinization of Hospice: Charisma and Bureaucratization." *Social Science & Medicine* 34, no. 12 (1992): 1363–1375. doi:10.1016/0277-9536(92)90145-g.

Johnson, Byron, Matthew Lee, Maria Pagano, and Stephen Post. "Positive Criminology and Rethinking the Response to Adolescent Addiction: Evidence on the Role of Social Support, Religiosity, and Service to Others." *International Journal of Criminology and Sociology* 5 (2016): 172–181. doi:10.6000/1929–4409.2016.05.16.

Kastenbaum, Robert J. *Death, Society, and Human Experience.* 10th ed. Boston: Allyn & Bacon, 2009.

Keyes, Corey L., and Barrett, Michalec. "Viewing Mental Health from the Complete State Paradigm." In *A Handbook for the Study of Mental Health: Social Contexts, Theories, and Systems*, edited by Teresa L. Scheid and Eric R. Wright. Cambridge, UK: Cambridge University Press, 2010.

Kitwood, Tom M. *Dementia Reconsidered: The Person Comes First.* Buckingham, UK: Open University Press, 1997.

Kübler-Ross, Elisabeth. *On Death and Dying: What the Dying Have to Teach Doctors, Nurses, Clergy and Their Own Families.* New York: Touchstone, 1969.

Maller, Doreen. "Education and Kindness: Becoming a Mental Health Practitioner." In *The Praeger Handbook of Community Mental Health Practice*, edited by Doreen Maller and Kathy Langsam, 1–18. Vol. 1. Santa Barbara, CA: Praeger, 2013.

McNamara, Beverley, Charles Waddell, and Margaret Colvin. "The Institutionalization of the Good Death." *Social Science & Medicine* 39, no. 11 (1994): 1501–1508. doi:10.1016/0277-9536(94)90002-7.

Mitchell, Gary, and Joanne Agnelli. "Person-Centred Care for People with Dementia: Kitwood Reconsidered." *Nursing Standard* 30, no. 7 (2015): 46–50. doi:10.7748/ns.30.7.46.s47.

National Hospice and Palliative Care Organization. "Palliative Care." Accessed February 18, 2017. http://www.nhpco.org/palliative-care-4.

Nouwen, Henri J. M. *Out of Solitude: Three Meditations on the Christian Life.* Notre Dame, IN: Ave Maria Press, 1974/2004.

Rivas, Lynn Rae. "Invisible Labors: Caring for the Independent Person." In *Global Woman: Nannies, Maids and Sex Workers in the New Economy*, edited by

Arlie Hochschild and Barbara Ehrenreich, 70–85. New York: Henry Holt and Company, 2004.

Ronel, N., N. Frid, and U. Timor. "The Practice of Positive Criminology: A Vipassana Course in Prison." *International Journal of Offender Therapy and Comparative Criminology* 57, no. 2 (2011): 133–153. doi:10.1177/0306624x11427664.

Saunders, Cicely M. *Watch with Me: Inspiration for a Life in Hospice Care*. Sheffield: Mortal Press, 1965/2003.

Saunders, Cicely M., and David Clark. *Cicely Saunders: Selected Writings 1958–2004*. Oxford, UK: Oxford University Press, 2006.

Seale, Clive. *Constructing Death: The Sociology of Dying and Bereavement*. Cambridge, UK: Cambridge University Press, 1998.

Shield, Renee Rose. *Uneasy Endings: Daily Life in an American Nursing Home*. Ithaca, NY: Cornell University Press, 1988.

Stoddard, Sandol. *The Hospice Movement: A Better Way of Caring for the Dying*. New York: Vintage Books, 1978.

Villet-Lagomarsino, Ann. "Hospice Vs. Palliative Care." Hospice Vs. Palliative Care. 2016. Accessed February 28, 2017. http://www.caregiverslibrary.org/caregivers-resources/grp-end-of-life-issues/hsgrp-hospice/hospice-vs-palliative-care-article.aspx.

Walter, Tony. "Modern Death: Taboo or Not Taboo?" *Sociology* 25, no. 2 (1991): 293–310. doi:10.1177/0038038591025002009.

Walter, Tony. *The Revival of Death*. London: Routledge, 1994.

World Health Organization. "Mental Health: Strengthening Our Response." World Health Organization. April 2016. Accessed February 26, 2017. http://www.who.int/mediacentre/factsheets/fs220/en/.

CHAPTER NINE

Culture-Centered Hospice Care: Welcoming Our African American Elders Home

Denise Boston

We came from a culture of tremendous order, which provided us with a viable belief system, and which guided behavior and moral interrelationship. Family closeness, sharing life with the community and friends, participation in communal structures, sacred rituals, communion with our ancestors, and contact with the ancestral land meant everything. We came from a morality ordered, spiritual universe, where the practical business of life, where science and technology, were always grounded within a sacred and religious framework. (Ani, 1997, 13)

Although hospice and palliative care professionals and advocates have made tremendous inroads in bringing awareness to end-of-life concerns and advance care planning, studies have indicated that racial disparities and underutilization of hospice care among diverse cultural groups still persists (Crawley et al., 2000; Rhodes, Teno, and Connor, 2007). For Americans of African descent, a group historically underrepresented in hospice care, there has been a complex interplay of factors attributed to these disparities such as distrust of the medical system, financial disincentives, negative perceptions, and biases and discrimination in the health care environment (Pullis, 2011). This chapter focuses on the application of a culture-centered hospice care approach with an emphasis on the integration of traditional cultural values and art-based practices into the delivery of hospice and palliative health care.

I have been reflecting, over the last eight years, on my dad's end-of-life home care hospice experience. As an elder black man, my father took great pride in how well he overcame many societal obstacles and racial inequities in his lifetime. He worked tirelessly to achieve social mobility, established a middle-class lifestyle for his wife and children, and maintained a healthy physical and mental regime until he was diagnosed with lung cancer in his seventies. When chemotherapy was no longer effective in battling his disease, he was told by his physician that he had less than six months to live and was referred to hospice services. My father wanted to die in the safety and comfort of his own home, and chose the hospice in-home care option.

The hospice team (all white) was very skilled in their palliative and patient support; however, I walked away from his end-of-life experience not only with a huge personal loss, but also with a sense of deep dissatisfaction in the lack of cultural humility and the ways in which the team interacted with my father and our family. In the process of providing hospice care, there was no attempt by anyone on the hospice team to learn about who my dad was, his feelings about hospice care, or who we were as a family unit. The entire process was very business-like, and although the hospice practitioners exhibited compassion and physical comfort for my father, they did not solicit any collaboration from my mom, who was the primary caregiver, or his children. For me, what was most disturbing was their inability to incorporate our family values and rituals into the hospice experience in order to create meaning and connection for all of us. As a psychology educator and researcher, this personal experience initiated a deep curiosity to examine hospice experiences of other Americans of African descent. I also wanted to examine whether research or initiatives were being conducted across the United States to improve hospice and palliative care with the African American population.

Studies indicate that African American elders enroll in hospice less often than their white counterparts. Research also demonstrates that factors such as the racial, historical, cultural, economic, and medical issues affect attitudes toward acceptance of, access to, and utilization of palliative and hospice care (Rhodes et al., 2007). While research in the United States adds a growing body of knowledge on the disparities associated with the end-of-life care among African Americans, very little investigation has been done on innovative ways to enhance consideration of end-of-life care using race-conscious hospice models with Americans of African descent (Watts, 2003. The purpose of this chapter is three-fold: one, to discuss the relevance of integrating an African-centered and race-conscious worldview into hospice and palliative care; two, to explore ways in which expressive arts and ritual can create meaning and connection; and three, to provide practical recommendations for the therapist and service providers.

Hospice and Palliative Care in the United States

Hospice in the United States is an interdisciplinary form of end-of-life care, which emphasizes comfort, pain relief, and emotional and spiritual support for patients with life-limiting illness. According to Beernaert et al. (2015), Palliative care is effective for patients at the end of life, with the aim to relieve suffering as well as addressing the multiple needs of patients with terminal illnesses and their families, including psychological, social, and spiritual aspects. The hospice team comprises a physician, a nurse, a psychologist, a social worker, a clergy, and trained volunteers. The concept began in the United States in the 1970s. Between 2013 and 2030, older adults 65 years and older of racial/ethnic populations is projected to increase by 123 percent (Han, Tiggle, and Remsburg, 2007). Hospice care can be provided at either a patient's home, a nursing center, a hospital, or a hospice facility.

The end-of-life process, as proposed by hospice and palliative care practitioners, should focus on creating an environment that allow patients to experience comfort, dignity, and the best quality of life possible. Interdisciplinary hospice teams are able to provide patients and families comprehensive care when they integrate diverse expertise. However, statistics from the National Hospice and Palliative Care Organization (2015) specify that African Americans represent 8 percent of patients who participate in hospice care, as compared with 76 percent whites. According to Crawley et al. (2000), barriers to end-of-life care for African Americans are shaped by various historical and contemporary events. They also state that the legacy of slavery, abuses in medical experimentation, economic injustices, and racial profiling practices have led to a loss of credibility of many institutions including the health care system. Thus, in order to achieve the aforementioned goals of comfort, dignity, and optimal quality of life, integration with African American patients' cultural values and historical legacies is critical. Culture should be a core and central element in the service delivery of end-of-life care, as it facilitates how we understand, experience, and respond to death (Becker, 1975).

African-Centered Worldview

An African-centered theoretical perspective attempts to define how Africans on the continent and in the diaspora, across time and space, struggle to bring about peace, harmony, balance, and justice in the midst of continuous social and civil injustice (Carruthers, 1999). African-centered scholars place African ideals at the center of any analysis that involves African culture and behavior (Akbar, 1999 Azibo, 1989; Myers, 1993). In terms of applying an appropriate culture-centered approach with African American terminally ill patients, an African-centered worldview is congruent in understanding the psychology of African Americans, their lived experiences, and their meaning of death and dying. It also provides a framework for understanding the psychological impact of long-term exposure to racial disparities and the psychosocial behavior patterns of elder Americans of African descent (Kambon, 1992). The framework encompasses the holistic, cultural, sociohistorical, and collective value system of black people. Nobles (1986) states that from an African perspective, the personal self is indistinguishable from the self that is derived from membership in the African community. Ani (2004) asserts that in understanding the traditional African worldview, one is able to explain the African diasporic ethos in response to the dominant culture.

The African American culture is extremely diverse in its social context. The focus of this chapter is on those who are descendants of enslavement in the United States. Many of their stories emanated in the deep South with variations in structures of black families—the nuclear, extended, and augmented (Billingsley, 1988). Billingsley states that:

> In every Negro neighborhood of any size in the country, a wide variety of family structures will be represented. This range and variety does not suggest, as some commentaries hold, that the Negro family is falling apart, but rather that these families are fully capable of surviving by adapting to the historical and contemporary societal and economic conditions facing the Negro people. (21)

In his groundbreaking research, Billingsley (1988) urged other researchers engaged in understanding black Americans to be more sensitive to the importance of structural characteristics when reaching conclusions about black families. The migration of African American from the South between 1915 and 1970 also provides a valuable description of how blacks have carried cultural values, traditions, and beliefs with them all over the country. In *The Warmth of Other Suns*, Isabel Wilkerson (2011) provides vivid stories of migration journeys that black people made to the North, Midwest, and West, in order to escape the impact of traumatic and threatening acts and experiences such as lynching, incarceration, and the Ku Klux Klan. An African-centered framework in the hospice field would assist hospice teams in understanding the ways in which Americans of African ancestry in the United States experienced stressful events associated with racism and adverse social conditions as well as their perspectives of religion, unity, death/immortality, and the ways in which kinship were maintained in black families in America (Nobles, 1986). It will offer a cogent awareness of the effects enslavement, racism, and oppression on African Americans and the unique historical, societal, and cultural factors that have helped shaped their personalities and behaviors (Akbar, 1999; Azibo, 1989; Kambon, 1992; Myers, 1993).

Hospice: A Place for Expressive Arts Therapists

One significant aspect of hospice care is that the multidisciplinary care team provides relevant end-of-life care professionals, psychosocial professionals, pastoral counselor and spiritual professionals, and well-trained volunteers from the community. Additional clinicians such as massage therapist, Reiki practitioner, acupuncturist, and others may join the team at the request of patient and/or family (Krout, 2003). Studies indicate that clinical psychologists in hospice and palliative care needed to build another level of skill sets in order to improve professional ability. Fan, Lin, and Lin (2014) contend that therapists have a passion for the field and willing to engage in the work, be flexible, and do self-reflection. There is also a new direction toward interventions such as expressive arts designed to improve the patient's sense of life purpose and self-worthiness, and creativity is a collaborative act between the patients/family and the expressive arts therapist.

Levy et al. (1995) suggests that expressive arts therapies are applicable to trauma and loss as well as the reflexivity of the various modalities of creative writing, music, dance and movement, visual arts, and multimodal approaches for specific populations. The inclusion of meaning-based intervention is also being considered in helping patients and their loved ones explore new and meaningful understanding, and approach to death and dying. Creative expression can be a salient intervention in assisting hospice patients and families in meaning-making as it relates to psychosocial needs such as helplessness, hopelessness, and meaninglessness (Safrai, 2013).

However, for U.S. patients of African descent, in search of meaning and purpose, there exists a worldview that includes historical, racial, and societal implications. Emotional adjustment may be dependent on reflecting on critical experiences. An African-centered therapeutic approach has been influential in the development of authentic and culturally relevant models for understanding human existence (Jamison and Carroll, 2014). According to Mariette, (2013), "Delivering culturally congruent African-centered services and programming to . . . Africans in Diaspora must include treating their Spirit as affected by contextual antecedents and historical legacies, current experience of living, and the meaning of being human" (267). Team-based care, which includes an arts-focused therapeutic component with an awareness of cultural underpinnings, can enhance the expressions of grief and honor the lived experience and meaning construction. In the next section I will offer three art modalities—music, visual arts, and narrative—to concretely illustrate strategies to understand, assess, and incorporate expressive interventions conducive to African American elder hospice patients. The last area of understanding is the role expressive arts plays in the area of aesthetic response and the counselor's therapeutic experience with the patient and family.

Expressive Arts Strategies in Hospice Care

Romanoff and Thompson (2006) suggest that for many patients and families, the diagnosis of terminal illness requires a revision of the assumptions that have ordered a guided experience and requires the construction of a new life story. The authors go on to state that hospice practitioners can play an important role in helping individuals reconstruct their lives and create meaning at the end of life. Aldridge (1999) contends that creativity has the potential of assisting terminally ill patients in transcending the moment of suffering, and a new consciousness is created.

Expressive arts therapy is a nascent therapeutic field. It is the practice of using music, writing visual arts, poetry, movement music, rituals, drama, song, storytelling, and other art forms in an integrated way. The process of creativity and creating offers resources such as self-expression, self-exploration, and connection with ritual and community (Richardson, 2016; Somé, 1994). For many indigenous cultures, the arts have been a way of life and survival.

Each art form is a field of its own, and honors specific structural expectancies. However, for the expressive arts therapist, all art forms are available to the client for personal expression for whatever purpose (Levy et al., 1995). Expressive arts interventions that encourage nonverbal exploration are especially helpful to individuals who are in the final stage of their lives and whose feelings are inaccessible through words or gestures. Understanding life experiences of African American elders through storytelling, music, visual arts, dance, songs, drama, rituals, and poetry is a language of illumination and honoring. The first arts modality that will be discussed is music and its ability to decrease depressive symptoms and social isolation as well as increasing communication, self-expression, reminiscence, and life review (Clements-Cortes, 2004).

Art Modality: Music

According to Whitehead (2011), "Music therapy is one of the most popular forms of complementary therapies for hospice and palliative care programs in the United States and Canada" (697). She states that the purpose of music therapy at the final stage of life is to improve the quality of the experience by relieving symptoms, addressing psychological needs, offering support, and meeting spiritual needs. The music intervention also provides care for caregivers and family members by addressing their coping and communication skills and grief.

Music has been shown to have a significant role in the healing ceremonies for many African people in the diaspora. Barker (2015) provides a critical theory of music and resistance and contends that music was used to provide intimations of freedom for slaves living in the United States. In his examination of forms of resistance in slave songs, he identified two intersecting tendencies: freedom as material practice and freedom as the aesthetic imagination. Therefore, he suggests that the historical roots of music for many enslaved people provided "a vital means through which material freedom could become enjoined with the practices of everyday life" (379). Studies have shown that the memory of the song stays with us longer than regular memories (Brotons, Koger, and Pickett-Cooper, 1997). The following music therapy techniques would be applicable when working with African American patients and caregivers to bring about a particular change, whether that change is therapeutic, emotional, or spiritual.

Designing a Playlist of Favorite Music

1. Have a conversation with patients regarding the role music played in their life; allow patients to share as far back as they remember.

2. Ask if the patient was a member of a church, temple, or mosque and the style of religious or spiritual music he or she enjoys (e.g., praise/worship, gospel, sanctified).

3. Once you have identified the patient's music choices, actively engage family members to be involved in assisting you with the development of a playlist of the music shared by the patient. Gather other stories from the family about the patient's selection of songs and what the music means to them.

4. The playlist will become a part of the patient's care setting and used as background music.

5. In the course of the therapeutic session with the patient, select a song on the list and initiate a conversation about a story connected to the song.

6. Encourage family members to learn a song on the list and sing it during a visit.

Art Modality: Visual Arts

The practice of art therapy can be a great tool for the counselor to help hospice patients and their families construct meaning in the light of impending loss. The imagination is engaged through artistic expression to enhance healing and growth. Attig (2000) asserts that in the realm of grief and bereavement counseling, the use of artistic discipline may be a new way for the bereaved to communicate when words seem inadequate. Americans of African descent have used the aesthetic to respond to every aspect of their lived experiences in the United States. Bereavement support is particularly essential for African American families who have witnessed traumatic deaths through homicide, premature loss of loved ones, and diminished lifespan (Genevro, Marshall, and Miller, 2004). The arts-based intervention that follows provides a supportive space for family members to reflect on their experiences of loss and to create intentional memorials that encourage them to hold on to memories of strength, endurance, and resilience.

Memory Boxes or Altar-Making

A memory box is a great place to keep photos, artifacts, poems, drawings, meaningful items, and other keepsakes of the patient and family. Collecting mementoes of the elder and putting them in one place can be very helpful to them and the family in the final stages of life. It also helps confine the memories to one area of the home environment. The family should schedule three 2-hour sessions with the expressive arts therapist to create and decorate a memory box, altar, or both.

Session 1: Discussion on the therapeutic benefits of creating a memory box as a way to memorialize their loved one in any way they choose. Generating ideas of the box design and dimensions. The homework assignment is for everyone to bring in a memorable object that remind them of the person or events they shared together.

Session 2: Supplies are brought in to begin building the box as well as various art materials for decorating (fabric, ribbons, flowers). If an altar is selected, the family determines where they would like to arrange the table. Everyone begins gathering memorabilia and writing poetry or letters if desired. On the table, objects may include photos, statues, food, drink, flowers, poetry, candles incense, and favorite items of the patient.

Session 3: The last session involves placing objects strategically in the memory box or on the altar and celebrating the final product with food, stories, and testimonials.

Note: The creation of smaller memory boxes can be made as gifts to the patient or keepsakes for family members to remember their loved one for many years following the transition.

Home altars can also provide a sacred space for meditation, reflection, and prayer. Using representations of the patient's life and various memorable family artifacts can reconnect the family with their historical past in a personal and spiritual way. The process of creating the altar is a reflective experience and can generate stories related to the objects and memories selected for the table.

Narrative Therapy

Narrative therapy invites clients to explore the human experience through stories. Together, the client and the therapist examine all the richness and meanings that they hold. These stories are instrumental in the approach a person constructs his or her life around. One of the main tenets in narrative therapy is externalizing the problem (Denborough, 2014; White, 1989; White and Epston, 2015). Narrative therapists view these problem-saturated stories as standing in the way of the clients. In relation to end-of-life experiences, Romanoff and Thompson (2006) contend that:

> All patients have stories to tell, and most are eager to tell their stories. For many, illness and impending loss tears the coherence of the life narrative, disrupting daily activities, identities, and imagined futures. The linear structure of the modern mythic story, the culturally shared assumptions by which we live our lives, is derailed . . . The challenge for the patient and family is to construct and reconstruct a meaningful tale, to write a new chapter of the life story that accommodates a changed reality and lived experience. (310)

For clients of diverse cultural backgrounds, the cultural contexts contain forces that often limit psychological growth (Sue and Sue, 1999). Therefore, the focus in culture-centered narrative counseling is not only on helping clients tell their stories, but also to find strategies for resisting internalization of negative cultural messages (Semmler and Williams, 2000). In a continual search to find creative and innovative approaches of supporting those who are in end-of-life care, the use of narrative therapy is congruent with the search for meaning for African American elders.

Tree of Life

The tree of life is a narrative-based approach to working with any people of any age who have experienced trauma, social inequities, or health challenges. This concept was codeveloped by Ncazelo Ncube (REPSSI) and David Denborough (Dulwich Centre Foundation) initially to assist colleagues to work with children affected by HIV/AIDS in South Africa (Denborough, 2014). This approach has been replicated all over the world with various populations. It is a strength-based process that enables people to speak about their lives in positive and affirming ways. The narrative strategies below will illustrate how empowering this intervention is in highlighting the interconnections of the past, present, and significant relationships along the way.

The tree of life project takes 2–3 days. Following are directions for two different processes—the first with the patient and the second with the caregiver and family. The basic structure involves drawing a tree with the following eight areas mentioned below and filling each of the areas with relevant information.

The Roots—hometown, place of birth, cultural background

The Ground—present experiences

The Trunk—skills, values, talents

The Branches—hopes, dreams, wishes

The Leaves—names of those who are significant in your life (past and present)

The Fruits—gifts that you have received from others (attributes, material gains)

The Seeds and Flowers—the legacies you wish to leave to others

Tree of Life with Hospice Patient

Session 1: Have the tree already drawn on large paper, unless the patient requests to drawing it instead. Post the explanation for each area of the tree for easy access for the activity. Explain the process, and if you are completing the tree for the patient, ask questions about each of the areas on the tree. Proceed with deep listening skills and make sure that your response matches those of the patient's. Try to complete the roots, ground, and branches during the first session.

Session 2: Complete the remaining areas of the trees. If the patient is not well enough, the activity can be expanded for a third day. At completion, assess how the process was for the patient and what they discovered about themselves after the tree was done.

Note: Incorporate within this conversation what their perceptions are of death and dying as well as life purpose.

Tree of Life with Caregiver and Family

Session 1: Explain the process and allow each participant 45 minutes to draw and complete their tree. Family members can continue to work on tree between sessions.

Session 2: Each family member is given an opportunity to share what they discovered in the process of completing their tree of life. Post all of the trees around the room and include the patient's tree in the "forest" of trees. Have the family explore the other trees and share their response about what they discovered about themselves as a family, gifts they received from the elder, and the legacy that will be carry into the future.

Note: Altars and narratives associated with the process can take 1–2 sessions.

Counselor's Aesthetic Response to family Experience

Many hospice care providers state that they feel called to hospice work and that caring for hospice patients, caregivers, and families is a fulfilling, enriching, and meaningful experience (Jones, 2005). End-of-life care offers opportunities to work with the broad spectrum of end-of-life experiences. Providing care for African American hospice patients, caregivers, and families enables professionals to experience a personal and unique insight into the complexity of their historical journey and lived experiences, which include, in some cases, disrespectful treatment by society and distrust of the medical system. Lack of trust has initiated resistance to, and underutilization of, hospice care services. However, once trust is established and an authentic culture-centered approach has been consistently delivered in the hospice service, families will be motivated to see the benefits of hospice care. When invited by expressive arts therapists to share personal stories of their lived experiences through art-based interventions, black patients and families may feel supported in sharing deeply held stories that impacted their lives.

> I saw myself not as an authority in expressive arts, but as a companion in the process of the client's self-discovery . . . I saw my role as one of creating a trusting environment in which the client would be heard at the deepest level, and where various means of self-exploration would be available. (Rogers, 1995, 106)

According to Richardson (2016), "In the field of expressive therapies, the therapist is in the role of witness, by virtue of being in the presence of clients, their art, and their process of creating art" (25). Hearing these stories can be stressful, overwhelming, and impactful for professionals of a different cultural background as well as care providers from similar racial backgrounds. Exposure to repeated losses, traumas, and the intensity of the stories can cause compassion fatigue, secondary trauma, grief, and depression (Showalter, 2010). Inserting an aesthetic response component in hospice care must be an integral aspect of practice. Aesthetic responses and self-care may include practicing a personal art modality such as dancing, poetry, or improvisation. An aesthetic response may also be in the form of an artistic offering to the client and/or family that exemplifies a visual testimony of the impact of the relation established during the therapy visits. This response connects the therapist and the client and the potential of increased attunement in the relationship (Richardson, 2016).

Conclusion

In order to truly design and deliver respectful, comfort, support, and the best quality of end-of-life care possible for African American terminally ill elders, hospice care providers must consider the role that cultural values, historical and racial injustices, and inequities play in the lives of elder Americans of African descent. A culture-centered approach that includes the family, extended family, friends, and community of the hospice patient is aligned with the African ritual of "welcoming the spirit home." As hospice and palliative care models begin to bridge the racial divide to end-of-life care service with African American populations, considerations of African-centered therapies and *race consciousness*, which is described as an awareness of the historical journey of the group and a self-appraisal of one's attitudes and biases toward the group, offer an integral aspect of professional growth for culturally competent health professionals (Watts, 2003). Watts enlists guidelines to begin the process of incorporation of race consciousness as a component of cultural competence professional development. They consist of the following:

1. Conducting a self-appraisal of racial and ethnic heritage that includes:
    - Place of birth
    - Length of time in country and history of migration
    - Ethnic affiliation and identity

- Primary and secondary languages
- Style of communication
- Religion
- Food preferences
- Health beliefs and health practices
- Customs around transitions, such as birth and illnesses
- Self-appraisal of attitudes, feelings, and beliefs toward African Americans and persons of color

2. Launching a culture interest group with a focus on African American health concerns

    - Assemble a coalition of colleagues to assist you with this initiative
    - Conduct a survey to examine the racial/ethnic diversity within the group
    - Establish a routine time for group sessions
    - Use different strategies to get to know the other person, e.g., conduct a culture health history on a colleague
    - Gather data about the problems of race and ethnicity in your setting with use of surveys or questionnaire
    - Design a strategic plan for increasing culture competence of colleagues and staff
    - Launch a lecture series on race and African American health care issues
    - Obtain a list of potential experts to discuss issues of race, disparities in health, and the black experience
    - Build partnerships with families and community leadership
    - Develop a reference library of resources on aspects of race, culture, competency, and health disparities of staff
    - Develop a timetable to evaluate the efficacy of your efforts

3. Participating in continuing education/professional development programs to increase knowledge about minority issues with specific emphasis on the African Americans

4. Developing a philosophy of lifelong learning[1]

Although a culture-centered approach may require an in-depth and concerted effort to collaborate with African American families and African-centered mental practitioners, this process is necessary if indeed there is a commitment to provide an environment where the patient can live and die with dignity and authentic support. For African Americans, being appreciated and honored during the final stage of their lives may be our last act of compassion and restorative justice for a people who were brought to the Americas against their will over 400 years ago. This act of honor and respect is owed to many generations of African descendants who deserve a quality end-of-life hospice care experience that provides comfort, support, and, more importantly, cultural humility.

Note

1. Republished with permission from Watts, R. J. "Race Consciousness and the Health of African Americans." *Online Journal of Issues in Nursing*. 2003. Accessed February 23, 2017. https://www.ncbi.nlm.nih.gov/pubmed/12729454. Permission conveyed through Copyright Clearance Center, Inc.

References

Akbar, N. *Know Thyself*. Tallahassee, FL: Mind Productions & Associates, 1999.

Aldridge, David. *Music Therapy in Palliative Care: New Voices*. London, UK: Jessica Kingsley Publishers, 1999.

Ani, Marimba. *Let the Circle Be Unbroken: The Implications of African Spirituality in the Diaspora*. New York: Nkonimfo Publications, 1997.

Attig, Thomas. *The Heart of Grief: Death and the Search for Lasting Love*. New York: Oxford University Press, 2000.

Azibo, D. A. Y. "African-Centered Theses on Mental Health and a Nosology of Black/African Personality Disorder." *Journal of Black Psychology* 15, no. 2 (1989): 173–214. doi:10.1177/00957984890152008.

Barker, Thomas P. "Spatial Dialectics." *Journal of Black Studies* 46, no. 4 (2015): 363–383. doi:10.1177/0021934715574499.

Becker, Ernest. *The Denial of Death*. New York: Free Press, 1975.

Beernaert, K., L. Deliens, A. De Vleminck, D. Devroey, K. Pardon, L. V. D. Block, and J. Cohen. "Is There a Need for Early Palliative Care in Patients with Life-Limiting Illnesses? Interview Study with Patients about Experienced Care Needs from Diagnosis Onward." *American Journal of Hospice and Palliative Medicine* 33, no. 5 (2015): 489–497. doi:10.1177/1049909115577352.

Billingsley, Andrew. *Black Families in White America*. New York: Simon & Schuster, 1988.

Brotons, M., S. M. Koger, and P. Pickett-Cooper. "Music and Dementias: A Review of Literature." *Journal of Music Therapy* 34, no. 4 (1997): 204–245. doi:10.1093/jmt/34.4.204.

Carruthers, Jacob H. *Intellectual Warfare*. Chicago: Third World Press, 1995.

Clements-Cortes, A. "The Use of Music in Facilitating Emotional Expression in the Terminally Ill." *American Journal of Hospice and Palliative Medicine* 21, no. 4 (2004): 255–260. doi:10.1177/104990910402100406.

Crawley, L., R. Payne, J. Bolden, T. Payne, P. Washington, and S. Williams. "Palliative and End-of-Life Care in the African American Community." *JAMA*, The JAMA Network. November 15, 2000. Accessed February 23, 2017. http://jamanetwork.com/journals/jama/fullarticle/193262.

Denborough, David. *Retelling the Stories of Our Lives: Everyday Narrative Therapy to Draw Inspiration and Transform Experience*. New York: W.W. Norton & Company, 2014.

Fan, S.-Y., W.-C. Lin, and I.-M. Lin. "Psychosocial Care and the Role of Clinical Psychologists in Palliative Care." *American Journal of Hospice and Palliative Medicine* 32, no. 8 (2014): 861–868. doi:10.1177/1049909114543492.

Genevro, J. L., T. Marshall, and T. Miller. "Report on Bereavement and Grief Research." *Death Studies* 28, no. 6 (2004): 491–575. doi:10.1080/07481180490461188.

Han, B., R. B. Tiggle, and R. E. Remsburg. "Characteristics of Patients Receiving Hospice Care at Home versus in Nursing Homes: Results from the National Home and Hospice Care Survey and the National Nursing Home Survey." *American Journal of Hospice and Palliative Medicine* 24, no. 6 (2007): 479–486. doi:10.1177/1049909107305654.

Jamison, D., and K. Carroll. "A Critical Review and Analysis of the State, Scope, and Direction of African-Centered Psychology from 2000–2010." *Western Journal of Black Studies* 38, no. 2 (2014): 98–107.

Jones, S. H. "A Self-care Plan for Hospice Workers." *American Journal of Hospice and Palliative Medicine* 22, no. 2 (2005): 125–128. doi:10.1177/104990910502200208.

Kambon, K. *African-Black Psychology in the American Context: An African-Centered Framework*. Tallahassee, FL: Nubian Nation Publication, 1992.

Krout, R. E. "Music Therapy with Imminently Dying Hospice Patients and Their Families: Facilitating Release Near the Time of Death." *American Journal of Hospice and Palliative Medicine* 20, no. 2 (2003): 129–134. doi:10.1177/104990910302000211.

Levy, Fran J., Judith Pines Fried, and Fern Leventhal. *Dance and Other Expressive Art Therapies When Words Are Not Enough*. New York: Routledge, 1995.

Mariette, G. "International Healing and Collaborative Structures." *Journal of Black Psychology* 39, no. 3 (2013): 261–268.

Myers, L. *Understanding an Africentric Worldview: Introduction to and Optimal Psychology*. Dubuque, IA: Kendall/Hunt, 1993.

National Hospice and Palliative Care Organization, "Facts and Figures on Hospice Care in America." 2015. doi:10.1037/e614232011–001.

Nobles, W. *African Psychology: Towards Reclamation, Reascension, and Revitalization*. Oakland, CA: Black Family Institute Publication, 1986.

Pullis, Bridgette. "Perceptions of Hospice Care among African Americans." *Journal of Hospice & Palliative Nursing* 13, no. 5 (2011): 281–287. doi:10.1097/njh.0b013e31821adb18.

Rhodes, Ramona L., Joan M. Teno, and Stephen R. Connor. "African American Bereaved Family Members' Perceptions of the Quality of Hospice Care:

Lessened Disparities, but Opportunities to Improve Remain." *Journal of Pain and Symptom Management* 34, no. 5 (2007): 472–479. doi:10.1016/j.jpainsymman.2007.06.004.

Richardson, Carmen. *Expressive Arts Therapy for Traumatized Children and Adolescents: A Four-phase Model.* New York: Routledge, 2016.

Rogers, Carl R. *A Way of Being.* Boston: Houghton Mifflin, 1995.

Romanoff, B. D., and Thompson, B. "Meaning Construction in Palliative Care: The Use of Narrative, Ritual, and the Expressive Arts." *American Journal of Hospice and Palliative Medicine* 23, no. 4 (2006): 309–16. doi:10.1177/1049909106290246.

Safrai, M. "Art Therapy in Hospice: A Catalyst for Insight and Healing." *Art Therapy: Journal of the American Art Therapy Association* 30, no. 3 (2013), 122–129.

Semmler, Pamela Lucey, and Carmen Braun Williams. "Narrative Therapy: A Storied Context for Multicultural Counseling." *Journal of Multicultural Counseling and Development* 28, no. 1 (2000): 51–62. doi:10.1002/j.2161-1912.2000.tb00227.x.

Showalter, S. E. "Compassion Fatigue: What Is It? Why Does It Matter? Recognizing the Symptoms, Acknowledging the Impact, Developing the Tools to Prevent Compassion Fatigue, and Strengthen the Professional Already Suffering from the Effects." *American Journal of Hospice and Palliative Medicine* 27, no. 4 (2010): 239–242. doi:10.1177/1049909109354096.

Somé, Malidoma Patrice. *Of Water and the Spirit: Ritual, Magic, and Initiation in the Life of an African Shaman.* New York: Penguin, 1995.

Sue, Derald Wing., and David Sue. *Counseling the Culturally Different: Theory and Practice.* New York: John Wiley & Sons, 1999.

Watts, R. J. "Race Consciousness and the Health of African Americans." *Online Journal of Issues in Nursing.* 2003. Accessed February 23, 2017. https://www.ncbi.nlm.nih.gov/pubmed/12729454.

White, M. *Selected Papers.* Adelaide: Dulwich Center, 1989.

White, Michael, and David Epston. *Narrative Means to Therapeutic Ends.* Auckland, NZ: Royal New Zealand Foundation of the Blind, 2015.

Whitehead, Phyllis. "Music Therapy for End-of-Life Care." *Clinical Journal of Oncology Nursing* 15, no. 6 (2011): 697–698. doi:10.1188/11.cjon.697-698.

Wilkerson, Isabel. *The Warmth of Other Suns: The Epic Story of America's Great Migration.* New York: Random House, 2011.

CHAPTER TEN

Aging and the Law: The Legal Aspects of Aging and Care Provision

Pamela Zimba

The Aging Population

The population of the world, and of the United States, is aging. By 2020, the number of Americans 65 and older is expected to reach 54 million, which is approximately 18 percent of the population (Frolik and Barnes, 2007). By 2030, this age group will represent 20 percent of the population, and almost 22 percent by 2050 (Frolik and Barnes, 2007). The United Nations has estimated that one in five people (approximately 2 billion) will be 60 years of age or older by 2050 (Moskowitz, 2003). In the United States, people 80 and older are the fastest growing age group (Moskowitz, 2003).

When considering legal obligations for elder care and consideration, most applicable laws are state laws as opposed to federal. This chapter is written considering information related to the state of California. Should you reside elsewhere, please use this chapter as a guide, but check with specifics of your state of residence. In California, "elder" means any person who is 65 years of age or older. The California Welfare and Institutions Code Sections 15600–76 (hereinafter referred to as the "Elder Abuse Act") defines "abuse of an elder" as "physical abuse, neglect, financial abuse, abandonment, isolation, abduction, or other treatment with resulting physical harm or pain or mental suffering" (Cal Welfare & Inst. Code

§15610.07(a)) "or the deprivation by a care custodian of goods or services that are necessary to avoid physical harm or mental suffering" (Cal Welfare & Inst. Code §15610.07(b)).

Recent estimates of elder abuse cases in the United States show a total of 5,961,568, reported cases, which is 9.5 percent of the overall population. Women represent 67.3 percent of persons over 60 subjected to abuse and neglect The median age of the elder abuse victims is 77.9. In 66 percent of the incidents of elder abuse, the perpetrator is an adult child or spouse. The breakdown of reported elder abuse cases includes neglect, 58.5 percent; physical abuse, 15.7 percent; financial abuse, 12.3 percent; and emotional abuse, 7.3 percent (Statistic Brain, n.d.). The fastest growing and most vulnerable are those 80 years and older, who are abused two to three times more than those 60 and older (Moskowitz, 2003).

This chapter will outline the requirements and considerations for reporting incidences of elder abuse as well as other legal and ethical issues that may impact on the care of elders in a therapy practice. As discussed later, pursuant to the Elder Abuse Act, marriage and family therapists (MFTs), interns and trainees are considered to be mandated reporters when evidence of elder abuse is present. These laws are governed by the Elder Abuse Act, which was created to include: (1) providing increased protection to a vulnerable population (Cal Welfare & Inst. Code §15601); (2) requiring health practitioners, care custodians, clergy members, and employees of county adult protective services agencies and local law enforcement agencies to report known or suspected cases of abuse of elders and to encourage community members in general to do so (Cal Welfare & Inst. Code §15601(a)); (3) gathering information on the numbers of abuse victims, discovering the circumstances surrounding the acts of abuse, and obtaining other data that will aid the state in establishing services to aid all victims of abuse (Cal Welfare & Inst. Code §15601(b)); and (4) providing for legal protection for persons who report suspected cases of abuse, provided that the report is not made with malicious intent (Cal Welfare & Inst. Code §15600(c)).

Ethical Standards for Marriage and Family Therapists

The board of directors of the California Association of Marriage and Family Therapists (CAMFT) publishes the Code of Ethical Standards for MFTs (2011). Members of CAMFT are expected to be familiar with and abide by these standards and applicable California laws and regulations governing the conduct of licensed MFTs, supervisors, educators, interns, applicants, students, and trainees. There are a multitude of approaches, techniques, modalities, and methods of treating a client. The standards discussed here are to be utilized as a guide for your ethical behavior. Although there may not be a specific prohibition against a particular type of conduct, this should not be interpreted as meaning that such conduct is deemed ethical or unethical. The standards are not exhaustive. If you are unclear or uncertain about your ethics as they relate to an anticipated course of action, it is important to seek counsel from attorneys, supervisors, colleagues, consultants, or other appropriate authorities.

If your professional association (for instance, and noted herein, American Association of Marriage and Family Therapists—AAMFT) (2015) prescribes a standard higher than that required by law, you must meet the higher standard of its code of ethics. Lack of awareness or misunderstanding of an ethical standard is not a defense to a charge of unethical conduct. The purpose of this section is to discuss, in brief, certain of those code sections that may be applicable to your work with an elder. If you have additional questions, please consult your professional association's code of ethics for further clarification. Applicable code sections are discussed in the following paragraphs:

Section 1.2 addresses the issue of informed consent in a therapeutic setting. Although state law does not provide significant guidance regarding the content of an informed consent agreement, a therapist needs to engage with her client in the informed consent process or risk discipline. Basically, the process includes describing to your client the treatments that will be used and the purpose of those treatments. The process should also include a discussion about fees and billing practices. The language used in the agreement should be reasonably understandable to the client. The concept of client's right to self-determination is a cornerstone of the process and a focus needs to be placed on the client's right to choose for herself what treatment to take part in and the goals to pursue.

When persons, due to age or mental status, are legally incapable of giving informed consent, therapists may be able to obtain informed permission from a legally authorized person, if such substitute consent is legally permissible. The content of informed consent may vary depending upon the client and treatment plan; however, informed consent generally necessitates that the client: (1) has the capacity to consent; (2) has been adequately informed of significant information concerning treatment processes and procedures; (3) has been adequately informed of potential risks and benefits of treatments for which generally recognized standards do not yet exist; (4) has freely and without undue influence expressed consent; and (5) has provided consent that is appropriately documented (AAMFT, 2015, Section 1.2(a)–(e)).

The California case of *Cobbs v. Grant* (1972) sets forth four principles of informed consent. They are: (1) clients do not usually have the same expert knowledge as health care providers; (2) clients have the right to control their participation in treatment, including the right to choose whether to participate in treatment; (3) the client needs information, particularly about the benefits and risks of treatment, to make an effective decision about whether to participate in treatment; and (4) the client relies on the health care provider to give her the information in terms that the client can understand (*Cobbs v. Grant*, 1972).

Section 1.3 addresses the issue of "Multiple Relationships" and provides in part that: "Therapists . . . make every effort to avoid conditions and multiple relationships with clients that could impair professional judgment or increase the risk of exploitation. Such relationships include, but are not limited to, business or close personal relationships with a client or the client's immediate family." When the risk of impairment or exploitation exists due to conditions or multiple roles, therapists document the appropriate precautions taken. If the client provides you with permission, you are allowed to break the confidentiality requirement. A written "Release of Information" form should be prepared by you, reviewed with the client, and signed by the client, thereby entitling you to share information from the therapy with a specific third party (AAMFT, 2015, Section 1.3). Verbal agreements are not considered protective or admissible, even those notated; only proper written authorization is admissible (Benitez and Kashing, 2012).

Mandated Reporting Laws

California Welfare and Institutions Code Section 15630 addresses the issue of mandated reporters. It states, in part, that any person who has assumed full or intermittent responsibility for the care or custody of an elder is a mandated reporter. This includes "administrators, supervisors, and any licensed staff of a public or private facility that provides care or services for elder or dependent adults, or any elder or dependent adult care custodian, *health practitioner*, clergy member, or employee of a county adult protective services agency or a local law enforcement agency" (Cal Welfare & Inst. Code §15630(a)). Therapists are required to familiarize themselves with laws regarding elder abuse reporting and the specifics of the state of practice. Remember that when practicing under supervision, it is important to advise and consult with your supervisor regarding case concerns.

Once it is determined that a report may be necessary, the following mandates apply: Any mandated reporter, while in her professional capacity or within the scope of her employment, who observes or has knowledge of an incident that reasonably appears to be physical abuse, abandonment, isolation, abduction, financial abuse, or neglect *shall* report the known or suspected instance of abuse by telephone or through a confidential Internet reporting tool (as authorized by Section 15658 of the Elder Abuse Act) immediately or as soon as practicably possible. If reported by telephone, a written report shall be sent, or an Internet report shall be made through the confidential internet reporting tool (as established in Section 15658) within two working days (Cal Welfare & Inst. Code §15630(b)(1)). This reporting responsibility includes situations in which the mandated reporter is told by the elder or dependent adult that she has experienced behavior, including an act or omission, constituting physical abuse, abandonment, abduction, isolation, financial abuse, or neglect, or reasonably suspects that abuse, shall report the known or suspected instance of abuse (Cal Welfare & Inst. Code §15630(b)(1)).

The Internet report, which is a confidential report (hereinafter "confidential report") that is not subject to public disclosure, asks for information about: (1) name of the victim, (2) name of suspected abuser and his or her relationship to the elderly person, (3) name of reporting party and whether the party is waiving confidentiality, (4) incident information, (5) type of abuse being reported, (6) reporter's observations, beliefs, and statements by the victim if available; this section also seeks information as to whether the alleged perpetrator still has access to the victim and whether or not the allegation involves a serious bodily injury; it also asks that the reporter provide information about any known potential dangers for the investigator, (7) other persons believed to have knowledge of abuse, (8) family member or other person responsible for victim's care, (9) telephone report made and to whom, and (10) written report made and to whom.

In most instances, the mandated reporter shall report to the adult protective services agency or the local law enforcement agency immediately, or as stated above, as soon as practicably possible. If reported by telephone, a written or an Internet report shall be sent to adult protective services or law enforcement within two working days. The laws regarding mandated reporting in instances in which the suspected or alleged abuse occurred in a long-term care facility are complicated. In the event you are working in a long-term care facility, which does not include a state mental hospital or a state developmental center, you should review the code, consult the "General Instructions" that are attached to the confidential report, and/or speak with your supervisor for further guidance on your reporting requirements.

The Elder Abuse Act provides relief for any mandated reporter who reports a known or suspected instance of abuse of an elder. The mandated reporter cannot be held civilly or criminally liable for any report required by this section (Cal Welfare & Inst. Code §§15634, 15634(a)). In addition, if an action is brought against such a person, the code is designed to limit the financial hardship the person may incur as a result of fulfilling her legal responsibilities. As such, the mandated reporter may "present to the California Victim Compensation and Government Claims Board a claim for reasonable attorney's fees incurred in any action against that person on the basis of making a report required or authorized by this article if the court has dismissed the action upon a demurrer or motion for summary judgment made by that person, or if he or she prevails in the action" (Cal Welfare & Inst. Code §15634(c)). California attorneys are specifically exempted from these mandatory reporting requirements because of the attorney–client privilege (Cal Welfare & Inst. Code §15632(b)).

If a mandated reporter fails to report suspected abuse, that reporter could be charged with a misdemeanor (Cal Welfare & Inst. Code §§15630, 15622.5).

In the event the elder tells you directly that he or she is the victim of behavior constituting physical abuse, abandonment, abduction, isolation, financial abuse, or neglect, the law is specific that you must report the abuse even if you do not believe it is true, unless these three provisions exist: (1) You are not aware of any independent evidence that corroborates the statement that the abuse had occurred, (2) The elder has been diagnosed with a mental illness or dementia, or is the subject of a court-ordered conservatorship because of a mental illness or dementia, and (3) In the exercise of your clinical judgment, you reasonably believe that the abuse did not occur (Cal Welfare & Inst. Code §15630(b)(3)(A)). Pursuant to the code section, you are not required to investigate a known or suspected incident of abuse. However, this provision does not lessen or restrict any existing duty that you have to report (Cal Welfare & Inst. Code §15630(b)(3)(B)).

It is recommended that, in the event of elder abuse or the belief that elder abuse exists, the mandated reporter read Welfare and Institutions Code Sections 15630 et seq in order to determine the need to report.

Elder Abuse as Defined in the California Welfare and Institutions Code

Section "F" of the confidential report requires the mandated report to explain, in writing, his or her observations, beliefs, and statements made by the victim (if available). Given the type of information required, it is important that the therapist have a basic understanding of the different types of abuse and the definition of each, as set forth in the Elder Abuse Act (Cal Welfare & Inst. Code §§15600–15676).

The Elder Abuse Act defines *physical abuse* as any of the following: (1) assault, (2) battery, (3) assault with a deadly weapon or force likely to produce great bodily injury, (4) unreasonable physical constraint or prolonged or continual deprivation of food or water, (5) sexual assault (Cal Welfare & Inst. Code §§15610.63(e)(1)-(9)), and (6) use of physical or chemical restraint or psychotropic medication (Cal Welfare & Inst. Code §§15610.63(a)-(e)). *Serious bodily injury* means an injury involving extreme physical pain, substantial risk of death, or protracted loss or impairment of function of bodily member, organ, or mental faculty, or requiring medical intervention, including, but not limited to, hospitalization, surgery, or physical rehabilitation (Cal Welfare & Inst. Code §15610.67).

Neglect can be difficult to determine in certain situations, particularly in a situation where the elder is neglecting his or her own care. The Elder Abuse Act defines *neglect* as either (1) the negligent failure of any person having the care or custody of an elder (Cal Welfare & Inst. Code §15610.23) to exercise that degree of care that a reasonable person in a like position would exercise (Cal Welfare & Inst. Code §15610.57(a)(1)) or (2) the negligent failure of an elder to exercise that degree of self-care that a reasonable person in a like position would exercise (Cal Welfare & Inst. Code §15610.57(a)(2)). If you are unsure whether or not "neglect" exists in any given situation, it is important to consult with colleagues, and, where applicable, with a supervisor to help determine whether a report is required.

Neglect includes, but is not limited to, all of the following: (1) failure to assist in personal hygiene, or in the provision of food, clothing, or shelter, (2) failure to provide medical care for physical and mental health needs, (3) failure to protect from health and safety hazards, (4) failure to prevent malnutrition or dehydration, and (5) failure of an elder to satisfy the needs for himself or herself as a result of poor cognitive functioning, mental limitation, substance abuse, or chronic poor health (Cal Welfare & Inst. Code §§15610.57(b)(1)-(5)). Any individual responsible for the care of an elder must ensure that these areas listed above are being appropriately addressed. If not, the caregiver can be reported for neglect. When it comes to self-neglect, it is not the intent of the law to penalize the elder who is unable to care for him- or herself; instead, the intent is to make sure that the elder's needs are being met. Reported types of abuse also includes *self-neglect*, which involves issues such as the elder's lack of physical care, medical care, health and safety hazards (risk of suicide or unsafe environment), malnutrition and/or dehydration, and financial self-neglect.

The term *mental suffering*, means "fear, agitation, confusion, severe depression, or other forms of serious emotional distress that is brought about by forms of intimidating behavior, threats, harassment, or by deceptive acts performed or false or misleading statements made with malicious intent to agitate, confuse, frighten, or cause severe depression or serious emotional distress of the elder" (Cal Welfare & Inst. Code §15610.53).

The code defines *abandonment* as the desertion or "willful forsaking" of an elder under circumstances in which a reasonable person would continue to provide care and custody by anyone who has this responsibility (Cal Welfare & Inst. Code §15610.05).

Isolation has many meanings under the code. It includes (1) acts that prevent an elder from receiving his or her mail or telephone calls; (2) telling a caller or visitor that an elder is not present, or does not wish to talk with the caller, or does not wish to meet with the caller when this is false, contrary to the express wishes of the elder, and is made for the purpose of preventing the elder from having contact with family, friends, or concerned persons. The elder's competency or lack thereof is irrelevant; (3) false imprisonment of the elder; and (4) physical restraint that is intended to prevent the elder from meeting with visitors (Cal Welfare & Inst. Code §§15610.43(a)(1)-(4)). Keep in mind that the acts set forth above do not constitute "isolation" if performed because of a reasonably perceived threat of danger to the property and/or the physical safety of the elder (Cal Welfare & Inst. Code §15610.43(c)).

In the Elder Abuse Act, the term *financial abuse* is utilized and is found to occur when a person or an entity does any of the following to an elder: "(1) takes, secrets, appropriates, obtains, or retains real or personal property of an elder . . . for a wrongful use or with intent to defraud, or both, (2) assists in taking, secreting, appropriating, obtaining, or retaining real or personal property of an elder . . . for a wrongful use or with intent to defraud, or both, or (3) takes, secretes, appropriates, obtains, or retains, or assists in taking, secreting, appropriating, obtaining, or retaining, real or personal property of an elder by undue influence" (Cal Welfare & Inst. Code §§15610.30(a)(1)-(3)).

A person or an entity shall be deemed to have taken, secreted, appropriated, obtained, or retained property for a wrongful use if, among other things, the person or entity "takes, secretes, appropriates, obtains, or retains the property and the person or entity knew or should have known that this conduct is likely to be harmful to the elder" (Cal Welfare & Inst. Code WIC§15610.30(b)). Additionally, a person or an entity "takes, secretes, appropriates, obtains, or retains real or personal property when an elder . . . is deprived of any property right, including by means of an agreement, donative transfer, or testamentary bequest, regardless of whether the property is held directly or by a representative of an elder" (Cal Welfare & Inst. Code §15610.30(c)).

Confidentiality and the Mandated Reporting Requirements

So that the client can feel safe in therapy, generally the law requires you to avoid making public any information about your client. The CAMFT Code of Ethics states, "The overriding principle is that MFTs respect the confidences of their patient(s)" (CAMFT, 2011, Part 1, Section 2.1). However, this ethics code also sets forth some exceptions to the general principle. Section 2.1 provides, in part:

> Marriage and family therapists do not disclose patient confidences, including the names or identities of their patients, to anyone except (1) as mandated by law (2) as permitted by law (3) when the marriage and family therapist is a defendant in a civil, criminal, or disciplinary action arising from the therapy (in which case patient confidences may only be disclosed in the course of that action, or (4) if there is an authorization previously obtained in writing, and then such information may only be revealed in accordance with the terms of the authorization.

An issue arises when the mandated reporting requirements, set forth above, conflict with your ethical and legal duty to maintain confidentiality. California Business and Professions Code Section 4982(m) defines *unprofessional conduct* as the failure to maintain confidentiality of all information that has been received from a client in confidence during the course of treatment and all information about the client that is obtained from tests or other means, except as otherwise required or permitted by law (Cal Bus. & Prof. Code §4982(m)).

Any failure to adhere to the business and professions code could result in possible disciplinary action, civil liability, and/or criminal liability. Specifically, California Business and Professions Code Section 4983 provides, in part, that an individual who is in violation of Section 4982(m), or other provisions set forth in this chapter, is guilty of a misdemeanor that is punishable by imprisonment in the county jail not exceeding six months, or by a fine not exceeding $2,500, or by both (Cal Bus. & Prof. Code §4983).

When confronted with a reporting situation involving elder abuse, remember that Section 2.1(a) provides for an exception when the reporting is mandated by law. As discussed above, the mandated reporting laws specifically define the various types of abuse that must be reported, as well as the timing, the methods for reporting the abuse, the immunities that come with reporting, and the penalties that may attach for failing to report (Cal Bus. & Prof. Code 4983.2(a)). It is also important to keep in mind that any disclosures that are made should not exceed the boundaries of the reporting requirements as set forth in the confidential report.

Any information that is not subject to the mandated reporting requirements remains confidential. You would not want to provide any additional information such as the client's course of therapy and his or her treatment goals, if the information is not relevant to the specific incident of abuse being reported. Remember, all releases should be issued in writing and maintained in the client file (Pelchat, 2012).

Psychotherapist–Patient Privilege

Privilege relates to specific client–therapist relationships as recognized by state law; "simply put, privilege is the right to withhold testimony" (Pelchat, 2012) should you be called as a witness to appear in court. Evidence Code Section 912 provides in part that your right to claim a privilege is waived with respect to a communication protected by the privilege if any holder of the privilege, without coercion, has disclosed a significant part of the communication or has consented to disclosure made by anyone. Confidential communication between patient and psychotherapist means information, including information obtained by an examination of the patient, transmitted between a patient and her psychotherapist in the course of that relationship and in confidence by a means which, so far as the patient is aware, discloses the information to no third persons other than those who are present to further the interest of the patient in the consultation, or those to whom disclosure is reasonably necessary for the transmission of the information or the accomplishment of the purpose for which the psychotherapist is consulted, and includes a diagnosis made and the advice given by the psychotherapist in the course of that relationship (Cal Evid. Code §1012) is considered to be confidential. Consent to disclosure is manifested by any statement or other conduct of the holder of the privilege indicating consent to the disclosure, including failure to claim the privilege in any proceeding in which the holder has legal standing and the opportunity to claim the privilege (Cal Evid. Code §912(a)). When two or more persons are joint holders of a privilege, a waiver of the right of a particular joint holder of the privilege to claim the privilege does not affect the right of another joint holder to claim the privilege (Cal Evid. Code §912(b)). It is important to remember that a disclosure in confidence of a communication that is protected by a privilege, when disclosure is reasonably necessary for the accomplishment of the purpose for which the therapist was consulted, is not a waiver of the privilege.

Evidence Code Section 1014 provides that the "holder of the privilege" or a "person who is authorized to claim the privilege by the holder of the privilege" has a privilege to refuse to disclose, and to prevent another from disclosing, a confidential communication between a psychotherapist and her patient (Cal Evid. Code §1014(a) and (b)). The "holder of the privilege" refers to either the patient when she has no guardian or conservator or a guardian or conservator of the patient when the patient has a guardian or conservator (Cal Evid. Code §1013(a) and (b)).

There are several exceptions to this privilege. The patient's mental condition may be applicable in situations such as a petition for conservatorship. This section states that there is no privilege as to a communication relevant to an issue concerning the mental or emotional condition of the patient if the issue has been brought by the patient or any party claiming through or under the patient (Cal Evid. Code §1016(a) and (b)).

A HIPAA (Health Insurance Portability and Accountability Act of 1996) authorization and waiver should be signed by the client as part of informed consent. It provides authorization for health care providers to release information concerning the client's otherwise confidential medical information to each other and to the individuals who have been designated to act in the event of disability. The client has the right to withdraw permission for the release of information or can revoke the authorization at any time. Any revocation must be made in writing and will not affect information that has already been released. The person or entity receiving the confidential medical information does not have authority, unless otherwise provided, to further use or disclose this information to others. The client must identify the persons or entities authorized to receive the information.

Protective Orders and Elders

Business and Professions Code Sections 6125 and 6126 discuss the unauthorized practice of law, which includes consulting with and/or providing legal advice without a license to practice law in the state of California. A finding of guilt for violating the code constitutes a criminal misdemeanor with a penalty of up to six months in the county jail and/or a fine of up to $1,000, for a first offense. In situations in which your elderly client seeks your advice regarding options of dealing with an abusive situation, there are suggestions that can be made to your client without crossing over the line into the unauthorized practice of law.

While it is the mandate of the therapist to report suspected abuse, legal practices may or may not include the therapist as they are enacted. Although you may not be involved in the hearing on a restraining order, you may be asked to continue providing emotional support for the elder and/or the family should they elect to stay in your practice after a confidential report is provided and/or an application for a restraining order is filed with the court. In addition, it may be necessary, in certain situations, to suggest to your elderly client that a restraining order be obtained. This may be an extremely sensitive topic for any number of reasons. For example, the alleged abuse may involve a family member, and/or the family member lives with the elder, or the elder lives with the family member, or the elder is dependent upon a non-family member who is the primary caregiver, or the elder is not aware of the abuse (particularly in situations in which the family member and/or caregiver is responsible for the elder's finances). For anyone or more of these reasons, the elderly client may not be willing to file a restraining order.

As such, a basic understanding, for educational purposes, of the process for obtaining a restraining order is helpful in situations in which you are called upon to provide ongoing emotional support to your elderly client.

The Elder Abuse Act provides that an elder who has suffered abuse may apply for a protective order (Cal Welfare & Inst. Code §15657.03). Unlike the application for a domestic violation restraining order, there is no requirement that a family relationship exist between the elder and the alleged abuser. The elder may file a petition or it may be brought on behalf of an abused elder by a conservator or a trustee of the elder or an agent under a durable power of attorney, or any other person legally authorized to seek such relief (Cal Welfare & Inst. Code §15610.30(b)).

In certain instances of abuse, a temporary restraining order may be issued, without notice if reasonable proof exists of past act or acts of abuse against an elder (Cal Welfare & Inst. Code §15657.03(c)). The order may exclude a party from the elder's residence when specific factors exist: upon a showing that (1) the party who will stay in the residence has a right to possession of the property (Cal Welfare & Inst. Code §15657.03(d)(1)), (2) the party to be excluded has assaulted or threatens to assault the elder (Cal Welfare & Inst. Code §15657.03(d)(2)), and (3) physical harm or emotional harm would otherwise occur (Cal Welfare & Inst. Code §15657.03(d)(3)). The temporary order will remain in effect for 25 days. A hearing for a permanent restraining order should take place before the lapse of the temporary order (Cal Welfare & Inst. Code §15657.03(b)(3)). Both orders can include requests (1) to stop a party from abusing, intimidating, molesting, attacking, striking, stalking, threatening, sexually assaulting, battering, harassing, telephoning, destroying personal property, and contacting the elder (Cal Welfare & Inst. Code § 15657.03(b)(3)(A)); (2) to exclude a party from the elder's residence, unless title is in the name of the party to be excluded (Cal Welfare & Inst. Code §15657.03(b)(3)(B)); and (3) to stop a party from specified behavior that the court determines is necessary (Cal Welfare & Inst. Code §15657.03(b)(3)(C)).

In the state of California, to initiate a request for a protective order, the elder or a person on his or her behalf files a form entitled "Request for Elder or Dependent Adult Abuse Restraining Order" (Judicial Council Form EA-100). This form asks the elder to provide information about the instances of abuse and when and how it happened. If the abuse was solely financial, the elder must indicate that on the form. If there are prior instances of abuse, the elder should also provide that information.

The form also asks the elder to tell the court what he or she wants the court to order the respondent to do. This includes refraining from physically abusing, financially abusing, intimidating, molesting, attacking, striking, stalking, threatening, assaulting, hitting, harassing, destroying personal property, disturbing the peace of the elder, and/or contacting the elder either directly or indirectly. Stay away orders are also available, as are requests for move-out orders. In certain instances, the court will grant a temporary restraining order within 24 hours of the elder requesting it (Judicial Council Form EA-100-INFO).

In a hearing on a permanent restraining order, a support person (which may be the therapist) may accompany the elder to court, and if the elder is in pro per, the support person may sit at the table with the elder. The support person is there to provide moral and emotional support for the elder who alleges that she is a victim of abuse. The support person may not provide legal assistance, but may assist the elder in feeling more confident that she will not be injured or threatened by the respondent during the hearing (Cal Welfare & Inst. Code §15657.03(j)). The respondent may file a response that explains and/or denies the alleged abuse (Cal Welfare & Inst. Code §15657.03(g)). No filing fees are needed to obtain a protective order. The duration of an order is no more than five years and is subject to termination or modification by further order of the court (Cal Welfare & Inst. Code §15657.03(h)).

Durable Power of Attorney, Advance Health Care Directive, and Conservatorships

One of the biggest challenges may be the care and management of the elder's legal and medical needs if the elder lacks the ability to do so. In instances in which the elder is experiencing diminished capacity or has lost capacity for self-care, a petition for a conservatorship may be initiated and, when approved, allows others to take legal responsibility for the elder's financial and health care needs. It is important to note that less drastic measures, such as the preparation of a durable power of attorney for financial management and/or an advance health care directive, are preferred when possible. The discussion contained in this chapter is for the purpose of providing you with basic information about the conservatorship process. It is not intended as a comprehensive explanation. It is recommended that if and/or when additional information is needed, you should consult with an attorney.

A durable power of attorney for management of property and personal affairs (DPOA) is a very important document. By signing a DPOA, the client (referred to as the "principal") is authorizing a person (referred to as the "agent") to act on behalf of the principal. There are several types of powers of attorney, which are (1) a special DPOA that gives the agent authority to carry out specific actions, as stated by the principal, and usually for a specific and limited period of time; (2) a general durable power of attorney, which gives the agent authority to act immediately upon the signing of the DPOA, and (3) a springing durable power of attorney, which requires declarations signed by two of the principal's physicians confirming that the principal lacks capacity, after which this DPOA becomes effective (it may be reversed if it can be shown that the principal has regained capacity). The DPOA requires a notary's acknowledgment or it must be signed by two independent witnesses. A DPOA that will affect real property should be notarized. The DPOA can be amended or changed so long as the principal has the capacity to do so. The same formalities must be adhered to as those required in the signing of the original DPOA.

Among other things, the DPOA may grant to the agent (1) the power to manage, dispose of, sell, and convey real property, personal property, and stocks and bonds; (2) the power to manage the principal's banking and other financial matters, business transactions, insurance and annuity transactions, claims and litigation, personal and family maintenance, retirement plans, tax matters; and (3) the power to manage the principal's benefits received from social security, Medicare, Medicaid, civil or military service, and/or other governmental benefits (Cal. Prob. Code §§4400–4465).

The powers conveyed to the agent continue to exist unless specified by time limitations or the principal terminates the agent's authority. Additionally, the DPOA continues to exist even if the principal can longer make his/her own decisions regarding the management of assets. The agent is entitled to receive payment for the time incurred in serving as the agent.

The agent has two primary legal duties, which are (1) to act solely in the interest of the principal and to avoid conflicts of interest and (2) to keep the principal's property separate and distinct from any property owned or controlled by the agent. In addition, the agent may not transfer the principal's property to herself without full and adequate consideration and specific authority that permits such a transfer. An agent who violates any of these requirements may be prosecuted for embezzlement and in the event the principal is 65 years of age or older, the agent may also be prosecuted for elder abuse and violations of the Elder Abuse Act (Cal. Penal Code § 368). Upon the death of the client, a DPOA is no longer effective (Cal. Civil Code §2357; Cal. Prob. Code §4152). A DPOA gives authority to someone who will have/could have full access to the client's assets. It is extremely important that the client exercise caution in designating someone to act as the agent.

An advance health care directive (AHCD) provides the principal with the opportunity to designate someone to make medical decisions in the event the principal becomes unable to do so (Cal. Prob. Code §§4605, 4629, 4682). In the AHCD, the principal may include instructions to the agent, which include the ability to (1) consent or refuse consent to any care, treatment, service, or procedure to maintain, diagnose, or otherwise affect a physical or mental condition; (2) select or discharge health care providers and institutions; (3) approve or disapprove diagnostic tests, surgical procedures, and programs of medication; (4) direct the provision, withholding or withdrawal of artificial nutrition and hydration and all other forms of health care, including cardiopulmonary resuscitation; and (5) make anatomical gifts, authorize and autopsy, and direct disposition of remains (Cal. Prob. Code §4701).

The AHCD must be signed and dated by the principal, and it must be signed by two qualified witnesses or acknowledged before a notary public. If the principal is a patient in a skilled nursing facility, the AHCD must also be signed by the "Patient Advocate" or "Patient Ombudsman"; generally, the principal should provide a copy of the AHCD to the primary care physician.

In a conservatorship, the court appoints someone (the conservator) to care for the elder (proposed conservatee) who is unable to care for herself or manage her own money. California has two types of conservatorships: probate and lanterman-petris-short. The probate conservatorship is more commonly used in California and will be discussed briefly in this chapter.

In a probate conservatorship, the petitioner applies to be appointed as the conservator for the elder. This may include a conservatorship of the person, in which the petitioner is requesting the right to make decisions about the elder's medical and health-related needs and/or a conservatorship of the estate, in which the petitioner is requesting the right to manage the finances and make legal decisions for the elder. Although it is possible for interested persons to file a petition in pro per, generally, due to the complexity of the petition and the process of appointing a conservatorship, an attorney will be needed to assist with the process. It can be a lengthy process, particularly if the capacity (or lack thereof) of the elder becomes adversarial. In addition, it is an expensive process. Most important, it is typically implemented when the elder has lost the ability to make decisions for herself, which means that the elder's rights are being restricted through a court order. More information on conservatorships is available in the *Handbook for Conservators* (2016).

Additional Miscellaneous Information

Elders are entitled to government support programs that can grant them access to health care, including mental health care and financial assistance. A person who has reached full retirement age—66 or 67—may receive *social security* benefits and continue working. A person who waits until age 70 to collect benefits will receive a larger monthly benefit check regardless of any additional earnings. However, if a person starts receiving benefits before full retirement age and continues to earn additional income, the benefits will be reduced if the earnings exceed a certain amount. For more information, a local social security administration office should be contacted.

Medi-Cal (in California) and *Medicaid* (in the other 49 states) may provide additional assistance for the cost of a nursing home if an individual qualifies. Legal advice should be obtained before making any decisions regarding Medi-Cal qualifications. Generally, an applicant may not have more than $2,000 in assets (excepting those assets that are characterized as "excluded" from consideration). An application must be filed and the reviewer will determine whether the elder has "given away" or "transferred" any assets for less-than fair market value over the last 30 months from the date of application. A penalty will be assessed for any assets transferred within this period, which will probably result in a period of ineligibility based on the total amount of the assets given away or transferred.

Medicare may pay up to 100 days of nursing home expenses, but only if the elder was hospitalized for 3 consecutive days and then required skilled nursing care. Medicare will fully cover the cost for the first 20 days. After that the elder will be required to make a co-payment.

Conclusion

With more seniors entering into and staying involved in live-long mental health support services, it is incumbent on the therapist to stay abreast of the legal and ethical requirements specific to this population. While working with the additional statutes and considerations might at first feel daunting, this chapter's goal was to clearly define the additional requirements needed when working with this vulnerable population. Similar to our working with minors, working with elders requires additional knowledge and support, and therapists are encouraged to check in with supervisors, their professional organizations and seek consultation should it be necessary to best serve the needs of their clients.

References

American Association of Marriage Family Therapists. "Code of Ethics." January 1, 2015. Accessed April 7, 2017. https://www.aamft.org/iMIS15/AAMFT/Content/Legal_Ethics/code_of_ethics.aspx.

Benitez, Bonnie R., and Sara Kashing. "Authorization to Release Information." *The Therapist*, June 2012. Accessed April 8, 2017. http://www.camft.org/COS/The_Therapist/Legal_Articles/Bonnie/Authorization_to_Release_Information.aspx.

Cal Business & Professions Code §4982–3, 6125–6.

Cal Civil Code §2357.

Cal Evidence Code §912–1016.

California Association of Marriage and Family Therapists . . . "Code of Ethics." June 11, 2011. Accessed April 7, 2017. http://www.bing.com/cr?IG=4906C045ADF74EE19B93707E111DC16E&CID=15DD1F080F9A63D1290515550E0A62D2&rd=1&h=lIedoWp6nNtGbH-Dp-qjuUa2VYDLH0IXTwMzTu8An94&v=1&r=http%3a%2f%2fwww.marincamft.org%2fResources%2fDocuments%2fCAMFT%2520Code%2520Of%2520Ethics.pdf&p=DevEx,5061.1.

Cal Penal Code §368.

Cal Probate Code §4152; 4400–4465, 4605, 4629, 4682, 4701.

Cal Welfare & Institutions Code §15600–76.

Cobbs v. Grant (1972) 8 Cal. 3d 229.

"EA-100-INFO Can a Restraining Order to Prevent Elder or . . ." Accessed April 7, 2017. http://www.bing.com/cr?IG=64D5502ECBDC4D469042DB849FE20397&CID=2F72674D1B426E790FD76D101AD26F2E&rd=1&h=oUDAwbk_gsrsuLplkS_FVdXNl_fhnBH0PN82sl9as5g&v=1&r=http%3a%2f%2fwww.courts.ca.gov%2fdocuments%2fea100info.pdf&p=DevEx,5061.1.

"EA-100 Request for Elder or Dependent Adult Abuse . . ." Accessed April 7, 2017. http://www.bing.com/cr?IG=F93CADC4CC7A4BCA9B98AF3EFD FE6A32&CID=092D188ECF256B2E3D3512D3CEB56A80&rd=1&h=a OqtroZ7CH2jhYantDufjZgvriJ4Sjwiv_G1RUaPm6I&v=1&r=http%3a%2 f%2fwww.courts.ca.gov%2fdocuments%2fea100.pdf&p=DevEx,5061.1.

Frolik, Lawrence A., and Alison McChrystal Barnes. *Elder Law: Cases and Materials*. New Providence, NJ: LexisNexis, 2007.

Handbook for Conservators—Judiciary of California. Accessed April 7, 2017. http://www.bing.com/cr?IG=DEB9632E98464E339BAF7AFA147C5F6D&CID= 03E387E2382D61DB23D08DBF39BD60E7&rd=1&h=aZPP7YNWO8e CjGiHI5Hu1n20Tp2jnII0ePFZ_cHAtY4&v=1&r=http%3a%2f%2fwww .courts.ca.gov%2fdocuments%2fhandbook.pdf&p=DevEx,5068.1.

Moskowitz, S. "Golden Age in Golden State: Contemporary Legal Developments in Elder Abuse and Neglect." *Loyola of Los Angeles Law Review* 36 (2003): 589–66.

Pelchat, Zachary. "Psychotherapist-Patient Privilege Your Special Relationship in the Law." *The Therapist*, August 2012. Accessed April 8, 2017. http://www .camft.org/COS/The_Therapist/Legal_Articles/Zach/Psychotherapist_ Patient_Privilege_Your_Special_Relationship_in_the_Law.aspx.

"Statistic Brain." Statistic Brain. Accessed April 7, 2017. http://www.statisticbrain .com/elderly-abuse-statistics.

CHAPTER ELEVEN

Supervision: Competencies and Special Issues

Kathy Langsam

At the start of my clinical career, I made a very conscious decision that I wanted to specialize in working with children, adolescents, and families. I quickly learned that when working in community mental health you don't get to pick your clients. My caseload comprised many older adults. In the process of working with elders, I was forced to recognize and deal with my stigma, ageism, countertransference, fear of chronic illness, fear of death, mortality, and insecurities of what a 30-something newly licensed clinician had to offer to an 80-plus-year-old client.

This chapter explores the need for a trained workforce to provide services for older adults and their families, how specific competencies can be acquired, and how supervision can be an asset in the development of those competencies, while identifying practitioner bias and exploring the impact on the therapeutic relationship and therapy.

Vast evidence supports the need for more practitioners to provide mental health services to older adults, typically 65 years of age and older. Population projections indicate that, by 2030, when the last of the "baby boomers" (born between 1946 and 1964) reach retirement, older adults will comprise more than 20 percent of the U.S. population (Ortman, Velkoff, and Hogan, 2014). Within this growing segment of the population, those experiencing mental disorders are expected to reach 15 million by 2030; this will be the largest cohort of any age group (Jeste et al., 1999).

It is important to recognize that this segment of the population is also growing in diversity, increasingly composed of racial and ethnic minorities (Karel, Gatz, and Smyer, 2012). Aging patterns also vary by localities (Karel, Gatz, and Smyer, 2012).

Despite the ongoing growth of the population, the work force has not kept up with the demand. Recent analysis of data from 2001 to 2003 indicates that during a 12-month period, an estimated 20.4 percent of adults 65 years of age and older met the diagnostic criteria for a mental disorder, including dementia (Karel, Gatz, and Smyer, 2012). Up to 45 percent of older adults, age 85 and above, meet the criteria for cognitive impairment, including dementia (Orozco et al., 2014). An American Psychological Association study revealed that up to 63 percent of older adults with a mental health disorder do not receive services they need, while only 3 percent of older adults report seeing a practitioner (APA, 2003; Qualls et al., 2002).

Mental health statistics also reveal that older adults have high rates of suicide among all age groups, older white men in particular (Office of the Surgeon General, 2012). Co-morbidity of mental health and medical conditions contributes to the high rate of suicide, along with bereavement, loss of physical and cognitive abilities, substance use, retirement, and other life changes (Peralta, 2010). There is a tendency for older adults and the general population, as well as clinicians to view mental health problems (e.g., depression, anxiety, cognitive impairment) as part of normal aging (Laganà and Shanks, 2002). The interaction between mental health and medical conditions and myths regarding older adults make recognition, diagnosis, and treatment of the conditions complex (APA, 2011).

The American Psychological Association identified geropsychology as a specialty in 2010 (APA, 2011), which "applies the knowledge and methods of psychology to understanding and helping older persons and their families to maintain well-being, overcome problems and achieve maximum potential during later life. Professional geropsychology appreciates the wide diversity among older adults, the complex ethical issues that can arise in geriatric practice and the importance of interdisciplinary models of care" (APA, 2016).

The specialty of geropsychology has identified the following biopsychosocial problems encountered by older adults and their families:

- Mental disorders such as depression and anxiety
- Dementia and related behavioral/lifestyle changes
- Changes in decision making or everyday living abilities
- Coping with and managing chronic illness
- Behavioral health concerns such as insomnia and pain

- Grief and loss
- Family caregiving strains
- Adjustment to aging-related stresses including marital/family conflict, changing roles
- End-of-life care

(APA, 2016)

Despite the status of specialty of geropsychology, very few PhD, PsyD, or master-level specialized programs exist. Further, students' graduate education is "generalized," lacking specific courses in working with older adults (Qualls et al., 2002). Specific issues regarding older adults are typically addressed in required graduate courses, life span and family systems plus elective courses in aging and grief. Both students and practitioners report little interest in taking these electives or obtaining continuing education focusing on older adults and ultimately working with older adults (Quails et al., 2002; Rosen, 1995).

Unless students receive specialized training in practicum sites specializing in providing services to older adults, specific skills are acquired "on the job" and through supervision (Norman et al., 2001; Quails et al., 2002). Supervisors aid both students and new practitioners in developing competencies to work with older adults.

Competencies

While most older adults receive adequate clinical services by "generalists," professional organizations have identified competencies for working with older adults. In 1990, the American Counseling Association published ten minimum essential competencies. These are as follows:

1. Focuses on counselor attitudes and knowledge; exhibits positive, wellness-enhancing attitude
2. Demonstrates knowledge of the unique considerations in establishing and maintaining relationships with older people
3. Sensitivity to sensory and physical limitations
4. Understanding that older adults represent a unique group with unique counseling needs based on social and cultural foundations
5. Understanding life span developmental issues
6. Awareness of group counseling with older adults
7. Lifestyle and career issues

8. Competence in later life including psychological, social, and physical factors
9. Currency of research in later life
10. Knowledge of informal and formal referral sources

(Orozco et al., 2014; Myers and Sweeney, 1990)

The Pikes Peak Model for training in professional geropsychology has been developed to identify specific competencies (Knight et al., 2009). This model is an outgrowth of the APA Guidelines for Psychological Practice with Older Adults, first developed in 2004, and revised in 2014 (APA, 2004, 2014). The model takes the position that additional competencies are needed when working with older adults where issues are often more complex and specialized. Knight et al. (2009) cites examples of potential presence of dementia, complications from comorbid medical problems, assessment of decision-making capacity, and nursing home consultation (206). Pikes Peak Model goes beyond the foundation of geropsychology to identify five categories: (1) attitudes; (2) general knowledge of adult development, aging, and older adults; (3) assessment; (4) intervention, consultation, and other service provision; and (5) continuing education regarding older adults (Knight et al., 2009, 208). These competency areas apply to supervisors as well as supervisees, and provide a framework to think about attitudes, knowledge, and skills.

The Pikes Peak Model emphasizes the importance of didactic and supervised experiential training to develop geropsychology competencies (Karel et al., 2014).

Attitudes

A survey of PhD and PsyD training directors in geropsychology reveal the following attitudes required for interns:

- Emotional maturity, empathy, warmth, patience, and a sense of humor
- Ability to be flexible and adapt therapy for the needs of elders (e.g., using visual aids with elders who are hearing impaired, shortening session lengths for those unable to tolerate longer sessions)
- Engage elderly clients ambivalent about therapy
- Expect different attitudes and beliefs

(Paules, 2012)

In developing attitudes, it's also important to be aware of individual diversity in all manifestations, including how gender, ethnicity, language, religion, socioeconomic status, sexual orientation, gender identity, disability status, and urban or rural residence interact with attitudes and beliefs about aging for both the practitioner and the client (Knight et al., 2009). It is essential for practitioners to understand the ways in which age and birth cohort membership affect client's experience of other sources of diversity (Knight, 2011).

Supervision provides the opportunity for practitioners to explore client experience of growing up in the 20th century in the United States as well as countries of origin, and how this shaped their individual diversity. Unique experiences include gender roles, ethnic minorities, religion, and LGBTQ (Knight, 2011). Cultural values may be shaped by experiencing the Great Depression, World War II, Korean War, Summer of Love, and Vietnam War (Orozco et al., 2014). These experiences may contribute to an older adult's attitudes regarding dependency versus independence, resiliency, and self-disclosure (feelings) and ultimately affect the therapeutic relationship.

Knowledge

Knowledge about working with older adults needs to go beyond conventional wisdom, and the practitioner's own personal and familial experience of aging (Knight, 2011). It includes an understanding of adult development (biological, psychological, emotional, and social development) and aging. In addition, practitioners need an increased understanding of the effects of neurological and health problems in later life, cognitive changes, functional changes, and specific psychopathology including comorbidity. The unique psychopathology points to the need for specific assessment methods and instruments suitable for older adults (Knight et al., 2009).

Skills

Practitioners are respectful of older adults and aware of one's own ageist biases. One of the most effective ways to combat biases is to acquire an understanding of normative aging and have contact with older adults who are successful in the process.

The model also identifies specific clinical skills: (1) understanding and application of aging-specific aspects of informed consent, confidentiality, capacity and competency, end-of-life decision making, and elder abuse and neglect; (2) understanding of cultural and individual diversity to assessment, intervention, and consultation; (3) working within multi- and interdisciplinary teams; (4) knowledge of evidence-based treatments for older adults, including individual, group, and family treatments; and (5) awareness of special issues that may arise in clinical, community, or residential settings (Knight et al., 2009).

Researchers have developed a tool to measure practitioner competencies outlined in the Pikes Peak Model (Karel, Emery, and Molinari, 2010; Karel et al., 2012). The Pikes Knowledge and Skill Assessment Tool (available at: http://www.copgtp.org) may be the most useful in structured geropsychology programs where ongoing evaluation, self-assessment, and direct observation of the supervisee in numerous clinical settings are incorporated into the program (Karel et al., 2010).

Excellent sources of information on geropsychology practice, training, and supervision are available at http://www.copgtp.org; http://gerocentral.org.

Without a geropsychology training program, "generalist" practitioners develop their older adult competencies "on the job" with the support of clinical supervision.

Utilization of Clinical Supervision

Irrespective of the theoretical orientation that a supervisor adopts (e.g., developmental, competency-based, and interpersonal), "a good supervisory relationship is tied to supervisee confidence, clinical focus, feelings of safety, professional development, self-monitoring, ethical decision making, and insight into client dynamics" (Karel et al., 2014, 44). Clinical supervision and professional mentoring provide opportunities for supervisees to explore their self-awareness in terms of their attitudes, assumptions, biases, and countertransference about older adults (Karel et al., 2014; Knight, 2011).

Supervision Methods

Direct Observation

While supervisees report that direct observation of clinical work by live observation, co-therapy, and viewing view tapes is preferred, it is the least utilized in most clinical settings (Karel et al., 2014). Observing supervisor's participating in staff meeting, multidisciplinary teams, and consultations session is also reported as very helpful by supervisees (Karel et al., 2014).

Supervisor Self-Disclosure

Supervisees report that supervisor self-disclosure is helpful in strengthening the supervisory relationship and normalize the supervisee's experience of working with older adults and development of clinical skills (Karel et al., 2014). Helpful topics include supervisor's early struggles working with older adults; dealing with feelings about client safety, client's death, client's desire to die, and challenging aging family dynamics (Karel et al., 2014).

As a supervisor, it's also important to discuss how your views are affected by your age cohort, for example, baby boomer, and the timeframe when you received clinical training (Knight, 2011). This discussion highlights the importance of understanding the impact of a client's age cohort.

Didactic Training

Clinical supervision provides an opportunity to determine the practitioner's grasp of understanding normal aging, which is the foundation for developing clinical skills in working with older adults (Knight, 2011). Didactics include but are not limited to dementia, differential diagnosis, medication, common medical issues in old age, differentiating capacity versus competency, grief and loss, and death (Paules, 2012).

Specific clinical skills are also developed in this setting, including use of appropriate assessments for older adults, realistic treatment goals and interventions, participation on an interdisciplinary team, and understanding the impact on treatment based on the diversity of settings (e.g., medical, psychiatric, long-term care) in which services are provided (Karel et al., 2014).

Integrated models of care utilized in primary care and community health centers are where many older adults receive treatment for both mental health disorders and chronic medical conditions (Institute of Medicine, 2008; Karel, Gatz, and Smyer, 2012). These integrated models of care take the practitioner beyond the confines of the therapy room. Clinical supervision provides an opportunity for the practitioner to learn his or her role in working with other professionals; including psychiatrists, physicians, social workers, and case managers. Common areas discussed are how to communicate with other providers, participation on a multidisciplinary team, coordination of services, treatment plan, and advocacy (Karel et al., 2012; Partnership for Health in Aging, 2011).

This systems approach also requires an understanding of the services available to older adults, including hospitals, residential facilities, rehabilitation facilities, wellness centers, and adult daycare. Clinicians also provide resources for family caregivers, such as support groups, respite care, and how to navigate the complex system of care.

Self-Awareness

Supervision typically focuses on reviewing a difficult therapy session, so the supervisee may develop a better understanding of the client, of him- or herself, the therapeutic process, and possible alternative interventions (Moffett, 2009). The success of this technique depends on a strong and trusting supervisory relationship and that the supervisee will report difficulties. Unfortunately, novice supervisees may not be aware of difficulties. Furthermore, supervisors report that supervisees often overestimate their abilities (Karel et al., 2014).

Directed self-reflection protocols are another useful supervision technique that primes supervisees for problematic events before they occur and explores possible reactions (Moffett, 2009). The supervisor generates a list of questions that address issues that have been frequently problematic for supervisees working with a separate population and/or setting. The questions are phrased in terms of hypothetical situations. The questions cover personal and professional issues and are listed hierarchically. This is done so supervisees can identify their personal style and clarify their professional role and also develop empathy for a population they may be unfamiliar with (Moffett, 2009). The supervisee is to reflect and write answers; although the actual answers are not required to be disclosed, the issues raised through the assignment will be discussed in supervision (Moffett, 2009).

Examples of questions are:

"What would you think, feel, and do when . . . ?"

"Under what circumstances would you . . . ?"

"What do you do believe when you cannot perform a task as well as others expect you to?"

"Under what conditions would you give up on a difficult task or blame others for your difficulties?"

"Under what conditions would you ask for help from someone?"

"Under what conditions would you offer help to someone?"

"What do you think, feel, and do when someone is in distress?"

"What do you feel, think, and do when someone asks for help?"

"What do you think, feel, and do when your efforts to help someone don't work?"

"What do you want from the person you try to help?"

"What do you think, feel, and do when someone who has asked you for help begins to criticize you?"

"What do you think, feel, and do when you discover that someone who has asked for help is deceiving you?"

"What do you do when someone has ended an important relationship by leaving abruptly?"

"What are the acceptable ways for someone to express anger toward you?"

"What do you think, feel, and do when you are expected to follow rules that you don't agree with?"

"How do you decide whether to answer a client's personal questions?"

"How do you know what your client is thinking and feeling?"

"Under what circumstances do you accept a client's report of his or her past behavior as accurate?"

"Under what circumstances do you trust a client's judgment about predictions about future behavior as accurate?"

"How do you know if you helped a client?"

"Under what conditions would you terminate a relationship with a client?"

Topics addressed in self-awareness discussions are discussed in the following sections.

Ageism The term *ageism* was coined to account for prejudices and stereotypes applied to older adults based on age alone (Butler et al., 1998). The effect of ageism, like racism and sexism, is responsible for social avoidance, discriminatory practices and policies, and prohibiting older adults from living life in ways afforded to younger generations (Bennett, 2002).

Clinicians' bias to work with older adults has been identified in studies dating back to the 1960s (Kastenbaum, 1963). The reasons cited were: (1) fear of the lowered status associated with treating older adults, (2) anxiety around personal fears of aging and death, and (3) concerns that it may be a poor investment to counsel an older adult because they will not benefit from therapy (Kastenbaum, 1963). Danzinger and Welfel (2000) found that practitioners across all disciplines (professional counselors, psychologists, clinical social workers) judged older adults as less competent and less likely to improve than younger clients. In addition, the study found that female clients, regardless of age, were believed to be less competent than male clients. These attitudes affect the clinicians' work with older adult clients, often reinforcing the clinicians' stereotypes of older adults (Danzinger and Welfel, 2000; James and Haley, 1995; Wolfe and Biggs, 1997).

It is also important not to discount the effect of positive stereotyping older adults, which can also cloud the practitioner's ability to assess and diagnose mental health and substance disorders (Knight, 2011).

Negative attitudes toward aging are common; it's not usual to hear practitioners make negative statement about themselves in terms of growing older and pessimism about old age. It's important for the supervisor to comment with advantages of aging, for example, retirement lifestyle or acquiring more mature coping styles and ability to regulate emotions (Knight, 2011). It's not enough to counter negative attitudes with positive attitudes on aging; to do this can result in ignoring real problems of aging (Knight, 2011).

Taken together, these negative attitudes toward older adults can result in creating barriers for treatment. Furthermore, such barriers are contradictory to the ethical standards of the mental health disciplines (Danzinger and Welfel, 2000). It is essential that all practitioners recognize older clients' rights to access services and support their autonomy in decision making while maintaining client confidentiality.

Numerous studies contradict the attitude that older adults do not benefit from therapy. In fact, several studies have provided empirical evidence that psychotherapy is just as effective with older adults as it is with the younger population (Knight and McCallum, 1998; Myers and Harper, 2004; Orozco et al., 2014; Scogin and McElreath, 1994; Thompson, Gallagher, and Breckenridge, 1987).

Other studies challenge the stereotype that mental illness is a normal part of aging (Cohen et al., 2004; Siegel, 2004). In reality, mental illnesses are no more prevalent in the elderly population than for other age cohorts (Orozco et al., 2014).

Evidence-based treatments (assessment, intervention, consultation) have been developed for older adults. There are numerous evidence-based treatments focusing on anxiety, depression, insomnia, schizophrenia, disruptive behaviors associated with dementia/neurocognitive disorder, distress in family caregivers, and life transitions such as widowhood, caregiving, and grandparenthood (Bartels et al. 2004; Karel, Gatz, and Smyer, 2012; Myers and Harper, 2004). The Substance Abuse and Mental Health Services Administration's National Registry of Evidence-Based Programs and Practices lists information about the various mental health and substance treatment relevant to older adults (http://www.nrepp.samhsa.gov).

Countertransference The traditional view of countertransference refers to the therapist's reaction to the client's transference onto him or her. It is equally important to examine the younger therapist's transference responses to older clients. Altschuler and Katz (1999) established a method to elicit countertransference reactions by supervisees in clinical settings with older adults. The authors constructed a sentence completion exercise to be both nonthreatening and stimulating to trainees. The sentences were designed based on major countertransference themes with older adults, client characteristics, common concerns of older clients, and specific content that typically evokes defensive reactions (Bennett, 2002). The sentence completion exercise comprises the following:

1. When I am with an old person, I . . .
2. To me, old means . . .
3. The thing I like best about old people is . . .
4. The thing I like least about old people is . . .
5. The secret to successful old age is . . .
6. One of the greatest fears of many old people is . . .
7. Sex over 65 is . . .
8. When an older person moves into a retirement home . . .
9. My grandparents . . .
10. When I think of being old I . . . (Altschuler and Katz, 1999, 84–85).

Altschuler and Katz (1999) identified the following countertransference themes:

1. **Overprotectiveness**—This may take the form of feeling that the older client is vulnerable, holding their arm when walking with them or having a sense of obligation to take care of him or her. In work with more frail clients, therapists may feel reluctant to share information that they feel the client could not handle.

2. **Wish to be a rescuer**—Clinicians may feel a need to rescue the older person from a terrible fate. Clinicians may share personal opinions based on unexamined countertransference reactions and unconsciously seek to influence the client and/or his or her family. As a result, the therapist's own rescue fantasies may unintentionally overlook the client's wishes and self-determination.

3. **Disgust**—Clinicians have feelings of disgust in relation to an older person's odor and overall hygiene. They also feel uncomfortable discussing sexuality in old age, often disgusted or repulsed by the idea of older adults having sex.

4. **Wish to restore youth and vigor**—Clinicians hold unrealistic expectations that may set the client up for inevitable failure.

5. **Unfinished**—Unfinished business with parents and/or grandparents affects treatment with older adult clients.

6. **Negative expectations and projections**—Clinicians' belief in stereotypes about older adults regarding physical and mental health, specifically, old age as a time of sickness, disability, hopelessness, isolation, and dependency, affects the care provided to older clients. This countertransference theme appears related to ageist views that fail to acknowledge the positive and healthy aspects of old age experienced by many older adults. The therapist's view that old age is a time of loss and grief should be explored to determine whether any personal grief issues might remain unresolved.

7. **Manifestation of sadness and fear**—This theme embodies general feelings of sadness and fear in relation to specific experiences of old age, such as Alzheimer's, physical debilitation, isolation, death of friends, and one's own mortality.

(Bennett, 2002, 34–37)

In a subsequent dissertation study (Bennett, 2002), supervisors identified similar countertransference themes explored in supervision: (1) younger therapists (under 65) experience profound existential responses when practicing psychotherapy with older adults (over 65): death anxiety, vulnerability, and inspiration; (2) younger therapists appear to respond to older clients with prominent ageist ideologies, sexuality, and frailty prevalent in Western culture; (3) younger therapists experience relational transference reactions based on their positive and/or negative fantasies/experiences with older family members (parents, grandparents), feelings of inadequacy, and a sense of overwhelm regarding the multiple roles of geropsychologists.

Supervisors have the responsibility of not only clarifying countertransference reactions, but also teaching supervisees how to incorporate this information into clinical practice (Altschuler and Katz, 1999; Bennett, 2002;). Supervision is the arena where these personal countertransference responses can be explored; if left unmonitored, it may profoundly affect the therapeutic relationship and treatment. It takes a skilled supervisor to determine when certain transference responses are appropriate to address in individual supervision, as opposed to work through in the supervisee's personal therapy.

Caring for the Family's Caregivers Whether the client is the older adult and/or his or her family, care for the "informal" caregiver is an important element of the therapy. An informal caregiver is an unpaid individual (spouse, partner, family member, friend, or neighbor) involved in assisting others with activities of daily living and/or medical tasks (Family Caregiver Alliance, 2017). The most common primary caregiver is an adult daughter,

daughter in-law, or other family relative. Care differs by ethnicity; Asians, African Americans, and Latina Americans are more likely to provide care than European Americans (National Alliance for Caregiving and AARP, 2015; Lee and Orozco, 2014).

A study by the National Alliance for Caregiving and AARP (2015) identified that approximately 34.2 million Americans provided unpaid care to an adult aged 50 or older (average age 69) in the past 12 months, which included approximately 15.7 million adult family caregivers care for someone who had Alzheimer's disease or dementia. Most caregivers are females (60%), with an average age of 49. Family caregivers spend an average of 24.4 hours per week providing care and nearly one out of four caregivers spends 41 hours or more a week providing care (National Alliance for Caregiving and AARP, 2015).

Practitioners should pay special attention to caregivers aged 75 or older. This demographic comprises approximately 7 percent of caregivers who are usually caring for a spouse/partner (National Alliance for Caregiving and AARP, 2015). While the study revealed that the oldest caregivers were not significantly experiencing more stress or strain than younger caregivers, they were more likely to be caregiving without other unpaid help. This often resulted in taking on numerous roles such as communicating with all care professionals and advocating for their recipient. These caregivers are less likely to be employed, on fixed income, and more likely to be managing household finances for themselves and the recipient (National Alliance for Caregiving and AARP, 2015).

While the older adult may be the client, it may be important for practitioners to assess the impact on family members' providing caregiving services. Practitioners can help family caregivers identify the range of responsibilities and issues, explore what they are prepared to take on, and identify additional resources to draw upon (Kampfe, 2014). Issues often arise regarding the reversal of caregiving roles and unresolved conflicts from the past. Challenges may arise regarding the ability to maintain the previous interpersonal relationship between the family caregiver and elder and new caregiver responsibilities. The caregiver's relationship with his or her own spouse/partner and children, home structure, finances, and employment may also be affected by this new role (Kampfe, 2014). It is not uncommon for caregivers to experience depression, anxiety, and "burnout" (Lee and Orozco, 2014). A helpful guide regarding caregiving is *A Complete Eldercare Planner* (Loverde, 2009).

Practitioners may provide referrals to family caregivers for individual therapy or recommend family therapy. Therapy is an opportunity for caregivers to express their feelings and worries in a safe environment where they are not judged (Kampfe, 2014). A key element of therapy is validation of everything the caregiver is doing, learning to give themselves credit while avoiding unrealistic expectations (Kampfe, 2014). Other topics may include strategies regarding balancing job responsibilities versus caregiving responsibilities and recognizing when it's time to ask for more help.

Caregiver family therapy (CFT) is a systems approach to treat families that care for an aging adult (Qualls and Williams, 2013). CFT comprises three phases: (1) identifying the problem, (2) structuring caregiver roles, and (3) ensuring caregiver self-care. Practitioners and/or case managers can also institute a less formal approach such as family meetings that include the elder to address significant decisions such as types of services that are needed to keep the elder in their home. It's also an opportunity for the primary caregiver to express his or her needs, and bring other family members in to share the burden. These conferences can also be done via Skype to include family members located in other regions (Kampfe, 2014). Regardless of whether formal family therapy or informal approaches are utilized, autonomy and self-efficacy of the elder must be respected and emphasized.

It's also not uncommon for practitioners to take on a case management role or help the family access this service. These responsibilities are time-consuming, and often irritating and frustrating (Kampfe, 2014). Case management services can include communication and paperwork with Medicare, Medicaid, or other insurance companies; identifying and contacting adjunct services such as nursing care, meals, exercise, nutritional counseling, other types of mental health therapy (music, art); medically related therapy (speech, physical, and occupational); and identifying and maintaining current support systems or specialists such as pharmacist, physician, religious organizations, neighbors, friends, and in-home help; the list can be endless (Kampfe, 2014).

The Family Caregiver Alliance is an organization that provides education, services, research, and advocacy for family caregivers (http://www.caregiver.org). This organization provides a wealth of information (in many languages) ranging from caregiving issues and strategies, fact sheets on health and legal topics, classes, to support groups in-person and online. It is vital that practitioners are aware of local community resources that may ease some of the burden for caregivers. These resources include local area agency on aging, paratransit, Meals on Wheels, daycare programs, respite care, hospice, and support groups.

Client Death It is common for practitioners to deal with death and dying when working with older adult clients and their families. It's even more common when practitioners are working in certain settings, for example, hospitals, long-term residential care, and hospice. While much has been written about how to work with clients regarding "end-of-life care," research and guidelines are sparse regarding how the experience impacts practitioners. Most of the research in this area is case specific or clinical case reflections from "generalist" practitioners (Foster and Vacha-Haase, 2013). Limited studies on nonsuicidal client deaths have identified common issues: countertransference, ambiguity in the therapeutic relationship, and feelings of guilt, denial, and avoidance (Foster and Vacha-Haase, 2013; Lardaro, 1988; O'Brien, 2011; Rubel, 2004; Schwartz, 2004; Veilleux, 2011).

Foster and Vacha-Haase (2013) conducted a qualitative analysis of the impact of client death on clinical geropsychologists. The study was small (10); all volunteer participants identified as European American/White; men were underrepresented; and most participants worked in long-term care facilities, 10 years average working with this population. The participants experienced client deaths ranging between 5 and 800.

The following five common themes were identified by 70 percent of the participants' narratives:

1. Development of a different mindset in geropsychology
   • Perceiving older adult client death as normal, inevitable, and expected
   • Developing personal concept of "good death" and death as positive experience
   • Becoming more comfortable with death and with personal reactions to death over time
   • Recognizing personal reactions to client death that include joy, relief, or neutral emotions as well as sadness and grief

2. Circumstances of memorable client deaths
   • Feeling connected to clients; feeling intimacy, closeness, genuine admiration, and liking
   • Watching clients make progress and achieve goals; experiencing professional satisfaction
   • Sharing experience of good death with clients
   • Feeling helpless or powerless during traumatic or painful client deaths

3. Personal/professional boundaries
   • Personal experiences with illness, death, and dying impact reactions to client death

- Experiences with client death lead to personal growth and reduced fear of death
- Personal beliefs about death and meaning in life impacted by client death
- Cognitive/emotional reactions to client death spill over into personal life

4. Impact of client death on clinical work
   - Immediate challenge of maintaining focus and managing emotional reactions
   - Long-term impact is overwhelmingly positive and improves quality of clinical work
   - Professional role expands to include end-of-life planning and advocacy, and increases knowledge and competence

5. Developing specific coping strategies
   - Giving oneself permission to be impacted and exploring reactions
   - Using cognitive and behavioral strategies to gain closure
   - Finding joy and meaning in clinical work with dying individuals
   - Seeking coworker and facility support when available

(Foster and Vacha-Haase, 2013, 418)

The very nature of the therapeutic relationship, including confidentiality, precludes practitioners from mourning their clients' deaths, for example, attending funerals and contact with deceased clients' families (Foster and Vacha-Haase, 2013). Doka (2002) identified this concept as "disenfranchised grief"—grief reactions that are not socially recognized, acknowledged, or sanctioned by one's social groups. The combination of disenfranchised grief and themes of development of a different mindset in geropsychology, circumstances of memorable client deaths, personal/professional boundaries, impact of client death on clinical work, and developing specific coping strategies provide avenues to explore in both individual and group supervision.

Burnout and Compassion Fatigue Researchers have argued that repeated experiences of client death, chronic illness, and end-of-life issues may lead practitioners to experience more pervasive problems such as burnout or compassion fatigue (Figley, 2002; Keidel, 2002). Practitioners' well-being is directly related to providing competent care to clients, it is not uncommon for practitioners to ignore their own self-care. Obviously, geropsychology practitioners are of greater risk in developing these syndromes.

Burnout is "a state of physical, emotional, and mental exhaustion caused by long term involvement in emotionally demanding situations" (Figley, 2002, 1436). The symptoms are categorized as follows:

- Physical—exhaustion, sleep difficulties, somatic problems
- Emotional—irritability, anxiety, depression, guilt, helplessness
- Behavioral—aggression, callousness, pessimism, defensiveness, cynicism, avoidance of clients, substance use
- Work-related—poor work performance, quitting the job, absenteeism, tardiness, work avoidance, risk taking
- Interpersonal—perfunctory communication, inability to concentrate, social withdrawal, lack of sense of humor, dehumanization, poor client interactions
                                                                            (Figley, 2002)

Compassion fatigue is a unique form of burnout affecting people in the caregiving professions (Keidel, 2002). The concept relies on the "assumption that empathy and emotional energy are the driving force in effectively working with the suffering in general, establishing and maintaining an effective therapeutic alliance, and delivering effective services, including an empathic response" (Figley, 2002, 1436).

Managing and treating burnout and compassion fatigue begins with educating practitioners about the syndromes. This may formally occur during graduate education, continuing education courses, and/or agency trainings. Supervisors have an obligation to integrate these concepts into their work with supervisees; it may take the form of general education, specific case discussions, and evaluation of supervisees' clinical skills/job performance.

Two excellent self-administered tools are available to monitor stress, burnout, and compassion fatigue: *the perceived stress scale* (http://www.psy .cmu.edu/~scohen/) and *compassion-satisfaction/compassion-fatigue* (http:// proqol.org/uploads/ProQOL_5_English.pdf).

The perceived stress scale (ProQOL), authored by Sheldon Cohen, is a 10-item measure that takes only 5 to 10 minutes at most (Cohen and Janicki-Deverts, 2012). It is the most widely used psychological instrument for measuring the perception of stress. It is a measure of the degree to which situations in one's life are appraised as stressful. The ProQOL is the most commonly used measure of the negative and positive effects of helping others who experience suffering and trauma and is available in more than 20 languages (Stamm, 2010). The ProQOL has subscales for compassion satisfaction, burnout, and compassion fatigue and is time-efficient. It has been in use since 1995 and is available for free. These scales can provide a good baseline for understanding of stress and compassion fatigue.

Self-care strategies are one of the best methods to mitigate the effects of burnout and compassion fatigue. A helpful tool to incorporate is a self-care assessment (Saakvitne and Pearlman, 1996; http://socialwork.buffalo .edu/content/dam/socialwork/home/self-care-kit/self-care-assessment.pdf). And in time, practitioners can watch stress levels drop and compassion satisfaction increase, utilizing self-care strategies.

Conclusion

In thinking about supervision of practitioners working with older adults, the term "parallel process" comes to mind. Many of the same issues that emerge in supervision are common themes in therapy with older adults and their families: specifically, the themes of stigma, ageism, transference/countertransference, fears, insecurity, loss/death, and self-care.

Supervisors have an opportunity to instill hope to practitioners working with older adults. That hope is based on the supervisor's own experiences. Common feelings of inadequacies tend to diminish as one gains experience in working with older adults. It is important to emphasize that meaningful and effective psychotherapy can occur with older adults, including those with significant cognitive and physical impairments.

References

Altschuler, Joanne, and Anne D. Katz. "Methodology for Discovering and Teaching Countertransference toward Elderly Clients." *Journal of Gerontological Social Work* 32, no. 2 (1999): 81–93. doi:10.1300/j083v32n02_07.

American Psychological Association. "Guidelines for Clinical Supervision in Health Service Psychology." *American Psychologist*, 70, no. 1 (2015): 33–46. doi:10:1037/a0038112.

American Psychological Association. "Guideline for Psychological Practice with Older Adults."*American Psychologist*, 59, no. 4 (2004): 236–260. doi:10.1037/0003.066x59.4.236.

American Psychological Association. "Guideline for Psychological Practice with Older Adults."*American Psychologist*, 69, no. 1 (2014): 34–65. doi:10:1037/a0035063.

American Psychological Association. "Mental Health Care and Older Adults: Facts and Policy Recommendations." 2003. http://www.apa.org/ppo/issues/older mhfact03.html.

American Psychological Association. *Psychological Geropsychology*. Washington, DC: Professional Psychological Association, 2016. http://www.apa.org/ed/graduate/specialize/gero.aspx.

American Psychological Association. "Recognized Specialties and Proficiencies in Professional Psychology." 2011. http://www.apa.org/ed/graduate/specialize/recognized.aspx.

American Psychological Association. "Resources for Psychological Practice with Older Adults and Their Caregivers." APA Office of Aging. (n.d.). http://www.apa.org/pi/aging/aging-resource-facts.pdf.

Bartels, S. J., T. E. Oxman, L. S. Schneider, P. A. Arean, G. S. Alexopoulos, and D. V. Jeste. "Evidence-Based Practices in Geriatric Mental Health Care." *The Journal of Lifelong Learning in Psychiatry* 2, no. 2 (2004): 268–281.

Bennett, M. A. "The Therapist's Transference: Younger Therapists Working with Older Adults." PhD diss., 2002. Available from ProQuest Dissertations & Theses Global. (305456290). http://0-search.proquest.com.library.ggu.edu/docview/305456290?accountid=25283.

Butler, Robert N., Myrna I. Lewis, and Trey Sunderland. *Aging and Mental Health: Positive Psychosocial and Biomedical Approaches.* 5th ed. Boston: Allyn & Bacon, 1998.

Cohen, Harriet L., Mark H. Sandel, Cecilia L. Thomas, and Thomas R. Barton. "Using Focus Groups as an Educational Methodology: Deconstructing Stereotypes and Social Work Practice Misconceptions Concerning Aging and Older Adults." *Educational Gerontology* 30, no. 4 (2004): 329–346. doi:10.1080/03601270490278858.

Cohen, Sheldon, and Denise Janicki-Deverts. "Who's Stressed? Distributions of Psychological Stress in the United States in Probability Samples from 1983, 2006, and 2009." *Journal of Applied Social Psychology* 42, no. 6 (2012): 1320–1334. doi:10.1111/j.1559-1816.2012.00900.x.

Danzinger, P. R., and E. R. Welfel. "Age, Gender and Health Bias in Counselors: An Empirical Analysis." *Journal of Mental Health Counseling* 22, no. 2 (2000): 135–149.

Doka, Kenneth J. *Disenfranchised Grief: New Directions, Challenges, and Strategies for Practice.* Champaign, IL: Research Press, 2002.

Family Caregiver Alliance. Caregiver Statistics: Demographics. 2017. http://www.cargiver.org.

Figley, Charles R. "Compassion Fatigue: Psychotherapists' Chronic Lack of Self-Care." *Journal of Clinical Psychology* 58, no. 11 (2002): 1433–1441. doi:10.1002/jclp.10090.

Foster, Amanda N., and Tammi Vacha-Haase. "Practicing Psychologists Working with Older Adults: A Qualitative Study." *Professional Psychology: Research and Practice* 44, no. 6 (2013): 415–423. doi:10.1037/a0034668.

Institute of Medicine. *Retooling for an Aging America: Building the Health Care Workforce.* Washington, DC: National Academic Press, 2008.

James, Joseph W., and William E. Haley. "Age and Health Bias in Practicing Clinical Psychologists." *Psychology and Aging* 10, no. 4 (1995): 610–616. doi:10.1037/0882-7974.10.4.610.

Jeste, Dilip V., George S. Alexopoulos, Stephen J. Bartels, Jeffrey L. Cummings, Joseph J. Gallo, Gary L. Gottlieb, Maureen C. Halpain, Barton W. Palmer, Thomas L. Patterson, Charles F. Reynolds, and Barry D. Lebowitz. "Consensus Statement on the Upcoming Crisis in Geriatric Mental Health." *Archives of General Psychiatry* 56, no. 9 (1999): 848. doi:10.1001/archpsyc.56.9.848.

Kampfe, Charlene M. *Counseling Older People: Opportunities and Challenges.* Alexandria, VA: American Counseling Association, 2014.

Karel, Michele J., Abby N. Altman, Richard A. Zweig, and Gregory A. Hinrichsen. "Supervision in Professional Geropsychology Training: Perspectives of Supervisors and Supervisees." *Training and Education in Professional Psychology* 8, no. 1 (2014): 43–50. doi:10.1037/a0034313.

Karel, Michele J., Erin E. Emery, and Victor Molinari. "Development of a Tool to Evaluate Geropsychology Knowledge and Skill Competencies." *International Psychogeriatrics* 22, no. 06 (2010): 886–896. doi:10.1017/s1041610209991736.

Karel, Michele J., Margaret Gatz, and Michael A. Smyer. "Aging and Mental Health in the Decade Ahead: What Psychologists Need to Know." *American Psychologist* 67, no. 3 (2012): 184–198. doi:10.1037/a0025393.

Karel, Michele J., Caitlin K. Holley, Susan Krauss Whitbourne, Daniel L. Segal, Yvette N. Tazeau, Erin E. Emery, Victor Molinari, Janet Yang, and Richard A. Zweig. "Preliminary Validation of a Tool to Assess Competencies for Professional Geropsychology Practice." *Professional Psychology: Research and Practice* 43, no. 2 (2012): 110–117. doi:10.1037/a0025788.

Kastenbaum, R. "The Reluctant Therapist." *Geriatrics* 19 (1963): 296–301.

Keidel, G. C. "Burnout and Compassion Fatigue among Hospice Caregivers." *American Journal of Hospice and Palliative Medicine* 19, no. 3 (2002): 200–205 doi:10.1177/104990910201900312.

Knight, Bob G. "Mentoring for Professional Geropsychology within a Doctoral Program." *Educational Gerontology* 37, no. 5 (2011): 378–387. doi:10.1080/03601277.2011.553559.

Knight, Bob G., and T.J. McCallum. "Adapting Psychotherapeutic Practice for Older Clients: Implications of the Contextual, Cohort-Based, Maturity, Specific Challenge Model." *Professional Psychology: Research and Practice* 29, no. 1 (1998): 15–22. doi:10.1037//0735-7028.29.1.15.

Knight, Bob G., Michele J. Karel, Gregory A. Hinrichsen, Sara H. Qualls, and Michael Duffy. "Pikes Peak Model for Training in Professional Geropsychology." *American Psychologist* 64, no. 3 (2009): 205–214. doi:10.1037/a0015059.

Laganà, Luciana, and Sheri Shanks. "Mutual Biases Underlying the Problematic Relationship between Older Adults and Mental Health Providers: Any Solution in Sight?" *The International Journal of Aging and Human Development* 55, no. 3 (2002): 271–295. doi:10.2190/1lte-f1q1-v7hg-6bc9.

Lardaro, T. A. "Till Death Do Us Part: Reactions of Therapists to the Deaths of Elderly Patients in Psychotherapy." *Clinical Gerontologist: The Journal of Aging and Mental health* 7, no. 3–4 (1988): 78–83.

Loverde, Joy. *The Complete Eldercare Planner: Where to Start, Which Questions to Ask, and How to Find Help*. New York: Three Rivers Press, 2009.

Moffett, Louis A. "Directed Self-Reflection Protocols in Supervision." *Training and Education in Professional Psychology* 3, no. 2 (2009): 78–83. doi:10.1037/a0014384.

Myers, Jane E., and Melanie C. Harper. "Evidence-Based Effective Practices with Older Adults." *Journal of Counseling & Development* 82, no. 2 (2004): 207–218. doi:10.1002/j.1556-6678.2004.tb00304. x.

Myers, J. E., and T. J. Sweeney. *Gerontological Competencies for Counselors and Human Development Professionals*. Alexandra, VA: American Association for Counseling and Development, 1990.

National Alliance for Caregiving, and American Association of Retired Persons. *Caregiving in the U.S.* Bethesda, MD and Washington, DC, 2015.

Norman, Suzanne, Karen Ishler, Lisa Ashcraft, and Marian Patterson. "Continuing Education Needs in Clinical Geropsychology." *Clinical Gerontologist* 22, no. 3–4 (2001): 37–50. doi:10.1300/j018v22n03_05.

O'Brien, John M. "Wounded Healer: Psychotherapist Grief over a Client's Death." *Professional Psychology: Research and Practice* 42, no. 3 (2011): 236–243. doi:10.1037/a0023788.

Office of the Surgeon General. *National Action Alliance for Suicide Prevention (US). 2012 National Strategy for Suicide Prevention: Goals and Objectives for Action: A Report of the U.S. Surgeon, General and of the National Action Alliance for Suicide Prevention*. Washington, DC: U.S. Department of Health & Human Services, 2012. https://www.ncbi.nlm.nih.gov/books/NBK109909/.

Orozco, L., W.M.L. Lee, J.A. Blando, and Bita Shooshani. *Introduction to Multicultural Counseling for Helping Professionals*. 3rd ed. New York: Routledge, 2014.

Ortman, J. M., V. A. Velkoff, and H. Hogan. "An Aging Nation: The Older Population in the United States." U.S. Census Bureau. 2014. https://www.census.gov/prod/2014pubs/p25-1140.pdf.

Partnership for Health in Aging. "Position Statement on Interdisciplinary Team Training in Geriatrics: An Essential Component of Quality Health Care for Older Adults." *Journal of the American Geriatrics Society* 62, no. 5 (2014): 961–965. doi:10.1111/jgs.12822.

Paules, A. E. *A Quantitative and Qualitative Examination of Graduate Level Clinical Geropsychology Training*. PhD diss., 2012. Available from ProQuest Dissertations & Theses Global. (1140342745). http://0-search.proquest.com.library.ggu.edu/docview/1140342745?accountid=25283.

Peralta, Hilary. *The Future of Mental Health: Graduate Student Education, Experience and Interest in Working with Older Adults*. PhD diss., 2010. Available from

ProQuest Dissertations & Theses Global. (741183250). http://0-search.proquest.com.library.ggu.edu/docview/741183250?accountid=25283.

Qualls, Sara Honn, Daniel L. Segal, Suzanne Norman, George Niederehe, and Dolores Gallagher-Thompson. "Psychologists in Practice with Older Adults: Current Patterns, Sources of Training, and Need for Continuing Education." *Professional Psychology: Research and Practice* 33, no. 5 (2002): 435–442. doi:10.1037//0735-7028.33.5.435.

Qualls, Sarah Honn, and Ashley A. Williams. *Caregiver Family Therapy: Empowering Families to Meet the Challenges of Aging.* Washington, DC: American Psychological Association, 2013.

Rosen, A., J. Pancake, and L. Richards. "Mental Health Policy and Older Americans: Historical and Current Perspectives." In *Emerging Issues in Mental Health and Aging,* edited by M. Gatz, 1–18. Washington, DC: American Psychiatric Publishing, 1995.

Rubel, Rena. "When a Client Dies." *Psychoanalytic Social Work* 11, no. 1 (2004): 1–14. doi:10.1300/j032v11n01_01.

Saakvitne, Karen W., and Laurie A. Pearlman. *Transforming the Pain: A Workbook on Vicarious Traumatization.* New York: W.W. Norton & Company, 1996.

Schwartz, R. *Therapists' Experience of Client Sudden Death: A Qualitative Study.* PhD diss., 2004.

Scogin, Forrest, and Lisa McElreath. "Efficacy of Psychosocial Treatments for Geriatric Depression: A Quantitative Review." *Journal of Consulting and Clinical Psychology* 62, no. 1 (1994): 69–73. doi:10.1037//0022-006x.62.1.69.

Siegel, R. J. "Ageism in Psychiatric Diagnosis." In *Bias in Psychiatric Diagnosis,* edited by P. J. Caplan and L. Cosgrove, 89–98. Lanham, MD: Jason Aronson, 2004.

Stamm, B. H. *The Concise ProQOL Manual.* 2nd ed. Pocatello, ID: ProQOL.org, 2010.

Substance Abuse and Mental Health Services Administration's National Registry of Evidence-Based Programs and Practices. http://www.nrepp.samhsa.gov.

Thompson, Larry W., Dolores Gallagher, and Julia S. Breckenridge. "Comparative Effectiveness of Psychotherapies for Depressed Elders." *Journal of Consulting and Clinical Psychology* 55, no. 3 (1987): 385–390. doi:10.1037/0022-006x.55.3.385.

Veilleux, Jennifer C. "Coping with Client Death: Using a Case Study to Discuss the Effects of Accidental, Undetermined, and Suicidal Deaths on Therapists." *Professional Psychology: Research and Practice* 42, no. 3 (2011): 222–228. doi:10.1037/a0023650.

Woolfe, Ray, and Simon Biggs. "Counselling Older Adults: Issues and Awareness." *Counselling Psychology Quarterly* 10, no. 2 (1997): 189–194. doi:10.1080/09515079708254171.

About the Editors and Contributors

Editors

Doreen Maller, LMFT, PhD, is a licensed marriage and family therapist and associate professor and chair of the Holistic Counseling Psychology Department of John F Kennedy University and a therapist in private practice in San Mateo, California. Her teaching focuses primarily on systemic and human relationships. Her publications include chapters in *The Sourcebook in Expressive Arts Therapy*, *Beyond the Burning Bra*, and *The Encyclopedia of School Crime and Violence*. She is the series editor for the *Praeger Handbook of Community Mental Health Practice* (2013). She has presented nationally and internationally on a variety of topics including family systems and addiction, trauma, neuroplasticity, and expressive arts. Dr. Maller made a midlife pivot from corporate leadership at Gap Inc. to study human systems; she holds a master's in counseling psychology and a PhD in transformative learning, both from the California Institute of Integral Studies. Dr. Maller is the 2017 recipient of John F. Kennedy University's Henry L. Morrison award for distinguished teaching.

Kathy Langsam, MA, LMFT, is a licensed marriage family therapist and is senior adjunct professor with Golden Gate University and adjunct professor with San Francisco State University where her teaching focuses on community mental health, psychopathology, evidence-based practice, and practicum. She was the 2016 recipient of Golden Gate University's Distinguished Adjunct Professor and, in 2013, the Psychology Department's Outstanding Adjunct Professor. She is the volume co-editor of *The Praeger Handbook of Community Mental Health Practice*. She has supervised and supported trainees, interns, and licensed staff in her various roles as director of clinical services, clinical director, director of training and internship program for 18 years and continues to consult with agencies and trains supervisors. She is a certified supervisor with the California Association of Marriage Family Therapists (CAMFT). In 2015, Kathy was named CAMFT Distinguished Clinical Member of the year. She holds a master's in clinical psychology from John F. Kennedy University.

Contributors

Darlingtina K. Atakere, MA, is a PhD candidate in the Department of Psychology and the Gerontology program at the University of Kansas. She received her master's degree in psychology from Arkansas Tech University. Her research examines social determinants of health and health outcomes among older minorities. In addition, an emerging area of interest for her is the examination of cultural ecological variations in eldercare, specifically looking at filial/felt obligation toward elderly parents with chronic illness.

Tamara A. Baker, PhD, is an associate professor in the Department of Psychology at the University of Kansas. She received her PhD from Penn State University in bio-behavioral health, and completed her postdoctoral training at the University of Michigan's School of Public Health. She is the editor of *Gerontology and Geriatric Medicine* (Sage Publications) and *Ethnicity and Health* (Taylor & Francis), and is Secretary for the Gerontological Society of America. Dr. Baker's research focuses the behavioral and psychosocial predictors and outcomes of chronic disease and pain in older adults from diverse race and ethnic populations. She also examines health disparities and disparities in pain management among older adults. Other emerging interests include understanding the role social determinants of health have on the physical and mental health and social well-being and adjustment of (minority) men.

John Eric Baugher, PhD, earned his PhD in sociology from Tulane University in 2001 and has since taught in various higher education contexts including Goucher College, the Evangelische Fachhochschule (Protestant University for the Social Sciences) in Freiburg, Germany, the State University of New York—New Paltz, University of Southern Maine, and the Maine State Prison. John's scholarship focuses on the application of contemplative perspectives and practices in health care, higher education, and leadership contexts. His recent projects include *Leading with Spirit, Presence, and Authenticity* (2014), *Creative Social Change: Leadership for a Healthy World* (2016), and *Compassion Unbound: Prisons, Hospice, and the Transformative Power of Contemplative Care* (forthcoming).

Bonnie Bernstein, MEd, MFT, BC-DMT, REAT, was mentored by pioneer dance/movement therapist Blanche Evan from 1970 to 1982. She is a licensed marriage and family therapist and adjunct faculty at J. F. Kennedy University in California. She has authored publications on dance/movement therapy for survivors of sexual trauma and on treating trauma within the global community. Throughout her life, she has researched world dance in indigenous cultures. Since 2008, she has led yearly month-long dance/movement therapy workshops for marginalized youth and survivors of sex trafficking in Kolkata, India. She was education director of an alternate route dance/movement therapy training program in California and South Korea. She is a CAMFT certified supervisor and internationally recognized dance/movement therapy educator and supervisor. Her private therapy practice is in Palo Alto, California.

Caroline D. Bergeron, PhD, is a program manager and evaluator at the Bexar County Community Health Collaborative in San Antonio, Texas. She has a doctorate in public health from the University of South Carolina, a master's in communications from the University of Montreal, and two bachelor's degrees in communications and in Spanish from the University of Ottawa. Dr. Bergeron's research focuses on healthy aging including falls, social participation, age-friendly and dementia-friendly communities, and chronic disease management. She has gained international experience in healthy aging working at AARP International, the Public Health Agency of Canada, and the World Health Organization.

Denise Boston, PhD, RDT, is the dean of Diversity and Inclusion at the California Institute of Integral Studies (CIIS). She is also professor and adjunct faculty in the School of Professional Psychology and Health, concentrating in expressive arts therapy and community mental health. Her current research interests revolve around art-based interventions, social and emotional learning, and cross-cultural applications. Additionally, her interests include investigating diversity, inclusion, and social justice initiatives in higher education. Dr. Boston has been a visiting lecturer at Yonsei University's International Summer School in Seoul, Korea, and Zhejiang University in Hangzhou, China. Her biggest passion and joy is mentoring African Diaspora scholars. Dr. Boston earned her PhD in counseling psychology from Walden University and MA in counseling and psychology from Goddard College.

Thomas Dirth, MA, is doctoral candidate in the University of Kansas social psychology program. He received his BA in psychology from

Wartburg College in Waverly, Iowa, in 2009 and his MA in psychology with a social emphasis at the University of Northern Iowa in Cedar Falls, Iowa, in 2011. His current research interests include how disability is represented socially, how people with disabilities formulate positive identity around their disability, and how this positive identification can mitigate stigma-induced health and well-being decrements. His research is heavily infused with disability studies perspectives, which work to reframe disability as a minority group identity and to question taken-for-granted assumptions of what is human ability.

Annie Fahy, RN, LCSW, is a writer, clinician, and trainer. She founded Annie Fahy Consulting in 2011 and trains nationally in motivational interviewing, harm reduction approaches, and other evidence-based practices that improve health care and assist providers in strategic empathy skills. She specializes in difficult patients and complex work settings. She has written a chapter on addiction for *The Praeger Handbook of Community Mental Health Practice* and in 2007, an article on addiction published in the *Journal of Social Work*: "The Unbearable Fatigue of Compassion: Notes from a Substance Abuse Counselor Who Dreams of Working at Starbuck's." Annie uses creative writing as a therapeutic practice for providers and clients. Annie is also a prizewinning poet. Her book *The Glass Train* is due in 2017.

Melissa Fritchle, MA, LMFT, is the author of *The Conscious Sexual Self Workbook*. She has a vibrant private practice in Santa Cruz, California, as a licensed marriage and family therapist and sex therapist, where she sees individuals, couples, and other relationship configurations. Her focus is holistic, always honoring the integration of the mind, body, and spirit; and sex positive, inviting people to define their own sexual boundaries, needs, and desires. She is adjunct faculty John F. Kennedy University and Sofia University and provides online trainings for AAMFT. A passionate educator and workshop leader, in 2011 she was awarded the Sexual Intelligence award for her groundbreaking work providing sex positive training for counselors and caregivers in Uganda. In 2014, she was invited to travel back to Africa to consult with the Catholic clergy there on creating better approaches to sexual issues within the clergy. She is a regular contributor for Psyched in San Francisco as well as other online media, such as *Huffington Post* and *PBS: This Emotional Life*, and a popular blogger on sex and relationships.

Alexandra Kennedy, MA, LMFT, is a psychotherapist in private practice (38 years) and author of *Honoring Grief, Losing a Parent, The Infinite Thread:*

Healing Relationships beyond Loss, and *How Did I Miss All This Before? Waking Up to the Magic of Our Ordinary Lives*. She has been an adjunct faculty member of John F Kennedy University (since 2003), the University of California Santa Cruz Extension, and the Institute of Transpersonal Psychology. She has been interviewed in *USA Today*, the *San Jose Mercury News*, the *San Francisco Examiner*, and the *Boston Herald* as well as on NPR's *Talk of the Nation*, CNN's *Sonja Live*, KQED's *Family Talk*, and *New Dimensions Radio*. Her articles, along with suggestions for grieving, appear on her website www.alexandrakennedy.com.

Araba A. Kuofie, BA, is a PhD candidate in the clinical psychology program at the University of Kansas. She received her BA in psychology at the University of Missouri—Kansas City and then served as an evaluation coordinator on two federal grants (Substance Abuse and Mental Health Services Administration and Human Resources and Services Administration), and as a research assistant on a National Institute on Minority Health and Health Disparities grant. Her research interests are in health disparities, and evaluating facilitators and barriers to health care accessibility. Other interests include examining the influence of cultural and societal factors on mental health stigma, and health promotion and awareness.

Martha McNiel, LMFT, TRI, ESMHL, is a licensed marriage and family therapist, PATH Intl. registered therapeutic riding instructor, and equine specialist in mental health and learning. For 17 years, Martha worked as a psychotherapist at the OMI Family Center, part of Community Behavioral Health Services in San Francisco, California. OMI is where she first became interested in animal-assisted therapy. For the past 15 years, she has directed and offered equine- and canine-assisted psychotherapy services at DreamPower Horsemanship, a nonprofit therapeutic horsemanship program in Gilroy, California. She is especially interested in working with military veterans and law enforcement officers and their families utilizing EMDR (eye movement desensitization and reprocessing) and animal-assisted therapies in the treatment of trauma.

Jacquelyn A. Minahan, MA, is a clinical psychology graduate student at the University of Kansas, specializing in both gerontology and health psychology. She received both her bachelor's degree in psychology and her master's degree in mental health counseling and behavioral medicine from Boston University. Her research interests are centered around chronic illnesses and chronic pain in older adults, specifically the effect of multimorbidities and pain on mood. She is also interested in the impact of social determinants of health within this chronically ill population.

Thomas Prohaska, PhD, is a professional with more than 30 years of experience in the health care field. He is the dean of the College of Health and Human Services at George Mason University and an emeritus professor of Public Health at the University of Illinois Chicago. He is on the board of trustees for the Retirement Research Foundation and is a technical advisor to the Pan American Health Organization Foundation. Dr. Prohaska has accumulated extensive expertise in diverse subject areas in aging and public health including physical activity, health psychology and behavioral health, long-term care, health disparities, and caregiving, among others. He has over 100 research publications including peer-review journal articles, book chapters, technical reports, and monographs in aging and public health.

Gerardo Rodriguez-Menendez, PhD, ABPP, MSCP, is the Department Chair of the Clinical Psychopharmacology Program at the Chicago School of Professional Psychology. He earned his PhD in clinical psychology, with a concentration in neuropsychology, from Albizu University. He completed his internship and part of his fellowship at the University of Miami Leonard M. Miller School of Medicine. Additionally, he earned a postdoctoral master of science degree in clinical psychopharmacology at Nova Southeastern University. He received his bachelor and master of science degrees in special education from Florida State University. Dr. Rodriguez-Menendez is a licensed psychologist in Florida, a board-certified psychologist with the American Board of Professional Psychology, and a Fellow of the American Academy of Clinical Psychology.

Matthew Lee Smith, PhD, MPH, CHES, FAAHB, is associate professor at the University of Georgia College of Public Health and adjunct associate professor at the Texas A&M School of Public Health. He has devoted his career to create synergistic partnerships and initiatives to encourage positive lifestyles and reduce rates of preventable morbidity and mortality. He has earned a national reputation as a falls expert and evaluator of evidence-based programs for older adults. His involvement in local, state, and national evaluation initiatives has been integral to foster understanding about the reach, adoption, implementation, effectiveness, and maintenance of different evidence-based programs targeting key populations in a variety of community, school, workplace, and health care sectors.

Vivien Marcow Speiser, PhD, BC-DMT, LMHC, NCC, is professor and director of the Institute for Arts and Health, GSASS, Lesley University. Her work has allowed her unparalleled access to working with groups across the United States, Israel, and internationally. She has used the arts as a way of communicating across borders and across cultures and believes in the power of the arts to create the conditions for personal and social change and transformation. As former founder and director of the Arts Institute Project in Israel, she has been influential in the development of expressive arts therapy in that country. Her current interests are in creative approaches to healthy aging, pastoral care, and cross-cultural conflict resolution through the arts and in the discipline of authentic movement.

Scott Valentine, MDes, works as an artist and LGBTQ senior advocate focused on the intersection of community development and social justice. His passion for storytelling often lends itself to working on extensive research projects that are meant to help elevate the awareness of vulnerable communities. He is currently working on multiple projects with LGBTQ seniors in order to further investigate the historic flashpoint of the Compton Cafeteria and Stonewall Riots. He has held research fellowships with Harvard's Joint Center for Housing Studies, New York City Department of Cultural Affairs, and the Fenway Institute for LGBT community well-being.

Pamela Zimba, JD, LLM (Tax), is an assistant professor of law and member of the Core Faculty at John F. Kennedy University College of Law in Pleasant Hill, California. She has been teaching law since 2007. In 2010, she developed the College of Law's Legal Clinic for Elders, and was appointed the director. The clinic's mission is to provide pro bono legal services to low-income seniors (60 years of age and older) in Contra Costa, Solano, and Alameda counties. Prior to becoming a full-time professor of law, Zimba was in private practice for 25 years. Her practice areas were elder law, estate planning, family law, and tax law. Presently, she maintains a small private practice, focusing primarily on elder law issues.

Index

Page numbers followed by *f* or *t* indicate figures or tables.

Lightning Source UK Ltd.
Milton Keynes UK
UKHW011611290119
336389UK00009B/486/P

9 781440 853340